GOING LOW

GOING LOW

HOW PROFANE
POLITICS CHALLENGES
AMERICAN DEMOCRACY

FINBARR CURTIS

Columbia University Press   *New York*

Columbia University Press
Publishers Since 1893
New York   Chichester, West Sussex
cup.columbia.edu

Library of Congress Cataloging-in-Publication Data
Names: Curtis, Finbarr, 1973– author.
Title: Going low : how profane politics challenges American democracy /
Finbarr Curtis.
Description: New York : Columbia University Press, [2022] |
Includes bibliographical references and index.
Identifiers: LCCN 2021049199 (print) | LCCN 2021049200 (ebook) |
ISBN 9780231205726 (hardback) | ISBN 9780231205733 (trade paperback) |
ISBN 9780231556132 (ebook)
Subjects: LCSH: Political culture—United States—History—21st century. |
Democracy—United States—History—21st century. |
United States—Politics and government—21st century. |
Political parties—United States—History—21st century. |
Nationalism—United States—History—21st century. |
Sports—Political aspects—United States—History—21st century. |
Freedom of speech—United States—History—21st century. |
Freedom of religion—United States—History—21st century.
Classification: LCC JK1726 .C87 2022 (print) | LCC JK1726 (ebook) |
DDC 306.20973—dc23/eng/20220206
LC record available at https://lccn.loc.gov/2021049199
LC ebook record available at https://lccn.loc.gov/2021049200

Cover design: Noah Arlow
Cover image: iStock Photo (dumpster), Shutterstock (fire)

For Susan and Maybelle

CONTENTS

ACKNOWLEDGMENTS

This is a weird book written in weird times. I want to thank my colleagues in the Department of Philosophy and Religious Studies at Georgia Southern University, who collectively braved in-person teaching during a pandemic. I especially wish to express my gratitude for the support of my department chair, Karin Fry.

I appreciate the invitations to introduce sections of this book through public lectures at the College of Charleston, North Carolina State University, the Norwegian University of Science and Technology, and Skidmore College. The perceptive questions from students and faculty helped to clarify my thinking and encouraged me to continue with the project.

I greatly benefited from feedback from those who read chapters from this text. I especially wish to thank Anna R. Alexander, Genevieve Banach, Sam Bauer, William Biebuyck, Anna Bigelow, Beena Butool, Jessica Johnson, Daniel Larkin, Jesse Lee, Gabriel Levy, Kathryn Lofton, Dana Logan, Dantrell Maeweather, Charles McCrary, Méadhbh McIvor, Kerry Mitchell, John Modern, Jenna Reinbold, Stefani Ruper, Elijah Siegler, Jack Simmons, Jennifer Sullivan, and Kyle Wagner. Jay Geller, William Robert, and Cheryl Beaver have also served as long-time conversation partners whose intellectual influence is present in everything I write. Thanks as well to the anonymous reviewers for their insightful readings and suggestions. I do not know if I succeeded in addressing their perceptive criticism, but I tried. Without Wendy Lochner at Columbia University Press, this book would not exist. I appreciate her encouragement and thoughtful suggestions for helping to focus this book's argument and finally get it published.

Going Low is dedicated to Susan and Maybelle, who showed up in the summer of 2016 and have been blissfully unaware of American politics. I envy them.

GOING LOW

INTRODUCTION

On January 8, 2021, Twitter suspended the account of Donald J. Trump. Anyone checking the president's tweets found instead an explanation that sounded like it was crafted by a newly sentient robot: "Twitter suspends accounts which violate Twitter Rules." This was no small blow to what had been dubbed the "Twitter Presidency."[1] Twitter provided a direct channel for the president to rally his supporters and insult his critics. Trump's detractors had long called for suspending the account, but Twitter was hesitant to interfere with its users' free speech. Trump finally crossed the line when his words incited a violent invasion of the capitol. Twitter's tipping point was not the offensive content of the president's speech but the violent actions it inspired.

This distinction between words and actions is a familiar feature of discussions of free speech, but it is unclear whether speech on social media is free. Twitter rules are not laws. They are corporate guidelines that claim to protect the public interest.[2] The Twitter ban raised questions about who could regulate public speech in a democratic polity. As a private corporation, Twitter is not bound by First Amendment protections. Citizens have a right to speak, but they do not have a right to be heard on social media. This raises further questions about democratic discourse in an age when so much political speech is funneled through corporations with virtual monopolies over their respective media. What rules govern speech, and who decides when these rules should be enforced?

Disputes over speech and offense are the focus of this book. Discussions of free speech in the United States often focus on legal debates about the First Amendment. *Going Low* addresses the law in part, but most of the attention is paid to arguments about rules and norms that govern civil discourse. These arguments are especially visible when liberal democratic institutions are under duress. Illiberal politics has adopted an offensive style that has tested the limits of liberal ideals of free speech. To understand these limits, *Going Low* brings together two overlapping themes: the rise of illiberalism and debates about offensive speech.

Offense is about more than hurt feelings. Giving offense can be a way of exerting dominance over others. It turns speech into contests over winning and losing. One way of winning is by profaning what other people hold sacred, especially when doing so intentionally and without regret. In Trump's case, his repeated refusals to apologize for giving offense show that he has triumphed over liberal norms of civility. The profane and offensive style of Trumpism effectively articulates the grievances of illiberalism.

One counterintuitive argument that this book proposes is that contemporary illiberalism is not antisecular. Rather, Trumpism's profane politics fits with secular distinctions between religion and the state. It is a profane politics that makes no public theological or moral arguments. This is a counterintuitive way of thinking about secularism, as the word *secular* is often taken to mean nonreligious. In this book, *secularism* describes institutions rather than persons. Secular liberals can be personally religious, but they insist that these convictions are private matters. I suggest that illiberal politics also classifies religion as private, but it seeks to expand the scope of privacy and shrink the public. Rather than resist religious privatization, illiberal secularism valorizes the private sphere in a process of superprivatization. Illiberal secularism protects markets from government regulation, reduces scientific authority to mere belief, and maximizes the sphere of religious freedom. It limits the scope of liberal democratic institutions in favor of a state defined primarily by the military and police.

The privatization of everything dovetails with attempts to destroy public civility and profane liberal pieties. Illiberalism's opponents are divided about what this offensive style means for free speech. Some hope to restore liberal civility. In her 2016 address to the Democratic Convention, for example, Michelle Obama exhorted the crowd not to stoop to the Republican nominee's level. As she reminded her audience, "When they go low, we go high." The best way to respond to politicians who went low was with a dignified refusal to engage. Rather than trade insults, Democrats were encouraged to keep the faith that civil discourse and a commitment to telling the truth would win out in the end. Critics from the left, however, have argued that civility is a pointless response to people who do not seek to be civil or included. These critics assert that illiberalism needs to be canceled. Debates about civility and illiberal offenses, then, reflect different evaluations of the threat that going low poses to American democracy.

SO MUCH WINNING

The Twitter ban added insult to the injury of the lost election. Twitter's decision to suspend Trump came at a moment when he was losing his grip on power. Losing was never the plan. In a 2016 campaign speech in Albany, New York, Trump prophesied: "We are going to win so much. We're going to win at every level. We're going to win with the economy. We're going to win with military. We're going to win with health care and for our veterans. We're going to win with every single facet. We're going to win so much you may get tired of winning and say please, please Mr. President. It's too much winning. We can't take it anymore."[3] The spectacle of winning was a gleeful performance of semantic excess. Trump's presidency promised so much winning, it could not be contained within the basic rules of grammar and propriety. Winning exuded a transgressive energy. It will be so much. It will be too much. Americans wanted to win, but winning might be more than some people can take.

The people who could not take it were the losers. According to Trump, losers were parasites within a culture of success. As he explained, "There are people—I categorize them as life's losers—who get their sense of accomplishment and achievement from trying to stop others."[4] Trump's losers were not necessarily those with fewer economic resources, although they sometimes were. Losing was about social status. Losers were weak and disrespected. They were driven by envy and resentment. The ledger of winning and losing kept score in a social world in which people cared a lot about what other people thought of them.

In Trump's America, losers tried to constrain successful men by making them follow rules. Losers abounded in zoning boards that would not let Trump build, journalists who refused to acknowledge his accomplishments, and above all, the guardians of civility who insisted time and again that Trump had gone too far. Trump was out of line when he gave offense, when he crossed uncrossable social lines by insulting some group or person with language ruled out of bounds within liberal public discourse. Perpetually vexing liberals, Trump had mastered the art of "owning the libs." The Twitter ban hit so close to home because it promised to make him the sort of loser who was forced to follow someone else's rules. It was a triumph for liberals who Trump took such pleasure in offending.

Winning and losing are familiar aspects of social life. However, Trump's brash reduction of politics to a no-holds barred contest between friend and enemy seemed extraordinary, surprising, and inexplicable to journalists and academic theorists. *Going Low* suggests that an analysis informed by the history of religions is well positioned to explain the appeal of transgressive rule breaking in politics. For one thing, religion is about rules. Under secular governance, religious rules are not explicitly penalized by law but rely instead on social norms followed by self-disciplining people who are governed by a sense of shame. A shameless person who gives offense without regard for social censure can exercise a potent form of charisma. A charismatic rule breaker exercises an unrestrained libidinal will that defies social taboos. Taboos define what lines cannot be crossed, what subjects cannot be discussed, and what behaviors cannot be tolerated. Someone who willfully violates taboos commits acts of profanation that are simultaneously dangerous and exciting.[5] The stakes for taboo violation can be especially high when not everyone agrees on the rules. Someone who laments profane behavior in one context can welcome deliberate acts of profanation that offend someone else. Arguments about offensive speech are contests to determine who gets to make rules, and the stakes for these contests are especially high when it is unclear who exercises rule-making authority.[6]

PROFANATIONS

Scholarship on religion and American politics often focuses on the political activity of groups conventionally classified as religious. In part, this book addresses religious subjects by considering defenses of Christian civilization, Islamophobia in American politics, evangelical identity formation, and responses to religious diversity. My goal, however, is to use ideas from the interdisciplinary study of religion to account for what makes things profane. I am interested in sentiments, ideas, and identities that do not belong in liberal discourse. Rather than a study of public debates, this is a study of public fights. Each chapter explores a public controversy to understand how feelings of honor, pride, dignity, envy, and shame affect how people argue with each other. The emphasis is on what happens when people trade insults and on how the visceral attachment to winning for the sake of winning has shaped American religion and politics.

The study of religion helps to understand offense in several ways. First, the feelings at stake in offensive speech are private sentiments that, like religion, are often excluded from secular public discourse.[7] Shame in particular poses problems for secular divisions between public and private spheres. People are expected to feel ashamed when their actions violate norms and break rules. The criteria for public shame are unclear, however, when there is no agreement upon the norms and rules because these are dependent upon diverse religious commitments that are classified as private. Shameless behavior, then, can be taken to be a symptom of the loss of religion's power to shape public norms that govern private behavior. One potential response to this loss would be to recover a sense of public religious decency. But another response is the deliberate and unapologetic performance of shameless behavior to dramatize the moral impoverishment of secular institutions. *Going Low* suggests that the shameless and profane character of Trumpism is part of illiberalism's appeal. Trump's staunchest supporters did not vote for him *despite* his offensive behavior but *because* of it. Going low is a defiant rejection of secular liberal attempts to replace Christian criteria for shame with norms and rules appropriate for a multireligious society.

Second, religious offenses play a prominent role in current debates about "identity politics." Like religious politics, identity politics complicates secular liberal models of public discourse. As a critique of unmarked liberal individualism, identity politics was imagined as an emancipatory project that hoped to resist overlapping forms of collective oppression. As Keeanga-Yamahtta Taylor explains, "But 'identity politics' was not just about who you were; it was also about what you could do to confront the oppression you were facing. Or, as Black women had argued within the broader feminist movement: 'the personal is political.'"[8] For some liberal commentators in the age of Trump, however, identity politics was a symptom of "tribalism" run amok. Some argued that leftist identity politics produced politically correct policing that bore responsibility for alienating white Trump voters.[9]

Like religions, identities are labels assigned to curious mixtures of sincere, intimate, and personal feelings that feel private but also mark membership in groups. This is not to say that identities are essentially religious because nothing is essentially religious. It is to say that the analysis of religion can help to inform the analysis of identity politics. By saying that nothing is essentially religious, I am following Jonathan Z. Smith's assertion: "While there is a staggering amount of data, of phenomena, of human expressions and experiences that might be characterized in one culture or another, by one criterion or another, as

religious—*there is no data for religion*. Religion is solely the creation of the scholar's study. It is created for the scholar's analytic
purposes by his imaginative acts of comparison and generalization."[10] This is a starting point for my scholarship. The idea that
religion is an invention of comparison and generalization is a
product of what I believe is Smith's theory of language.[11] In my
reading, Smith was informed by a pragmatist tradition that
teaches that words are not things in the world; they are concepts
that help to make the world intelligible. Words organize and
communicate information about the world within the conventions of language. There might be nonlinguistic things, but there
are no nonlinguistic words. Rocks might exist outside of language, but they do not call themselves rocks. People do use the
word *religion*, but religions are not people. In this sense, *religion*
is not a self-identified term. Lumping together diverse sets of
ideas, practices, and institutions as religious makes sense only
when people make observations and comparisons. This is not to
say that religion cannot be defined but that it can be defined in
multiple ways and for different purposes. There is no such thing
as a wrong definition of religion because there is no stable refer-
ent for religion that exists in the world. Rather than limiting or
constraining knowledge, this malleability allows for creative and
inventive interpretations of the stuff called religion.

One revision I would make to Smith's statement, however, is
that I substitute the word *people* for *scholars*. Everyone observes
and compares. To speak of religion is to enter a contested discursive field.[12] The legacy of these discursive contests means that
the label religion comes with historical and cultural baggage.[13]
This baggage is particularly prominent in secular divisions
between religion and politics. A distinction between religious
rules and political rules has not existed in all societies in all
times and places. The relatively arbitrary nature of these divisions

makes for fraught contests over which rules govern everyone and which rules are private concerns that arise from voluntary commitments in a multireligious society. Secular divisions can appear to marginalize the stuff called religion by restricting its public influence. But secular privacy can also help to invest the private sphere with an aura of sacrality in need of protection.

The need to protect the sacred points to a third reason for the relevance of the study of religion, which is that speech can register as offensive when it crosses contested boundaries between sacred and profane. By *sacred* I do not mean some persistent, timeless human essence. Sacred stuff does not need to be deep and heavy. It is, rather, a familiar part of social life in which some things are classified as set apart and therefore command reverence and respect. As the sociologist Émile Durkheim explains, "Sacred things are not simply those personal beings that are called gods or spirits. A rock, a tree, a spring, a pebble, a piece of wood, a house, in a word anything, can be sacred."[14] While identifying something as sacred might be arbitrary, the consequences of such classifications are significant. Following the rules for how to treat sacred things demonstrates respect for social authority. Deliberately breaking those rules challenges authority. Practices of producing, protecting, and profaning the sacred participate in drawing and redrawing rules.

Things marked as sacred are treated differently from ordinary things. Deliberate acts of profanation, in contrast, return the sacred to ordinary political life. As philosopher Giorgio Agamben explains, "If 'to consecrate' (*sacare*) was the term that indicated the removal of things from the sphere of human law, 'to profane' meant, conversely, to return them to the free use of men."[15] While sacred things should not be touched, the profane world is accessible.[16] Treating the sacred as ordinary can be a mode of political critique. In Marxist theory, capitalism profaned all that was holy by assigning everything a cash value. As *The Communist Manifesto* declares, "The bourgeoisie has stripped of its halo every occupation hitherto honoured and looked up to with reverent awe. It has converted the physician, the lawyer, the priest, the poet, the man of science, into its paid wage labourers."[17] In Karl Marx and Friedrich Engels's formulation, halos are not distinctive to priests. Physicians, lawyers, poets, and scientists could be stripped of their halos when they are treated as wage laborers whose professions commanded no special reverence. *Going Low* investigates speech that strips halos from a variety of social phenomena.

Lost halos also play a role in the Marxist contention that profanation reveals truth, as in the proclamation: "All that is solid melts into air, all that is holy is profaned, and man is at last compelled to face with sober senses his real conditions of life, and his relations with his kind."[18] Actors from across the political spectrum feel that there is something about profanation that reveals the "real conditions of life." For this reason, profane speech can be upsetting to some while appearing to others to be especially honest, true, and real. This equation between giving offense and telling the truth is especially prominent in the illiberal logic of owning the libs. By refusing to constrain his speech according to liberal norms, Trump seems to his supporters to be refreshingly honest.

Whatever the intentions behind acts of profanation, keeping something sacred requires protection. When protections fail, this can animate passions ranging from excitement to anxiety to anger. These sentiments are prominent in the stuff labeled religion. Early usages of *religio* involved a range of feelings invoked by breaking rules that marked the sacred as off limits. These sentiments included "inhibition, scruple, fear, and the object that invoked those emotions: taboo, bond, obligation, oath, treaty, transgression, guilt of transgression, curse, etc."[19] These emotions can be aroused through deliberate acts of desecration or simply by treating sacred things as if they were ordinary.

To be clear, not all rule breaking is profanation. Profanation, for the purposes of this book, is a transgression that refuses to repair social damage through acts of contrition. It breaks rules without shame. Profanation poses a more formidable threat to the social order than sin does. A sinner might break a rule but can still demonstrate respect for the institutions that uphold rules by performing the proper rituals of penance. A perpetrator who apologizes or is punished is still bound by rules. An act of profanation that is allowed to stand precipitates a crisis of authority. In Trump's case, his repeated refusals to apologize after violating liberal taboos demonstrates that norms of civility are powerless to stop him.[20]

Trump's demonstration of liberalism's fragility fits with historian of religion Bruce Lincoln's observation that failure to prevent profanation marks a loss of social power. In a study of the exhumed and displayed bodies of priests and nuns during the Spanish Civil War, Lincoln argues that deliberate acts of desecration have a potent political message. In the Spanish case, demonstrating the ordinary humanity of supposedly sacred bodies challenged the authority of the Catholic Church. As he explains, profanation can "demonstrate dramatically and in public the powerlessness of the image and thereby . . . inflict a double disgrace on its champions, first by exposing the bankruptcy of their vaunted symbols and, second, their impotence in the face of attack."[21] In Lincoln's analysis, profaning dead bodies was a leftist challenge to organized religion. Profanation, however, is politically neutral and has been used to advance communism, fascism, conservativism, liberalism, and anarchism. What political uses have in common is that unrepentant profanation produces winners and losers.

LIBERALISM

Going Low is not primarily a study of Trump himself. This book takes the rise of Trumpism as a starting point for seven case studies set in a moment in which the norms of liberal civility were under duress. This state of duress led secular liberals to proclaim: "This is not normal!" The norms of secular liberalism expect politics to serve public goods and aspire to principles of fairness. Liberals do not know what to do when citizens unapologetically seek to gain power at the expense of vulnerable others.[22] The inability to come to terms with winning and losing arises from an internal tension within liberal views of private interests and public goods. Liberal theories of the state begin with self-interested actors who enter into social contracts to protect their property. These same people should then engage in disinterested discussions of public goods with a diverse population of strangers.[23] For citizens fighting to preserve religious, racial, and sexual hierarchies, however, the ideal of disinterested discourse is a preening, naive, and weak abdication of national sovereignty by globalist elites. In a world in which you are either a winner or a loser, you exploit the vulnerable or you become vulnerable yourself. For this reason, the people most energized by calls to "make America great again" were those who felt threatened by what they saw as eroding social power and national prestige. Trump's claim that losers are envious was ironic, or perhaps especially appropriate, as Trumpism oozed populist envy and resentment. As Pankaj Mishra remarks in his study of resurgent populist movements, "Seized by a competitive fever, and taunted by the possibility that they are set up to lose, even the relatively affluent become prone to inventing enemies—socialists, liberals, a dark-skinned alien in the White House, Muslims—and then blaming them for their own inner torments."[24] This is not to say that Trump supporters were objectively losing in a material sense. Trump drew a great deal of support from rural and suburban areas that were relatively safe, prosperous, and homogenous. What mattered was the perception that other people's gains were your losses. If you convinced yourself that your way of life was threatened, then liberal civility demanded dangerous concessions to the very groups who were gaining power at your expense.[25]

As a repudiation of dispassionate technocratic liberalism, Trumpism's populist aesthetic promised vitality by unapologetically embracing winning. Trump's unbridled sincerity and offensiveness promised to defeat the specter of "political correctness." For Trump supporters, political correctness was an insincere restriction of the ability of white Americans to "be honest." It offered apologies and shame in place of strength. The antidote to this coercive regime was "common sense," a realistic appraisal of the threats posed by racial, ethnic, sexual, and religious others. As political scientist Nadia Marzouki explains, "Populist leaders owe their success to an ability to present themselves as the voice of common sense. This makes them all the more effective when it comes to disparaging the discourse of the 'enemy'—be it trusts, the federal government, international socialism, the United Nations, and so on—as naïve, overly idealistic, and irresponsible."[26] Furthermore, compliance with liberal civility eroded the religious freedom of Christians. A corporation was forced to cover contraception for its employees despite its moral objections. A baker was forced to bake a cake for a same-sex wedding. A child was forced to learn about Islam. All of this was felt as a loss of a once-Christian nation.[27]

Liberal models of free speech and religious freedom make it difficult to reckon with the power of offense.[28] Rather than address the political potency of profanation, liberalism classifies religious convictions as interior. For this reason, religious offenses should do no real harm. In his *Notes on the State of Virginia*, for example, Thomas Jefferson proclaims: "The legitimate powers of government extend to such acts only as are injurious to others. It does me no injury for my neighbor to say there are twenty gods, or no god. It neither picks my pocket nor breaks my leg."[29] This classic defense of liberal toleration ties freedom of speech to freedom of religion. As matters of mind and spirit, neither speech nor religion cause injury because neither affects the property nor bodies of others. There are no winners or losers.[30]

Jefferson's assertions were at odds with a Christian history that saw great injury in offenses against God. Laws forbidding blasphemy or compelling sabbath observance protected a Christian society from infidelity and moral anarchy. Modern liberal ideals of freedom asserted that these threats were overblown. Thinkers like John Locke argued that not only were laws that compelled religious participation unnecessary, they undermined Christian sincerity by forcing people to become to hypocrites.[31] It was pointless to compel people to be religious because religion was an interior matter beyond the scope of civil institutions. Similarly, free speech allowed people to say what they wanted without fear of external coercion or reprisal from others.

The line between the interior and exterior, however, is not always so clear. At times religion is a private zone to believe whatever one wants. At other times religion endorses social norms that govern individual behavior. Speech should express sincere internal commitments, but it is also a vehicle for democratic participation in which citizens engage other members of the public. Postcolonial critics of secularism have drawn attention to internal tensions in liberal ideals of free speech and religion. Questioning the apparently apolitical quality of religious offenses, Saba Mahmood argues that secular liberal dismissals of the injury caused by speech reflect an "impoverished understanding of images, icons, and signs."[32] *Going Low* extends these critiques to develop an economy of offensive signs.[33] In this case, the economy of offensive speech governs an unequal playing field in which some people's gains are other people's losses. Winning and losing are core features of capitalist economics, and speech under capitalism can help to produce, challenge, or fortify inequalities. Politically contested speech would not be so controversial if it simply let people express themselves. As literary critic Stanley Fish asserts, few people believe in free speech for the sake of freedom itself: "Free speech arguments are never made in the name of the abstraction itself but in the name of some agenda to which free-speech rhetoric has been successfully attached, and when the argument is won, the victor will not be free speech but that agenda."[34] To get ahead in a speech economy, you must compete for resources with others who are left behind. The question, then, is who wins and who loses by classifying some speech as free.

Talking about liberalism can be a daunting task because there is no unified or consistent liberalism. Rather than simplify this complexity by stipulating a precise, technical definition, this book tries to make sense of contemporary usages of liberalism. To this end, I stay as close as possible to describing liberals as invoked by the snarling two-syllable pronunciation of the word often heard in the American south. Contemporary liberalism is the product of a tradition that begins with the defense of rights found in people like Locke and Jefferson but over time has reckoned with more complex relationships between freedom and equality.[35] As social movements such as organized labor and civil rights transformed liberalism, freedom changed. Movements like these recognized that social forces other than the state could constrain personal freedom, and liberal reformers sought to use democratic institutions to advance public goods. Protecting rights without ensuring the ability to exercise rights drew criticism for creating negative peace.

Criticism of negative peace also shaped the liberal principles of inclusion that are focal points of the controversies in this book. To be liberal is to take seriously the difficult and often inconsistent demands that inclusion makes. Indeed, a liberal is someone who spends a lot of time taking things seriously.[36] Aspirations toward diversity, equity, and inclusion require attention to changing sensibilities about what language and imagery is offensive. According to religious studies scholar Donovan Schaefer, these changing sensibilities ask for self-criticism on the part of people who benefit from different forms of inequality: "Bodies that once felt like unchallenged masters of their space—white bodies, male bodies, cis bodies, straight bodies, rich bodies, citizen bodies—are being confronted, more and more, with a demand to respond to the violence in the wake of the comforts and pleasures they enjoy." Schaefer argues that these confrontations become more frequent in the increasingly mediated world that amounts to "an increasingly saturated shame panopticon."[37] It is unclear, however, what shame contributes to liberal ends. Ashamed white liberals can be more preoccupied with assuaging their own feelings than with seeking practical solutions to institutional inequality. White conservatives reject the premise that they have anything about which to be ashamed, and they see liberalism as a weak system that calls for their self-loathing.

Tying offense to inequality raises sociological questions about what bodies are unchallenged masters of their space. Liberals are divided about whether offensive speech should be assessed by the subjective intentions of speakers or by objective sociological and historical conditions. In the latter case, offense causes harm because it discursively reinforces social inequalities. There is an economy of speech, then, that mirrors economy in the financial sense of the word. Arguments about what is offensive often rest on evaluations of unequal distributions of wealth or unequal protection under the law. Many who defend free speech absolutism are those who personally benefit from viewing speech as mere words. In this way, leftist challenges to unrestrained free speech come from both within and without the liberal tradition.

ILLIBERALISM

The changing rules governing offense frustrates Americans who identify as conservative. They are tired of hearing that they should be ashamed.[38] They want someone to fight back, to rescue them from what Schaefer calls a "state of shame exhaustion, in which it becomes easier to repudiate shame altogether than respond to the moral demands placed on them."[39] In some ways, conservatism is a variant of liberalism and, with its emphasis on individual rights, is closer to the classical liberalism of the eighteenth century. American conservatives have been more comfortable with naked assertions of self-interest. Rather than see a tension between freedom and equality, they accept that social resources will be distributed unequally and hope that they win more than they lose. According to the conservatives who voted for Trump, contemporary liberalism has made too many compromises and has been naive in the face of threats. Trumpism is the response to the fear that someone somewhere is threatening to take something that is rightfully yours. As a vigorous response to threats, Trump's illiberalism makes his supporters feel safe.

Where things get tricky is that conservatism prides itself on respecting norms and the rule of law. This raises the question of whether Trumpism is conservative or whether it marks a turn toward fascism or ethnonationalist populism. Liberalism does not know how to reckon with illiberal movements labeled populist. As a self-proclaimed billionaire from New York, Trump would have been the enemy of nineteenth-century populists.[40] Populism in the twenty-first century, however, has come to describe any movement where the people fight back against perceived elites. Populist movements can be found on the left or right but are rarely in the middle. Populism echoes liberal critiques of the unequal distribution of power and resources. While liberalism sees the problem of inequality as a matter of contractual fairness among parties with different interests, populists argue that the people should have what is rightfully theirs. This depends on who speaks for the people. Populists claim to speak for the people, but the people are not simply the collection of citizens who happen to live in a particular place. Rather, appeals to the people invoke organic forms of identification and solidarity.[41] For this reason, populism and what has become labeled identity politics go hand in hand.

Unresolved anxieties about identity politics are often at the crux of what liberalism deems offensive. While direct insults toward individuals are hardly welcome, they do not have the taboo quality of bigoted language that insults members of groups. Liberals are more likely than conservatives to see social privileges as unearned advantages that contribute to unfair distributions of power. Offensive speech reinforces these privileges and exacerbates inequality in a way that goes beyond personal feelings.

Rejecting liberal sociology, conservative rhetoric claims to treat everyone as individuals responsible for their own lot. Conservatism in practice, however, seeks to shore up families, churches, nations, and markets as regulating institutions that keep individuals in check.

Right-wing populism is especially vexing to liberalism when, unlike conservative individualism, it explicitly affirms identifications based on bloodline, heritage, or civilization. What makes Trump so honest is that he told the truth that some people are born better than others and should have nothing for which to apologize. Aspects of this attitude have always been present within American politics. Trump's departure from more recent conservative rhetoric, however, is that he came out and said it in an age when liberals thought they had made progress. By going low rather than high, he revealed a profane truth about inequality at the heart of white Christian identity politics.

Like members of any social movement, Trump supporters are not a monolithic group. Many voters said they disliked Trump but voted for him because they disliked the alternative even more. The millions of people who voted for both Trump and Obama were not so obviously motivated by resentment of an African American president.[42] Not all of the arguments of this book apply to all Trump voters. The arguments do, however, wrestle with how liberalism stokes Trumpian resentment. *Going Low* suggests that, rather than any internally coherent political philosophy, Trumpism is illiberalism as an end in itself. Trump promised to turn liberals into losers. This means that the movement has no identity apart from liberalism. It requires liberalism to exist.

While Trumpism is illiberal, it is not antisecular. Indeed, Trumpism is more secular than secular liberalism. What makes this possible is that secularism has no fixed content. For the purposes of this book, secularism refers to processes of religious privatization that separate religion and state. Secularism is not irreligious; it prescribes the proper institutional space for religion. Liberalism is one way of being secular, but it is not the only way. There are, for example, authoritarian varieties of secularism. *Going Low* suggests that Trumpism's profane style is a more complete distillation of the secular distinction between religion and the state. It is a profane politics with no affirmative theological or moral content. This might seem counterintuitive as so many Trump supporters are Christian activists. Illiberal secularism is not mostly made of people who would describe themselves as secular. Illiberal secularists might prefer to live in a society governed by shared theological and moral convictions, but they believe that liberals destroyed this. Illiberalism makes a secular bargain that cedes control over public discourse in favor of protecting private institutional spaces.[43]

What I am suggesting is a redescription of what José Casanova calls the deprivatization of religion.[44] This redescription follows Casanova's understanding of secularization as a process of institutional differentiation between religion, state, economy, and science, but I invert his view that Christian political activism is a form of deprivatization and see it instead as a form of superprivatization. It is the privatization of everything consistent with what Patricia J. Williams calls the tyranny of the private.[45] Illiberal secularism celebrates free markets and the freedom of conscience as refuges from state regulation.[46] Whatever value the state might have is in the expansion of the military and police power at the expense of liberal democratic institutions. It is a state without a public. Valorizing the private sphere is consistent with conservative rhetoric that ties the American nation to faith and family.[47] As Lauren Berlant notes, conservativism protects the "sacredness of privacy" in a way that evacuates public engagement. As Berlant explains, "No longer valuing personhood as something directed toward public life, contemporary nationalist ideology recognizes a public good only in a particularly constricted nation of simultaneously lived private worlds."[48] Christian nationalism is consistent with illiberal secularism in that the nation, like religion, is privatized. The nation is pitted over and against liberal democratic institutions. In populist nationalism, the people have become dispossessed by a tyrannical government that hates their freedom. To be clear, illiberal secularism describes antigovernment rhetoric rather than the entirely of people's views about the good, the true, and the beautiful. Whatever theological or moral complexity exists in the lives of Trump supporters is flattened by illiberal secular politics. This flat secular space enables a motley crew of illiberal cobelligerents including evangelical pastors and QAnon conspiracy theorists to band together to defeat liberal enemies. Rather than see conservative Christians who support Trump as peculiarly and holistically religious, it makes more sense to see them as political actors making strategic choices to use secular political institutions to their advantage.

Illiberal secularism appeals to those who see politics as a dirty and profane business anyway and who abandon the public square to fortify private institutions against a nefarious government.[49] As Joshua Gunn explains, Trumpism takes a perverse pleasure in the failure of democratic institutions: "Collectively our speech and behavior evinces a perverse structure through a series of disavowals: the government is broken; Congress is dysfunctional; exogenous others are taking our jobs; or, of course, 'fuck it!'"[50] Illiberal secularism is the perverse fulfillment of secular processes of privatization. Disavowals of public goods lend themselves to an extravagantly vulgar style that delights in offending liberals. In this illiberal idiom, profane speech tells the truth.

Secular liberalism is vulnerable to this profane exposure because it is itself a belief system. Secular liberals care about public goods. They believe in human rights, scientific expertise, and shared commitment to civic norms that govern public life in democratic states. Illiberal secularism profanes these liberal pieties.

THE INTERNET

Once hailed as the information superhighway, the internet was supposed to be a free speech paradise. So much information would make censors powerless and national boundaries obsolete. Evgeny Morozov dubs this liberal optimism "cyber-utopianism." As he explains, "It's only now, as even democratic societies are navigating through this new environment of infinite content, that we realize that democracy is a much trickier, fragile, and demanding beast than we had previously assumed and that some of the conditions that enabled it may have been highly specific to an epoch when information was scarce."[51] It is easier to make speech free when there is not so much of it. The apparent stability of democratic institutions depends upon practical forms of regulation and discipline that can be at odds with abstract ideals of freedom. Secular liberals had more confidence in public discourse when they enjoyed editorial control over print and television media in a scarcer information age. In her study of the impact of social media on protest movements, Zeynep Tufekci observes that much of the anxiety about truth has to do with the loss of "trusted intermediaries" to sort through an overwhelming amount of information. These intermediaries, while imperfect, at least "provided boundaries of discourse and often delivered on at least some of their normative functions of investigative journalism, fact-checking, and gatekeeping."[52] Free speech flourishes when it is regulated by gatekeepers committed to liberal norms.

Social media skirts traditional gatekeeping and hands editorial control to a mixture of mob and algorithm.[53] People across the political spectrum can choose their own reality.[54] Trumpism flourishes on the internet, which is itself a profane space. For one thing, it allows for easy trafficking in profanity. Internet insults flout rules and norms in a mediated zone where nothing is sacred. The internet gives an outsized voice to those who can artfully insult and offend. As Jia Tolentino laments, "Today, on Facebook, the most-viewed political pages succeed because of a commitment to constant, aggressive, often unhinged opposition. Beloved, oddly warmhearted websites like *The Awl*, *The Toast*, and *Grantland* have all been shuttered; each closing has been a reminder that an open-ended, affinity-based, generative online identity is hard to keep alive."[55] Unhinged opposition is consumed with an ethos of winning that renders public concern quaint and unprofitable.[56] All of this serves as further validation of illiberal attacks on liberal public goods.

This is especially true of Twitter, Trump's favorite platform.[57] Its lack of personal accountability grants people the ability to insult without the interpersonal awkwardness that would result in face-to-face conversation. In some ways, Twitter is overrated. A study conducted by the Pew Research Center suggests that, of the 22 percent of Americans who use Twitter, about 10 percent produce the vast majority of tweets.[58] This skews perception of public opinion. Extremely online people saw their timelines as maps of the electorate and could not imagine possibilities like Trump as president in 2016 or Joe Biden as the Democratic nominee in 2020. Everything about Twitter is out of proportion, but this also contributes to its disproportionate impact on public discourse. The small percentage of the population made up by elite Twitterati is still an expansion over the tinier number of inside-the-Beltway pundits who shape opinion in television, radio, and print media.

In addition to undermining the special status of editorial gatekeepers, the internet has a spatial organization that challenges social norms that set something apart. The feeling of closeness without intimacy intensifies the spatial logic that the critical theorist Walter Benjamin saw in modern media in the 1930s. According to Benjamin, divisions between sacred and profane depend upon the careful organization and management of space and boundaries. The sacred qualities of art are profaned by mechanical reproduction because whatever special value is attached to an original work of art is eroded when it can be reproduced, distributed, and consumed in a variety of places or social contexts. This makes art accessible to more people in a process that is similar to how capitalism profanes all that was holy, but it also changes how art is perceived. The literal dislocation of images in a medium like film shocks the sensorium and transforms perception. As Benjamin explains, "The spectator's process of association in view of these images is indeed interrupted by their constant, sudden change. This constitutes the shock effect of the film, which, like all shocks, should be cushioned by heightened presence of mind."[59] While a heightened presence of mind should cushion these shocks, it is not clear this would be the case. Shock effects could be liberatory or reactionary, creating a new consciousness of collectivity or glamorizing a fascist leader.

Digital technologies that did away with repression in favor of exposure suited the Trump presidency. The internet was awash in shock. The surplus of shocking statements meant that the initial shock effects of each new outrageous story wore off and became a new normal. Many on both the left and right were left with a sense of disorientation that yearned for some imagined lost stability. As philosopher Achille Mbembe explains, "They genuinely long for a return to some sense of certainty, the sacred, hierarchy, religion, and tradition. They believe that nations have become akin to swamps that need to be drained and the world as it is should be brought to its end."[60] Those who felt lost were receptive to a message of winning. Trump's willingness to flout rules made him especially well-equipped to handle a world in which traditional rules were obsolete. As Mbembe suggests, "In this context, the most successful political entrepreneurs will be those who convincingly speak to the losers, to the destroyed men and women of globalization and to their ruined identities. In the street fight that politics will become, reason will not matter. Nor will facts. Politics will revert to brutal survivalism in an ultra-competitive environment."[61] Trumpism appeals to people who want a strong leader to protect them from the chaos of the very globalizing, digitally mediated world in which Trump flourished. Rather than recover lost public decorum, illiberal secularism hunkered down with private protections from an insecure world. Ironically, Trump's shocking internet presence produced the problem he promised to fix.

CHAPTER OVERVIEWS

The first three chapters discuss people who took pleasure in giving offense. The first chapter on Trump considers populist responses to politically correct liberalism. Trump's mastery of common sense enables him to be honest about racial and religious threats to American greatness, and this honesty requires offensive speech. To this end, the Trump presidency subscribed to a reality show ethos that stopped being polite and started being real. The spectacle of brazenly violating liberal taboos produced intense reverence for a powerful leader who liberated people from the shame of labels like racist or sexist. Trump's shameless behavior turned injunctions to be ashamed on their head by branding them as elitist liberal condescension. In a similar vein, he triumphed time and again over liberal fact checkers who challenged his version of reality. By gaining power from his performances as a profane man in a profane age, he was able to turn liberal frustration into political power.[62]

As someone who does not care about anyone's feelings, Steve Bannon has declared war on politically correct globalist elites. The second chapter analyzes how his confrontational style animates his work on behalf of populist movements that liberals decry as racist and Islamophobic. Islamophobia takes center stage in Bannon's imagined clash of civilizations between Islam and the West. Bannon's ironic use of incivility to defend civilization creates a crisis for liberal ideals of free speech and the truth. In what has been dubbed a "post-truth" era, reason and facts appear to be losing to populist passions. This raises questions about the efficacy of civil debates with illiberal actors who see liberal civility as the enemy.

The status of free speech within an imagined conflict between civilization and savagery is also the subject of the third chapter. Satirists who live by a credo that nothing is sacred insisted on drawing images of the Prophet Muhammad that they knew would offend Muslims. In the case of cartoon controversies, the purported clash of civilizations led to violence. In the United States, the threat of violence required a heightened commitment to private security in the form of guns. Although free speech promises peace, it protects insults that threaten violence. Offensive speech is one way that free citizens demonstrate their willingness to fight if necessary. Defending civilized nation-states, then, is ambiguous work. Civilization invokes images of cultivation, aesthetic sophistication, and restraint, but these virtues appear weak and effeminate when placed on the front lines of a war against barbarism.

Ambiguous values are the subject of the fourth and fifth chapters, both of which address responses to secular liberalism by people classified as "white evangelicals." Conservative Christians hope to rescue a sacred Christian nation profaned by sexual pollution. The fourth chapter considers the apparent hypocrisy of white evangelicals who make political decisions that overlook private sexual misbehavior. Evangelical support for Trump, for example, is taken to be a sign that Christians have abandoned their principles in favor of an irrational tribalism. Rather than a betrayal of evangelicalism, apparent hypocrisy is consistent with illiberal secular divisions between public and private. These divisions are evident in the rhetoric that frames Christian "values" as distinct from ordinary political views. While political views could be subject to public scrutiny and debate, values are sacred matters that make up fundamental aspects of private identities nurtured in families and churches. Attacking someone's values, then, could be cast as an offensive form of bigotry against Christians. Claiming that Christian values are under threat, then, is a strategic tool to protect private institutions from encroachments by a profane government.

Protecting private freedom shapes the legal arguments of the *Masterpiece Cakeshop* case, in which a Christian baker refused to bake a cake for a same-sex marriage. He argued that baking a cake would make him complicit with immoral practices that offended his conscience. The fifth chapter suggests that complicity claims provide a private refuge for Christians who have lost the legal power to regulate public morality. Legal arguments for protecting businesses from complicity abandon the pursuit of public goods in favor of empowering private institutions like families, churches, and corporations to regulate social life.

Public protests are the subjects of the sixth and seventh chapters, which focus on the challenge to liberalism posed by leftist protest movements that advocate for a more assertive response to illiberalism. Chapter 6 analyzes professional football players' refusal to stand for the national anthem in protest of police violence. This chapter assesses whether the refusal to honor civic symbols is a profanation of American civil religion that reveals a gap between the civic ideals of equality and the reality of police violence that enforces inequality. Black Lives Matter activists question American commitments to freedom, equality, and inclusiveness by asserting that racism is not a deviation from normal civic practices but is an ordinary feature of life in the United States.

Hostility toward protests is also the subject of the seventh chapter, which analyzes the uproar over "coddled" students and "cancel culture" on college campuses. One popular book in the coddling genre, Greg Lukianoff and Jonathan Haidt's *The Coddling of the American Mind*, argues that contemporary students suffer from an epidemic of "safetyism."[63] According to Lukianoff and Haidt, safetyism has an aura of sacrality. College students' desire to be safe treats offense as profanation. The proliferation of think pieces about coddling on college campuses offers psychological explanations of offense that deflect criticism of institutional inequality. By framing protests as an illiberal assault on free speech by hypersensitive students, liberal critics of coddling direct attention away from the discursive and physical policing necessary to ensure their own safety.

The chapters of *Going Low* address overlapping themes related to the rise of illiberalism and the rules governing speech, but they offer no single explanation of the relationships among religion, offense, liberalism, and free speech. This is because the rhetorical uses of free speech are selectively appropriated in different ways in different contexts. People make inconsistent arguments. Rather than attempt to identify a principle that ties together different usages of free speech, I argue that freedom is fundamentally unprincipled. Religious and political actors appear hypocritical, but this invites us to analyze the rationale behind inconsistent decisions made within particular contexts.

So it is by design that the first chapter makes a distinct argument about reality, exposure, and shame in the Trump presidency; the second chapter investigates what the so-called post-truth era means for liberal civility; the third chapter considers the violence latent in speech within contemporary gun culture; the fourth chapter examines white evangelical Christian nationalism as a form of illiberal secularism; the fifth chapter continues the discussion of Christian appropriation of secular categories by exploring the moral and theological impoverishment of complicity claims in the courts; the sixth chapter looks at how anthem protests function as a profanation of civil religion; and the seventh chapter examines so-called cancel culture on college campuses in terms of competing visions of safety. The goal in each chapter is to move away from an analysis that focuses on hurt feelings and to look instead at how boundaries are tested, rules are drawn and redrawn, and political power is distributed. The chapters do not prescribe resolutions to disputes about free speech. This book is not an argument for or against liberalism. It is a more modest attempt to figure out what is going on. One common theme among the chapters is that debates about offense are particularly fraught because liberalism never entirely realizes its aspirations to freedom, equality, and inclusion. In some sense, the eternal frustrations of liberal aspirations set the stage for Trumpism. The halo that many supporters bestowed on Trump was consistent with Michael Taussig's observation that acts of desecration produce new forms of sacrality by releasing a "strange surplus of negative energy."[64] This book seeks to understand how different actors respond when negative energy promises to become the raw material for so much winning.

1

THE REALITY OF
DONALD J. TRUMP

I n the beginning was the brand. And the brand was Trump. When it first aired in 2004, *The Apprentice* portrayed the quintessential mogul. While you watched the Trump name emblazoned on planes, buildings, and other shiny things, the introductory voiceover described a man who had conquered the urban jungle of New York City. Trump told a riches-to-rags-to-riches story of the consummate winner who fought back from the precipice of financial ruin. As he bragged, "I was seriously in trouble. I was billions of dollars in debt. But I fought back and I won, big league."

Many Americans felt that there was something unseemly about a reality television star as president. On National Public Radio, Mara Liasson observed: "Donald Trump promised to run the White House like a business, and that business appears to be a reality television production company."[1] The crass spectacle of the Trump White House was a double profanation of the dignity of the presidency. Not only did it turn the highest office of the land into a branding opportunity, Trumpism came from the kitschiest corner of the already kitschy world of mass media. Reality television governance had a penchant for drama designed to entertain a nation incapable of feeling shame. As conservative columnist George Will lamented, "Half or a quarter of the way through this interesting experiment with an incessantly splenetic presidency, much of the nation has become accustomed to daily mortifications. Or has lost its capacity for embarrassment, which is even worse."[2] Will feared that the Trump presidency had moved past national shame to the greater tragedy of a shameless nation.

Trump turned condescension to his advantage. His adviser Stephen Miller proclaimed that his boss was a "self-made billionaire [who] revolutionized reality TV and tapped into something magical that is happening in the hearts of this country."[3] A man of the people who scoffed at political correctness, Trump refused to abide by the decorum expected of elite politicians. Defying the establishment only intensified his support. Even Trump's bête noire the *New York Times* noted this appeal: "Mr. Trump has cast aside the mythology of a magisterial presidency removed from the people in favor of a reality-show accessibility that strikes a chord in parts of the country alienated by the establishment."[4] While the lack of presidential decorum scandalized Washington insiders, Trump's taste for fast food and his lowbrow tweeting habits made the office of the presidency less distant by removing its halo. As the *Times* explained, "That indifference to the way things have always been done has energized Mr. Trump's core supporters, who cheer his efforts to destroy political correctness, take on smug elites and smash a self-interested system that, in their view, has shafted everyday Americans."[5] Violating the norms that made the presidency special, Trump was a mogul with the relatability of a regular guy.

Trump spent decades cultivating the image of himself as a media master. As he bragged, "One thing I've learned about the press is that they're always hungry for a good story, and the more sensational the better. It's in the nature of the job, and I understand that. The point is that if you are a little different, or a little outrageous, or if you do things that are bold and controversial, the press is going to write about you."[6] His ability to work the press with stories that were bold or controversial was enhanced by the rise of social media, in which outrageous tweets could set the day's news agenda. According to his advisers, Trump's command of new media gave him a decided advantage over the hopelessly unsavvy Hillary Clinton: "If Donald Trump was Twitter, then Hillary Clinton was LinkedIn. Her online presence was filled with long descriptions of stances and policies. . . . Voters didn't want a scripted intellectual connection. They wanted a visceral one. That's what Mr. Trump gave them."[7] Mocking Clinton's "scripted intellectual connection" taunted earnest believers in good government who decried Trumpism's lack of policy substance. Rather than apologize, the Trump campaign doubled down on their embrace of the visceral and affective rhetoric that vexed those who believed that populist movements seduce ordinary people into voting against their own interests.[8]

Trump's visceral style is "popular" in a way that complicates political theories of populism. Trumpism is not the organic expression people's will as much as it is the creation of a publicist.[9] His image as a man of the people is a branding strategy rather than an appeal to shared economic interests. The most characteristically populist aspect of his presidential campaign was that he shared with his supporters a deep antipathy toward imagined elites.[10] Although a self-reported billionaire, Trump has long been derided as an outer boroughs denizen who lacks the refined tastes of Manhattan literati. In the 1980s the editor of *Spy Magazine* labeled the mogul a "short-fingered vulgarian."[11] The phallic subtext of the short-fingered jibe seemed to get under Trump's skin more than the many other insults directed at him.[12]

Some speculated that Trump's run for the presidency was a response to a 2011 White House Correspondents Dinner where he was ruthlessly insulted by President Barack Obama and comedian Seth Meyers. A rumored Trump presidential run was comedic material for the host. As Meyers joked, "Donald Trump has been saying he will run for president as a Republican—which is surprising, since I just assumed he was running as a joke."[13] Staring with a straight face throughout the barrage of insults, Trump did not look amused. According to fellow attendee Adam Gopnik, the 2016 campaign could be traced back to this moment. Trump's populist politics derived from his sense of wounded pride: "For the politics of populist nationalism are almost entirely the politics of felt humiliation—the politics of shame. And one can't help but suspect that, on that night, Trump's own sense of public humiliation became so overwhelming that he decided, perhaps at first unconsciously, that he would, somehow, get his own back— perhaps even pursue the Presidency after all, no matter how nihilistically or absurdly, and redeem himself."[14] Gopnik saw shame and resentment as motivations for Trump and his supporters. This assessment existed in ironic harmony with the diagnosis that Trumpism was shameless. But how can a movement be driven by both shame and shamelessness at the same time?

One answer is that shame and shamelessness went together because shameless behavior is one way of responding to shame. Trump supporters knew that media and educational elites thought they should be ashamed, but this illustrated liberal arrogance. After all, saying that other people are secretly ashamed was a bold and possibly arrogant assertion because you had to know what was going on in other people's heads. Claiming that someone was ashamed asserts that not only did you think they were wrong but that they also think they were wrong. Shame arose from hidden envy toward social betters. And envy was never good. As literary critic Sianne Ngai explains, "a person's envy will always seem unjustified, frustrated, and effete—regardless of whether the relation it points to is imaginary or not."[15] Identifying shame, resentment, or envy as motives for Trumpism rested on the premise that Trump's supporters were aware that they were out of line. As with jokes about a reality show presidency, however, Trump rebranded these explanations as elitist condescension. Shameless behavior demonstrated that there was no reason to be ashamed and that liberal critics were self-righteous do-gooders. Rather than apologize, Trump turned shame into a badge of honor.[16]

The closest approximation to shame that concerned Trump was embarrassment about a small crowd, a small amount of money, or a small penis. He was sensitive to appearing weak or unattractive. Weakness makes people losers, and there could be some shame in that. While it might be possible to embarrass Trump, the sense of shame that he lacked was any of the sensations that arise from guilt. Guilt requires remorse for some moral transgression or harm to others. If winning required breaking moral rules or hurting other people, it was all good.

Like all origin stories, however, the correspondents-dinner-revenge theory was the product of later recollections. Trump had toyed with running for president for decades.[17] On the *Oprah Winfrey Show* in 1988, he promised to get back at countries that were "screwing" the United States.[18] In 2000 he considered running on the Reform Party ticket. The correspondents' dinner story resonated, however, because there was something fitting about beginning the Trump presidency with insults, shame, and revenge. The path to presidential victory was the tale of a man who had been humiliated but then fought back and won.

This chapter suggests that there is something to the idea that shameless Trumpism was a response to efforts to shame Trump

supporters, but I am less convinced that this reflects an unconscious acceptance of liberal reality. Many of Trump's critics and
supporters share the conviction that their opponents secretly recognized reality for what it was but could not admit to it for fear
of the consequences. His critics imagine that Trump supporters
recognized their hero was racist but did not say this out loud.
His supporters believe that his critics really believed what he said
about racial and religious minorities but could not say so because
of political correctness. Therefore, Trump promised to reveal
what was real. To do this, the reality television presidency produced a narrative that felt real by playing to people's fears and
fantasies. This production flourished in an environment of relentless exposure and judgment of hidden vulnerability. Inventing
reality revealed profane truth when people stopped being polite
and started getting real. Trump's strategy for winning the
battle for reality depended upon a relentless profanation of
everything. For this project, it helps that he was an entirely
profane man.

COMMON SENSE

Rejecting the image of a showman without regard for truth or
decency, Trump supporters report that they were drawn to him
because he was refreshingly honest in a world of deceptive politicians. This is partly because if you believe that everything you
hear from traditional news outlets are lies, then you can believe
lots of things. But in addition to believing Trump's words, supporters saw honesty in an expressive style uninhibited by the
constraints of polite self-censorship. When liberal (and some
conservative) critics of Trump thought of honesty, they thought
of truth and falsehood. To be honest is to say things that are

consistent with other things one has said as well as to make statements that refer to some reality in the world. Trump's honesty, however, worked on an affective register. He articulated feelings and intuitions that affirmed his supporters' suspicions and prejudices.

Speech that validates prejudice is a good description of popular usages of "common sense." In some ways, Trump's penchant for conspiracy theories and his propensity for saying things that are demonstrably false would seem to be the opposite of common sense.[19] Trump's common sense, however, is a brand more than a coherent theory of language. At the Republican National Convention, his son bragged that his father's business philosophy was guided by people who "had doctorates in common sense."[20] Trump Jr.'s boast reveals an underlying tension, however. On one hand, common sense is a universal language. It requires no expertise and should be intelligible to everyone. On the other hand, common sense is an idiom and affective style recognized by some people and not others. As Nadia Marzouki observes, right-wing rhetoric ironically touts common sense as something that people do not hold in common, and this exclusivity undermines the ideal of the public as a common space for democratic deliberation: "The invocation of common sense is all the more ironic since it ends up opposing the very possibility of a *common* shared space for debate and social relations."[21] Common sense in this vein is something that everyone could have but some people lose. Or, more precisely, common sense is a viscerally perceived reality that educated liberals cannot acknowledge because they are cowed by political correctness.

In its philosophical usage, common sense asserts that language faithfully represents reality. In the eighteenth century, Scottish commonsense realism developed as a response to the idealists and skeptics who questioned the trustworthiness of sense perception. The philosopher Thomas Reid countered that if the counterintuitive arguments of idealistic philosophers seemed to contradict one's ordinary sense of reality, it was philosophy and not one's familiar sense of the world that was at fault. Those with no learning often knew far more than educated philosophers: "Poor untaught mortals believe undoubtedly that there is a sun, moon, and stars; an earth, which we inhabit; country, friends, and relations, which we enjoy; land, houses, and moveables, which we possess. But philosophers, pitying the credulity of the vulgar, resolve to have no faith but what is founded upon reason."[22] For Reid, it was absurd to throw out one's ordinary sense of the world because the speculations of philosophers could not explain it. Rather than an inadequacy of common sense, this was a failure of philosophy: "But if indeed thou hast not power to dispel those clouds and phantoms which thou hast discovered or created, withdraw this penurious and malignant ray; I despise Philosophy, and renounce its guidance: let my soul dwell with Common Sense."[23] Reid did not despise philosophy as such, but only philosophy that required a choice between abstract thought and everyday experience. Rather than disproving what people see, smell, hear, taste, and touch, philosophy should take this sensory data as trustworthy evidence from the real world.

While Reid argued that language could communicate reliable information about the sensory world, not all forms of communication worked in the same way. He divided language into "artificial signs" and "natural signs." Artificial signs were not false but were the products of human artifice and creation. They came from social conventions and had no necessary relationship to the things they signified. Anyone who spoke a particular language could understand what artificial signs said about the real world. But Reid argued that in addition to artificial signs, people were still able to communicate with the aid of natural signs. These were gestures and inflections that were intelligible to all human beings even if they did not share the same human language.

Natural signs did more than just communicate information in the absence of a common language; they conveyed subtlety and emotion in a way that changed the meaning of artificial signs. A tone of voice could convey anger even if one did not understand the literal meaning of the words in an irate tirade. Without the expected inflections and gestures that accompany anger, the simple statement "I am angry" would lack the force and significance of that same statement yelled at the top of one's lungs. Reid argued that natural signs made an immediate sensuous impression recognized by all human beings. Therefore, effective communication used the natural sign system common to all:

> It is by natural signs chiefly that we give force and energy to language; and the less language has of them, it is the less expressive and persuasive. . . . Speaking without the proper and natural modulations, force, and variations of the voice, is a frigid and dead language, compared with that which is attended with them; it is still more expressive when we add the language of the eyes and features; and is then only in its perfect and natural state, and attended with its proper energy, when to all these we superadd the force of action.[24]

When discussing natural signs, Reid stressed how overthinking could undermine the ability of human beings to know reality. Education could increase one's facility with arbitrary signs, but it could also diminish mastery of natural signs. The same infatuation with ideas that led philosophers to doubt their perception of the world could also lead to their inability to speak effectively.

While rational or dispassionate language may appeal to philosophers, it was unlikely to persuade ordinary people who drew on the full range of their senses to communicate. Philosophers were overcomplicated and boring.

While few Americans read Thomas Reid, the philosophy of common sense resonated with the American desire for democratic rule.[25] In his widely distributed pamphlet *Common Sense*, Thomas Paine argued for government based on ordinary wisdom: "I draw my idea of the form of government from a principle in nature, which no art can overturn, viz. that the more simple any thing is, the less liable it is to be disordered, and the easier repaired when disordered."[26] Casting off decadent aristocracy in favor of democratic simplicity, a new nation would be governed by ordinary people who possessed practical wisdom that eluded their social betters. Within a few decades of the American Revolution, Andrew Jackson embodied the common man in power. The practical sense of the Tennessee soldier was superior to educated reasoning because it cut through sophistry in favor of plain truths and preferred decisive action over dilettantish deliberation. Jacksonian populism combined a suspicion of political elites with a vigorous defense of white supremacy and national honor.[27] Placing a portrait of Jackson in his White House, Trump compared the condescension that both men received from established politicians. As he stated in a speech at Jackson's home in Tennessee, "Andrew Jackson rejected authority that looked down on the common people. . . . Jackson's victory shook the establishment like an earthquake. Henry Clay, secretary of State for the defeated President John Quincy Adams, called Jackson's victory mortifying and sickening. Oh boy, does this sound familiar."[28]

Reid's assertion that philosophers could lose the ability to perceive natural signs helps to explain why appeals to common sense can be a strategy to dismiss educated critics.[29] If people with excess education lost the capacity to recognize the affective quality of natural signs, then visceral appeals made sense to ordinary Americans while wonky Clintonians stuck to scripted intellectual connections.[30] Furthermore, as common sense was both a description of factual reality and a particular style, impressions became truth. This rhetoric of common sense turned precritical prejudices into empirical reality. This was further affirmed by the ubiquity of religious, sexual, and racial stereotypes across all forms of media. Mediated repetition made prejudices feel like they were based in reality. When Trump voiced these precritical prejudices, he made people feel good because he affirmed the intuitions and impressions that they used to orient themselves in the world, especially in relation to what was new and unfamiliar.[31] As preemptive judgments that make sense of unfamiliar persons or situations, prejudices make people feel safe and in grasp of reality. Trump's mastery of common sense came from his speaking the plain truth while making visceral and affective appeals to his supporters' precritical assumptions.

Common sense, then, was the preferred term to describe prejudices and generalizations ruled out of bounds by political correctness. For Trump's critics, prejudices were dangerous because unconscious assumptions produced bigotry. For those who applauded common sense, Trump stood up to liberal critics by honestly articulating his supporters' fears of religious, sexual, and racial others. Trump supporters were tired of hearing that their intuitions made them bad people. It was no fun when friends, coworkers, or even your own kids called you sexist or racist. As Donovan Schaefer notes, the liberal employment of shame was meant as progressive pedagogy: "Shame on the move—an openness to shame, a trafficking in shame—is how left wing politics feels. Leftist politics use shame to challenge not only the politics of others, but also themselves, grinding away their own sense of comfort in a relentless project to become more sensitive, more thoughtful, and more moral."[32] Such a pedagogy of shame was not directed at everyone but was specific to people whose identities came with sociological privileges. Identifying progressive politics with shame, then, could also have the effect of contributing to a visceral connection between liberalism and elite bourgeois whiteness. For Trump supporters, this meant that shame was unequally distributed and that they were condescended to by elite liberals. Grinding away their own sense of comfort was not welcomed by those who did not feel comfortable and felt instead that they were losing ground. As Lauren Berlant argues, Trump supporters wanted someone to tell them not to be ashamed when they felt vulnerable: "Mainly they seek freedom from shame. Civil rights and feminism aren't just about the law after all, they are about manners, and emotions too: those 'interest groups' get right in there and reject *what feels like* people's spontaneous, ingrained responses. People get shamed, or lose their jobs, for example, when they're just having a little fun making fun. Anti-PC means 'I feel unfree.'"[33] Trump's ability to offend elite sensibilities and get away with it felt like freedom. It liberated people from the shame of labels like racist or sexist while branding political correctness as its own form of elitism.

Joshua Hawley, a Republican senator from Missouri, provided an example of how this branding works when he argued that liberal elitism is a form of Pelagianism, a Christian heresy that taught that human beings could perfect themselves through their own free will. According to Hawley, liberal Pelagianism amounts to self-congratulatory posturing by wealthier people with better educations and cosmopolitan world views. He pits educated elite secular liberals against humble Christians. Secular liberals are so full of themselves that they no longer needed God. The defining feature of coastal liberals is that they are rich and successful: "Because if freedom means choice among options, then the people with the most choices are the most free. And that means the rich. And if salvation is about achievement, then those with the most accolades are righteous, and that means the elite and the strong. A Pelagian society is one that celebrates the wealthy, prioritizes the powerful, rewards the privileged."[34] Because Hawley's fusion of liberalism and Pelagianism is the eccentric creation of a conservative who relishes the role of contrarian political minority at prestigious universities, his essay reads less like an honest analysis than a counterintuitive negative argument by a college debater trying to fluster an opponent. One feature of Hawley's rhetoric that is typical of Trumpian populism, however, is that it erases racial, ethnic, and religious minorities from the Democratic Party in order to portray Trumpism's critics exclusively as affluent white secular liberals. This makes politically correct criticism into nothing other than elite liberal condescension toward white working-class Christian values.[35] Hawley frames liberal criticism as bigotry in an attempt to beat secular liberals at their own game.

Once political correctness is equated with elitism, Trump's racist, sexist, and Islamophobic statements can be rebranded as telling truth to power. Violating liberal taboos promises liberation from the tyranny of political correctness. The Twitter presidency, exhibiting an uncensored freedom from constraints of civility, truth, and grammar, is the perfect medium for this political combat.[36] Unconstrained thinking, feeling, and speaking excites a shared affective register otherwise concealed by the norms of liberal multiculturalism.

IT'S INSTINCTS, NOT
MARKETING STUDIES

According to Trump, intuitive reasoning leads to business success. When describing job interviews he conducted with prospective managers, he bragged: "Fortunately, we went through them fast, because I tend to size people up pretty quickly."[37] Sizing people up is a skill of salesmen who pride themselves on their ability to judge people by appearances and social cues. It is the opposite of withholding critical judgment until possessing more information. At the end of one round of interviews, for example, Trump described his hire as a guy named Irving: "You've got to understand that we are talking about a short, fat, bald-headed guy with thick glasses and hands like Jell-O, who'd never lifted anything in his life beside a pen, and who had no physical ability whatsoever. What he did have, however, was an incredible mouth."[38] Incredible mouth was Trump's way of expressing admiration for "one of the greatest bullshit artists I've ever met." Irving was the physically unfit but sharp-talking nerd that Trump needed.

Trump's speeches and writing are full of observations that highlight some typical aspect of people's ethnicity, race, religion, or gender. About a hotel manager named Patrick Foley, Trump states: "Pat has one of those great Irish personalities. He'll walk through the Hyatt Regency in Washington, D.C., or West Palm Beach, Florida, and he'll know everyone's name, he'll remember their families, he'll kiss the chef, tell the porter he's doing a great job, say hello to the lifeguard and the maids."[39] In another anecdote, Trump met a "a very smooth, attractive guy, an Italian who looked like a WASP."[40] When speaking to a Jewish Republican group in 2015, Trump appealed to common interests by asserting: "Look, I'm a negotiator like you folks; we're negotiators."[41] For Trump, these stereotypical judgments are signs of street savvy. Observations about bald-headed guys with thick glasses, smooth-talking Irishmen, attractive Italians, and Jewish negotiators are precritical judgments he uses to make quick and effective decisions.

In addition to a valuable management skill, the ability to effectively size up situations made Trump feel safe. For example, when he began to worry that his property in Cincinnati might lose money because of rising crime in the area, his gut feeling told him that trouble was brewing: "Again, it's instincts, not marketing studies. So I spent an extra two days in Cincinnati, and I rode around, and I saw that there was trouble brewing, that neighborhoods were getting rough."[42] Mastering criminological analysis by "riding around," Trump sized up a neighborhood by sight to know it was rough. Trump follows his instincts to keep his investments safe. This instinct also tells Trump that Mexicans are liars and rapists, African Americans are criminals, and Muslims are terrorists. For Trump supporters, to be honest about these threats is to say what everyone knows to be true but are too afraid to state out loud because they are afraid to give offense. One example of this reasoning is Trump's response to a New York prosecutor who sued him in the 1970s for refusing to rent apartments to African Americans. When speaking on the record, Trump called the accusations of discrimination outrageous. But in a private moment of candor, he appealed to the white lawyer's shared common sense about African Americans. As she recounted, Trump stated: "You know, you don't want to live with them either."[43] According to Trump's common sense, the prosecutor could not admit what Trump knew she knew because they were living in a legal and social environment where such sentiments were not publicly acceptable. Prosecutors afraid of telling the truth make New York dangerous. Backing away from offensive speech weakens defenses against threats like crime or terrorism. According to Trumpism, some of the most dangerous people are elite liberals whose education has destroyed their common sense and their competency to recognize threats. Fixing this requires a strong leader who can rescue the country from liberal losers.

I ALONE CAN FIX THIS

In his 2016 convention speech Trump announced that he would tackle a rising crime rate by proclaiming "I alone can fix this." This pronouncement brought together several prominent features of his public presentation: unapologetic self-promotion, playing to his audience's fears, and saying things that are false. His supporters did not care that statistics demonstrated that there was a decades-long decline in the crime rate. Trump's habit of inventing reality created new challenges for American news organizations tasked with figuring out what counted as objective or neutral journalism. During the presidential campaign, journalists trained to represent "both sides" of American political discourse while withholding their own commentary drew criticism for creating false equivalences between the technocratic policy statements of the Hillary Clinton campaign and Trumpian assertions that Obama was born in Africa, or that global warming is a hoax, or that unemployment rates among young African Americas exceeds 50 percent, or that Clinton had been fighting ISIS her entire adult life. In response to an announced press conference on the birther controversy that tricked news organizations into televising what amounted to a half-hour advertisement for the D.C. Trump hotel, a commentator in the *Washington Post* called it a "nothing burger full of falsehoods."[44] Trump himself tweeted a link to this article, titled "Donald Trump's Birther Event Is the Greatest Trick He Ever Pulled." Trump's endorsement of his own trickery indicated that he delighted in his power to get away with fantastic deceptions in plain view. In the face of statements that could be refuted with so little effort, journalistic fact-checking was a romantic, almost pointless exercise. Trump deliberately provoked the know-it-all fact-checkers of the *New York Times* and CNN. The more furious these fact-obsessed liberals became, the more audacious and exciting Trump's speeches felt.[45] Fact-checking Trump merely showed that someone who bragged about tricking you and getting away with it was indeed tricking you and getting away with it.[46] Rather than hurt the Trump brand, the futility of debunking only magnified his winning.

In *The Art of the Deal*, Trump tells stories about making grandiose promises that were at odds with reality in order to get what he needed. In one Atlantic City gambit, for example, he convinced construction workers to do meaningless work as show for a board of directors. Trump instructed the construction manager: "What the bulldozers and dump trucks did wasn't important, I said, so as long as they did a lot of it. If they got some actual work done all the better, but if necessary, he should have bulldozers dig up dirt from one side of the site and dump it on the other."[47] The scheme worked, and Trump bragged about his ability to manage a fake spectacle in order to produce reality. What earnest liberals saw as lying was for Trump the moral equivalent of bluffing in a game of poker. As Trump explained, outrage was a tactic: "I might make an outrageous comment in a meeting just to see whether the other people play along or take a stand and disagree. It's a good way of assessing the mettle of the folks across the table. Do they want to be liked? Are they comfortable with unpredictability? Are they capable of candor?"[48] He did not merely represent reality as it existed in the world; he played with reality in order to win.

Producing a convincing version of reality requires careful attention to people's fears and fantasies. As Trump explained, "I play to people's fantasies. People may not always think big themselves, but they can still get very excited by those who do. That's why a little hyperbole never hurts. People want to believe that something is the biggest and the greatest and the most spectacular. I call it truthful hyperbole. It's an innocent form of exaggeration—and a very effective form of promotion."[49] That Trump made up the phrase "truthful hyperbole" is in all likelihood an example of truthful hyperbole, as it was created by Trump's ghostwriter, Tony Schwartz. But this mattered little once it was branded by Trump. Therefore, there is something to the idea that Trump was the reality show president. The reality show style abandons any pretense that it is not trying to trick you. It allows you to enjoy the spectacle of do-gooder liberals tricked and bested time and again. Public trickery is an increasingly familiar feature of mediated reality. In her comparison between Trump and the moguliest of all reality moguls, Kim Kardashian, Kathryn Lofton notes that the culture of celebrity on reality television often features the "proud exposure of self-deception." As Lofton notes, "We know that you can simultaneously vote for Trump and believe he is an ass. We know, too, that fans can think him a hero simply because everyone else calls him an ass."[50]

Trump also shares with Kardashian a preternatural ability to leverage a personal brand for spectacular wealth. According to political theorist Corey Robin, Trump's success story illustrates the "moral emptiness of the market." Trump did not get rich because of his Puritan work ethic. He made his fortune by making deals in which he got the best of other people, and he is proud of this. As Robin explains, "The secret about Trump is that there is no secret. That is the truth about capitalism that is revealed in *The Art of the Deal*: there is no truth. It's a show about nothing."[51] Trump was not rewarded for working hard and playing by the rules. He conned people. Ironically, this message resonates with those who win as well as lose within capitalist markets. You can like Trump because he will protect your ill-gotten gains or because he is going to get back at the people who screwed you out of your job. The moral lesson is not the economy is fair but that it is unfair. Therefore, you are justified in doing whatever it takes to get ahead.

In addition to taking pleasure in deception, reality television overcomes people's sense of shame by fully exposing their hidden vulnerabilities. When the groundbreaking *Real World* first appeared on MTV in 1992, the introduction promised that the ubiquity of cameras would show what really happens "when people stop being polite and start getting real." Politeness masks reality. With total exposure, reality television promises a release from shame in exchange for the truth. There is a difference, however, between Trump and most reality stars. Arguing against the popular view that Trump was a reality show president, Lucas Mann notes that the *Apprentice* did not expect its host to start getting real. As a judge rather than a participant, Trump did not face the demands for vulnerability and exposure required of reality show contestants. His show placed him in the position of power over other people's vulnerability: "But the emotional crescendo of each episode, which involved offering up intimacy and vulnerability to hook the viewer, was provided by everyone on the show *but* Trump. His boardroom didn't change, the general tone of his dialogue didn't change."[52] Trump was not a contestant but a judge. He was the arbiter of winning and losing but never subject to its judgment. Trump's participation in the television medium was carefully crafted to make him seem powerful. The ever-inquisitive judge, the one who fires but is never fired, was free to act however he willed. Therefore, it came naturally to Trump to boast that he alone had superhero powers to eliminate crime. This was not a tangible policy proposal but a promise to be a strong leader who will do and say whatever it takes to invent a reality to match his supporters' fantasies. According to his former *Apprentice* producer, Mark Burnett, Trump's practice of saying whatever he wants is part of his winning ethos: "Donald will say whatever Donald wants to say. He takes no prisoners. If you're Donald's friend, he'll defend you all day long. If you're not, he's going to kill you. And that's very American. It's like the guys who built the West."[53] Like the guys who built the West, Trump is willing to kill whoever gets in his way. This is not politically correct, but it is an honest appraisal of the ethos of American settler colonialism.

By inventing an affective reality by saying whatever he wants while denouncing the fact-obsessed press as fake news, Trump could declare victory over facts as well as his enemies.[54] One gesture from his reality show days that Trump reenacted on the campaign trail was his habit of cocking his fingers into a gun gesture and announcing: "You're fired." The mix of executive power, decisive action, and implicit violence promised a new style of leadership that would dispatch corrupt politicians. As one analysis of Trump's repertoire of gestures explains, "When Trump uses the pistol hand as a boardroom executive on the Apprentice, it conveys arrogance, sovereign power, and commanding force. Trump is the kind of guy who will never admit his own failures and rarely gives others a second chance."[55] Refusing to admit failure and apologize is a part of Trump's relentless projection of strength. Apologizing for his role in promoting the birther theory, for example, would concede that his critics could be arbiters of reality. This is a characteristic of an authoritarian style of rule that seeks to discredit independent sources of information that could act as a check on power. By never apologizing, he concedes nothing to liberal fact-checkers.

According to Trump's advisers, this lack of humility made the president a more effective leader: "People say that Donald Trump never apologizes. There is some credence to that. In an interview, Frank Luntz once asked the boss if he ever asks God for forgiveness. 'I don't think I do,' Mr. Trump said, 'I just try to do better.'"[56] He never apologizes because he has nothing for which to apologize. Trump is neither apologetic nor weak. He equates contrition and humiliation in a tweet where he demands an apology from the *New York Times*: "I wonder if the New York Times will apologize to me a second time, as they did after the 2016 Election. But this one will have to be a far bigger & better apology. On this one they will have to get down on their knees & beg for forgiveness—they are truly the Enemy of the People!"[57] People who apologize are weaklings who get down on their knees to make a public admission of shame.

According to Representative Steve King, Trump's refusal to back down is a welcome change from the humiliating and effeminate weakness of Democratic leaders who apologize for American greatness: "I have described Donald Trump as 'the man who has mastered everything except humility.' He is good for America. We have had presidents that ran around and apologized. Bill Clinton did a contrition tour around the world, and Barack Obama did a contrition tour around the world, too."[58] Trump's refusal to apologize is most visible when he does not back down from giving offense. In his response to Clinton's critique of his referring to a former Miss Universe contestant as "Miss Piggy," for example, he explained that she had gained a lot of weight and that the label fit.[59] While these incidents hurt him with much of the electorate, sticking to his guns maintained credibility among supporters. He felt no shame, so they did not have to either.

FASCISM

Some critics characterize Trumpism—with its affective style, its unapologetic grandiosity, its violent rallies, its singular focus on a strong leader, and its appeal to romantic racialized nationalism that stoked fears of ethnic, religious, sexual, and racial others—as American fascism.[60] According to philosopher Jason Stanley, fascist regimes remake reality in line with the will of the leader: "A fascist leader can replace truth with power, ultimately lying without consequence. By replacing the world with a person, fascist politics makes us unable to assess arguments by a common standard. The fascist politician possesses specific techniques to destroy information spaces and break down reality."[61] Political analysts also note similarities between Trump's rise and other ethnonationalist, anti-immigrant movements. Trump himself welcomed such connections, anointing himself "Mr. Brexit" and refusing to distance himself from authoritarian leaders in Europe and elsewhere.

Fascist is an appealing label because it is not clear if Trump is correctly defined as a conservative.[62] Conservatism implies some deference to tradition along with a desire to conserve the status quo. As evangelical Trump critic John Fea insists, Trump is nothing like past conservative presidents who understood that the sanctity of the presidency "required them to respect the integrity of the office and the unofficial moral qualifications that come with it. Trump, however, spits in the face of this kind of historical continuity. This isn't conservativism. It is progressivism at its worst."[63] While *progressivism* was a polemical word choice that was hardly an accurate description of Trumpian illiberalism, Fea hoped to show that Trump has no interest in conserving traditional religious or political institutions. Trumpism abandons conservative impulses in favor of breaking rules.[64]

One feature of Trumpism that is different from past conservativism is its confidence in a singular leader exempt from the law. Trump supporters rallied behind a person who acted outside of limits and norms.[65] Rather than emulate Trump, evangelical supporters often defended their support for Trump by citing his exceptional nature. He got a pass from Christian judgment because someone needed to break rules in order to get things done.[66] As William Connolly explains, "One reason that the most ardent Trump supporters demand so little from him with respect to the values they themselves often propagate about marital life, church attendance, clean speech, and respect for the disabled is they are tempted to concur with his demand that the Leader be exempt from the limits ordinary people are called upon to acknowledge."[67] By violating taboos, Trump did extraordinary things necessary in a time where the rules were out of whack.[68] Strong leadership is a liberating alternative to establishment liberalism and conservativism, both of which symbolize the government's simultaneously inept and overreaching bureaucratic apparatus. This is especially true of white evangelical frustrations with establishment conservatism. As Jerry Falwell Jr. tweeted, "Conservatives & Christians need to stop electing 'nice guys.' They might make great Christian leaders but the US needs street fighters like @realDonaldTrump at every level of government b/c the liberal fascists Dems are playing for keeps & many Repub leaders are a bunch of wimps!"[69] Trump's populism challenges this corrupt system.[70] Seeking pure sovereign power unconstrained by democratic governance, Trumpism is suspicious of a decadent government and promises to restore power to an imagined racialized nation.

One problem with liberalism is that it is boring. To live with liberal democratic institutions means to learn to compromise with other people. No one ever really gets what they want. For that matter, liberals never eliminate social problems as much as they ameliorate them. Liberal ideals of freedom and equality always come up short when measured against political reality. As a set of unrealized aspirations, liberalism leaves most people frustrated. According to political theorist Ernesto Laclau, frustration with liberal institutions gives rise to populism on both the right and left:

> Since any kind of system is inevitably at least partially limiting and frustrating, there is something appealing about any figure who challenges it, whatever the reasons for and forms of the challenge. There is in any society a reservoir of raw anti-status-quo feelings which crystallize in some symbols quite independently of the forms of their political mobilization, and it is their presence we intuitively perceive when we call a discourse or a mobilization "populistic."[71]

While fascism does not have the democratic promise of leftist populism, it can tap into frustration with the status quo.

Unlike boring liberalism, fascism is exciting for some and terrifying for others. It promises total victory or total defeat. Neither American liberals nor conservatives have been able to deliver so much winning. In some ways Trump's triumph over establishment Republican conservatives was his most complete victory. Trump did not compromise or find common ground with Mitt Romney, Mitch McConnell, Paul Ryan, or Lindsey

Graham. He dominated them.[72] This exercise of raw power by a strong leader was exhilarating to supporters. The philosopher Alain Badiou suggests that Trumpism is a form of "democratic fascism" typical of European leaders like Silvio Berlusconi, Nicolas Sarkozy, Marine Le Pen, and Viktor Orbán. They gain power from their ability to "say publicly things that are unacceptable to a large portion of humanity today" but still work within the democratic system.[73]

Winning democratic elections while attacking democratic norms rejects the reasoned exchange of ideas in favor of the spectacle of the rally. Trump's rallies allow him to regale like-minded supporters with a litany of insults directed toward enemies. In describing the mixture of hatred and celebration, Jamelle Bouie compares the affect of Trump's rallies to lynch mobs. As Bouie explains, "If Trump has an unbreakable bond with his supporters, it's because he gives them permission to express their sense of siege. His rhetoric frees them from the mores and norms that keep their grievance in check. His rallies—his political carnivals—provide an opportunity to affirm their feelings in a community of like-minded individuals."[74] Liberal calls for civil discourse fall on deaf ears when people are convinced that they face a "state of siege." Trump's promise of winning resonates most deeply with people who feel like they have a lot to lose. But it also means that losing poses an existential threat to Trumpism. Authoritarian movements are structurally unprepared for the possibility of anything less than total victory. The counterpart to the rally, then, is the meltdown. At moments of greatest distress, Trump yells at the media and—before his account was removed from Twitter—angrily tweeted all-caps threats to his many enemies.

A political movement that suspends democratic norms in pursuit of total victory poses significant problems for the belief that free speech furthers democratic discourse. For Trumpism, free speech is a platform for unapologetic and shameless offense. Liberal ideals of free speech, however, call for listening to other people. Attempting to find common ground with people seeking total victory is a paradoxical goal. In an essay arguing against debating illiberalism, Laurie Penny states, "The discussion about whether free speech can stop fascism is not actually about free speech; it's a proxy for a rolling identity crisis among the political mainstream. About whether the mechanisms of state power can withstand fascist takeover. About whether good people with good ideas can stop bad people with worse ones. Which, right now, they cannot."[75]

Even among critics, not everyone agrees that Trumpism is fascist. Some theorists assert that Trumpism lacks the consistent ideology that fascism espouses.[76] Others object to the fascist label on the grounds that looking to European analogs ignores the ongoing presence of white supremacy in the United States. After all, the promise to "make America great again" appeals to a nostalgic American past. White supremacy has often been protected through extralegal tactics like voter suppression and lynching that create states of emergency by suspending democratic institutions. The lament that Trump was not normal and that he promised a novel form of fascism overlooked the normality of his ideas about religion, race, ethnicity, and gender in the longue durée of American history. As Badiou suggests, "Trump is positioned so that, for a moment, he can say that there is something new, namely 'Trump,' the name and the thing, whereas what he is saying, in its particulars, which are nationalistic, sexist, racist, and violently pro-private property, is anything but new."[77] Rather than a novel set of ideas, Trumpism appeals to long-standing American common sense.

Trumpism demonstrates that the faith in a fair set of rules to solve problems is more tenuous than liberals realized. Liberalism requires shared commitments to principles of freedom and equality that are never entirely achieved. Trump made a mockery of these commitments, and his own popularity demonstrates a gap between how liberals imagine their country and what its reality might be. According to Jasbir Puar, the shock of Trump has less to do with the novelty of Trumpism than with the exposure of this reality: "The jolt of Trump is not that he revealed something heretofore unknown, but that he has accelerated and vastly expanded the scale of disregard, extending precarity to, yes, your backyard: it's in your backyard."[78] By bringing illiberalism to your backyard, Trump exposed the limits of treating racism, sexism, homophobia, and Islamophobia as taboo subjects instead of ordinary features of everyday reality. Trumpism demonstrates the limits of liberal hopes that civility itself is a vehicle for diversity, and that liberal ideals of freedom and equality will suffice to address institutional inequalities. Trump's stereotypical reasoning about race, nation, ethnicity, sexuality, and religion are likely consistent with the views of the majority of white Americans for the majority of American history. In profaning liberal pieties to reveal the real sentiments of so many Americans, Trump's illiberal secularism serves as a revelation of American reality. This revelation calls for a self-reckoning among liberals who feel that American politics used to be civil and normal before Trump ruined it with offensive speech. It is one thing to criticize Trump because he hurt people; it is another matter to criticize Trump because he ruined your faith in the United States. Liberals fall into Trump's trap when they lament that he is not normal. Trump wanted to violate taboos in a way that made him exceptional.

It is possible that the people most ashamed of Trump are white liberals. As J. Kameron Carter notes, "Trump renders naked the ongoing solidarity of settler power, the incorporating yet exclusionary 'We' that has always been at the heart of the nation. The exposure of that nakedness has now incited more white melancholy and, at least for some white folks, has caused a certain embarrassment."[79] While white liberals may have been embarrassed by Trump, his supporters were not. The "ongoing solidarity of settler power" was especially visible in Trump's 2020 convention speech, which concluded with a rousing account of how "our ancestors" conquered the American frontier and built a nation. While the speakers of the four days of the Republican convention mimicked liberal inclusion, Trump's concluding historical sketch almost entirely excluded nonwhite people. As Trump narrated, "Americans built their beautiful homesteads on the open range. Soon they had churches and communities, then towns, and with time, great centers of industry and commerce. That is who they were. Americans build the future, we don't tear down the past!"[80] American was great. America was strong. America had a proud history. White settler colonialists won, and Native Americans lost. Recovering that spirit of winning would make America great again. This was a powerful and inspiring message to people who believed that overeducated liberals were ashamed to be American. As Trump supporters saw it, they had a choice between politicians who wanted them to be ashamed about the past and a man who told them to be proud of their great national and racial heritage.

Trump's speech is littered with references to God and Bibles, but these do not refer to a shared sense of reverence as much as they highlight an unapologetic commitment to illiberal exclusion. There is also nothing original about Trump's historical narrative. What is new about Trump is that he is an entirely profane man. This is an unusual trait among human beings. He is the rare person for whom nothing is sacred. For this reason, it does not quite work to call Trump a hypocrite. For him there is no gap between realism and idealism, or between private behavior and public norms. His reality is appearance all the way down. Collapsing reality with media spectacle speaks to people who have lost faith in their public power and instead settle for illiberal secularism. Replacing aspirations for public goods with an invented private reality makes them feel safe. By casting aside norms of civility that consider diverse sensibilities, a profane man who violates taboos promised to replace aspirations to fairness with the will to win.

LOSERS AND SUCKERS

If Trump had been 1 percent more popular in November 2020, he could have eked out another narrow Electoral College victory. He drew little solace, however, from knowing that over 10 million more Americans voted for him in 2020 than in 2016. When winning is everything, there is no consolation in fighting the good fight. Trump's disdain for losing may have hurt his electoral prospects. It did not help when he offended military veterans by disparaging fallen soldiers as "losers" and "suckers."[81] Furthermore, Trump's response to the COVID-19 crisis squandered a possible political opportunity. His first instinct was to play down the pandemic by promising easy victory. As he tweeted: "We are winning, and will win, the war on the invisible enemy."[82] Even after contracting the virus, he continued to minimize the threat. The preference for private freedom over public health led his supporters to attack mask and vaccine mandates. One irony was that public health crises can often bring political benefits. British prime minister Boris Johnson saw his popularity ratings rise after he got sick. Governors in multiple states benefited from a rally-around-the-leader effect. Trump, however, was unable to imagine that shared vulnerability could garner sympathy. Sickness was for losers.

It is not surprising that Trump refused to concede. He worked to manufacture a media narrative that the election was stolen in one last attempt to subject the presidency to the rules of reality television.[83] The resulting January coup was a final profanation of the dignity of the presidency.[84] Former Bush speechwriter Michael Gerson took offense at the insurrectionists' penchant for Christian language. As he lamented, the coup was a "desecration of democracy under the banner 'Jesus Saves.'"[85] Another offensive sign was a picture of an insurrectionist waving the Confederate flag in the U.S. Capitol, invoking an ongoing legacy of American resistance to the federal government. The Confederate flag also seems to be an appropriate symbol for people who feel that they have lost the power to shape American political life. As Jelani Cobb notes, "It was particularly fitting to see Wednesday's rioters bearing both Confederate flags and Trump banners as they stormed the Capitol. Trump is being transformed by his most fervent core of support into an embodiment of the Lost Cause. And at the center of a lost cause is a single difficult and immutably public fact: you lost."[86]

Trump did lose the election like the South lost the Civil War. The Confederacy, however, has never disappeared. The lost cause has remained a potent counternational force in American life. The legacy of the Confederacy has been a ubiquitous presence in defenses of white supremacy, states' rights, the sanctity of the armed private household, and resistance to the regulatory power of liberal democratic institutions. Trump played to people's fantasies that this vision might finally win, but the Capitol riot proved to be a spectacle of insurrection rather than a real plan for replacing the government. While the riot had very real effects on the lives of rioters as well as those who defended the Capitol, it was in no one's self-interest. It was an attack on the state as an end in itself. Rather than Christianize state institutions, the rioters dramatized that a white Christian nation was itself a lost cause. One significant victory for the rioters, however, was that liberal democracy did not really win either. If liberalism's losses were his gains, Trump could reasonably boast that he had fought back and won, big league.

2

STEVE BANNON AND THE
CLASH OF CIVILIZATIONS

Steve Bannon wants you to know that he does not give a shit. The self-styled "honey badger" (a reference to a viral YouTube clip of the animal in various states of doing whatever it wants) prides himself on his unbridled masculine will that acts without regard for your feelings.[1] As the former editor of *Breitbart News*, he presided over a website that offended liberals with headlines like "Why Equality and Diversity Departments Should Only Hire Rich, Straight White Men" and "Political Correctness Protects Muslim Rape Culture."[2] Saying what should not be said helps to make stories on *Breitbart* feel true while repurposing the label "fake news" to discredit mainstream media outlets that do not tell the truth about the threats posed by racial and religious others. Deliberately provocative and conspiratorial rhetoric unsettles any sense of a stable social order and then draws on this climate of instability and fear to call for a retrenchment behind clear national boundaries that protect white, masculinist, and Christian forms of identification. Offending others becomes a staple of right-wing populist rhetoric that rejects liberal ideals of diversity, equity, and inclusion. Pushing back against blurred religious, national, sexual, and racial boundaries, Bannon clarified lines between friend and enemy in preparation for a war in defense of Western Christendom.

In a speech delivered at the Vatican in 2014, he invoked the language of crisis to describe the "beginning stages of a bloody and brutal conflict" between the "church militant" and the forces of the "new barbarity."[3] The new barbarity was a combination of the external threats created by porous national boundaries and internal threats created by a weakened Christian identity. According to Bannon, liberal inclusivity leads to degenerate weakness that undercuts the strength of both American nationalism and Western civilization. A crusade for Christendom might seem like a holy war, a pushback against secularism to recover the religious roots of civilization. I suggest, however, that Bannon's rhetoric is better described as an illiberal secular program to combat secular liberalism. This battle is waged on profane ground.[4]

Bannon's rhetoric stirs up his devoted followers by using an unapologetic incivility to protect civilization. Fighting barbarism requires emergency measures of incivility.[5] While Bannon claims he is advancing the cause of Christendom, it is not clear that he has an evangelical desire to convert others. Illiberal secularism makes no attempt at inclusion. Rather, his insults shore up existing identities. Conservative media outlets do not give offense in order to convey uncomfortable truths to people likely to change their minds. Instead, sites like Breitbart warn an audience of like-minded people about barbarians at the gates.[6] This mediated clash of civilizations has had significant implications for the imagination of truth. Allying himself with the church militant did not mean that Bannon cared about doctrinal orthodoxy. Rather, telling the truth warned of the threats posed by enemies. If defending Christian civilization protected Christian persons rather than Christian truth, liberal ideals of religious inclusion could only weaken these defenses.[7] As Bannon's Christian civilization had no moral or theological content, its defense brought together a motley crew of self-identified religious and irreligious actors united by an illiberal secular opposition to the enemy.

Disagreements over the truth have not been limited to warnings against threats from others. Bannon's weaponization of politically incorrect truth-telling has revealed a more fundamental conflict about the rules governing political discussion.[8] In particular, sites like Breitbart have challenged the norms and rules that adjudicate truth claims in conventional media as well as academic disciplines. When conservatives have denounced "liberal media," they have asserted that the aspiration to objectivity is merely an ideological cover for undisclosed political biases. In Nicole Hemmer's account of the development of conservative media, activists she calls "populist elites" have long worked to undermine American confidence in mainstream media by mocking the ideal of objectivity as a marker of elitist pretension. As Hemmer explains, "Media activists weren't suggesting there existed a world of objective media that they rejected and a world of ideological media that they promoted. They were arguing there was no such thing as nonideological media, that objectivity was a mask mainstream media used to hide their own ideological projects."[9] Mainstream media organizations like the *New York Times* or the *Washington Post* base their reputation for integrity upon voluntary self-policing and a shared commitment to editorial rules. The brazen and shameless quality of illiberal media challenges this authority and then uses a different set of rules for assessing truth claims. Under Bannon's rules, the truth was a prize in a contest between friends against enemies. Within these contests, the most offensive statements were those that felt true because they were bravely willing to confront the enemy in a clash of civilizations. The question, then, was what sort of truth won a civilizational war.

POST-TRUTH

The headlines of right-wing news sites make clear that the world is in crisis. According to the political theorist William Connolly, fomenting outrage is a form of "shock politics." Shock politics works through disorientation. It feeds off the fear and insecurity of people unsure of what to believe in a world that is out of order. As he explains, "The idea here is to cauterize public outrage by allowing 'neutral parties' to now say that 'both sides' claim the same thing. The Big Lie as a strategy of public confusion and acceptance of authoritarian rule, linked to shock wave strategies of introducing new confusion."[10] In a world rocked by shock politics, truth is a power struggle. This has paved the way for an authoritarian leader who promised to win the struggle and repair the boundaries weakened by feckless democratic institutions. Decisive action could fix uncertain politics. In his account of the early days of the Trump presidency, journalist Michael Wolff suggests that Bannon had a kind of moral conviction that aligned shocking speech with bold action: "Bannon's strategic view of government was shock and awe. Dominate rather than negotiate. Having daydreamed his way into ultimate bureaucratic power, he did not want to see himself as a bureaucrat. He was of a higher purpose and moral order. He was an avenger. He was also, he believed, a straight shooter. There was a moral order in aligning language and action—if you said you were going to do something, you do it."[11]

Shock politics sorts through a complex and messy world by assigning clear identities to sources of confusion. Rather than the result of impersonal social forces, chaos comes from the malicious actions of bad people. This rhetoric offers both a clear explanation and a target for outrage.[12] As verbal competition, shock politics thrives when political debate is reduced to winning and losing. To many commentators confronting the rise of Trumpism, the waning of truth in favor of outrage is a sign of the times. Oxford dictionaries announced that the word of the year for 2016 was *post-truth*, which it defines as "relating to or denoting circumstances in which objective facts are less influential in shaping public opinion than appeals to emotion and personal belief."[13] Post-truth is an updated version of the neologism *truthiness*, coined by comedian Stephen Colbert to describe a "truth that comes from the gut, not books."[14] Some critics blame academic postmodernism for the rise in fact skepticism.[15] Postmodern analysis of the social construction of knowledge has convinced people that nothing is real and the truth is whatever they believe. This line of attack is an ironic improvement over the more familiar lament that postmodern philosophy is so obscure that no one can understand it. In the post-truth dispensation, French critical theorists had become so publicly influential that they elected the American president. As the pre-postmodern philosopher Daniel Dennett complained, "Maybe people will now begin to realise that philosophers aren't quite so innocuous after all. Sometimes, views can have terrifying consequences that might actually come true. I think what the postmodernists did was truly evil. They are responsible for the intellectual fad that made it respectable to be cynical about truth and facts."[16] Dennett's evaluation would seem to be perfectly realized when Trump adviser Kellyanne Conway cited "alternative facts" to argue that Trump's inauguration crowd was the biggest in history. As a skilled practitioner of the postmodern arts, Conway asserted that limiting discourse to one set of facts failed to tolerate alternative points of view.

The modifier "post" in post-truth, however, suggests that once upon a time people were convinced by objective facts rather than "appeals to emotion and personal belief" without specifying exactly when this was. The nostalgia for a time when truth was truth ignores the long-standing liberal suspicion of populist appeals to emotion.[17] For that matter, there is little evidence that people in the post-truth era have stopped caring about truth and facts. As one essay on fake news notes, "Such a loss of any anchoring 'reality' only makes us pine for it more. Our politics have been inverted along with everything else, suffused with a Gnostic sense that we're being scammed and defrauded and lied to but that a 'real truth' still lurks somewhere."[18] There are no bigger fans of facts than conservative media consumers, especially those who yearn for common sense. The post-truth world does not devalue facts; it places a fervent faith in facts understood as self-contained, self-evident pieces of information that lie outside of social contexts or human interpretation. Sites like Breitbart exist in an internet ecosphere in which conspiracy theorists and alt-right activists assert that they violate politically correct norms precisely because of their superior grasp of facts, logic, and reason.[19] As Aisling McCrea points out, there is often a gendered quality to this masculine willingness to fight for the truth. As she explains, "Specifically, these guys—and they are usually guys—love using terms like 'logic.' They will tell you, over and over, how they love to use logic, and how the people they follow online also use logic. They are also massive fans of declaring that they have 'facts,' that their analysis is 'unbiased,' that they only use 'reason' and 'logic' and not 'emotions' to make decisions."[20] The honey badgers of the world do not give a shit about how you feel because they do give a shit about facts. Their unflinching defense of reason makes them instinctively averse to what they see as the soft, feminine feelings that constrain politically correct speech. For logical men bravely willing to offend others by telling the truth, words like *facts, logic, reason,* and *rationality* are "thrown wherever possible at their 'emotional' and 'irrational' enemies: feminists, Marxists, liberals, SJWs [social justice warriors], and *definitely* the feminist Marxist liberal SJWs. You could call these men's way of viewing the world in simple 'me smart, you dumb' dichotomies Manichean, or even Derridean, if you really want to upset them by referencing a philosopher that they've heard is very bad."[21] As staunch opponents of Marxist critical theory, the denizens of post-truth media are more likely to be fans of Dennett than of French postmodernists.[22] Indeed, Dennett seems to be perfectly attuned to the style of guys who love logic when he decries the limits that radical feminism places on academic inquiry and free thinking. In his sarcastic evaluation, "Only women are qualified to do research on women (according to some radical feminists), because only they can overcome the *phallocentrism* that renders males obtuse and biased in ways they can never acknowledge and counteract."[23] According to Dennett, serious philosophers equipped with logic and facts needed to combat postmodern theories espoused by threatening women. While Dennett despises Bannon's politics, he does share the view that political correctness constrains the free exchange of ideas.

UNMASKED

Bannon's initial public forays into truth-telling and giving offense were in film. He got involved in the media business through his work at Goldman Sachs and eventually came to write, direct, and produce several documentaries. His cinematic oeuvre was shock politics perfected. As one critic who binge-watched all of Bannon's documentaries summarized, "If I learned one thing during this all-out assault on the senses, it was that the arc of the moral universe may be long, but it bends toward the guillotine.

Western Civilization as we know it is under attack by forces that are demonic or foreign—the difference between those is blurry—and people in far-distant power centers are looking to screw you."[24] Images of chaos abound in Bannon's films. Economic and political commentary is prefaced by ominous clouds, animals tearing each other apart, and angry mobs of shouting liberals.

The organizing theme of Bannon's 2011 documentary *The Undefeated* is that nothing makes Washington and Hollywood elites happier than banding together to screw over a good Christian mother.[25] The film begins with a montage of media figures who mock the intelligence and appearance of Sarah Palin. The Alaska governor was a small-town hockey mom who combined economic populism with a defense of Christian values to fight for the people against corrupt oil executives. According to the film, Palin posed an existential threat to the establishment of both the Republican and Democratic parties. Therefore, she faced ruthless opposition from economic elites in Alaska, cultural elites in Hollywood, and political elites in Washington. The title of the film suggests that while her vice presidential campaign did not lead to victory, her work for the Tea Party movement would win in the end.

The Undefeated was not entirely sure what to do with a strong woman as a protagonist. One function of the withering insults was that they feminized Palin as a mom as well as a victim, but the film does not suggest that the proper response to these assaults is to change gender norms to empower women. Rather, the attacks symbolize a crisis of masculinity. The film ends with Andrew Breitbart expressing his outrage at the inability of men to defend a woman's honor and repeatedly stating "I see eunuchs."[26] Men's failure to fight in defense of a Christian mother marks a loss of chivalry that is symptomatic of a civilization in decline.[27]

Civilization under attack is a central theme in the 2012 film *Occupy Unmasked*. Narrated by Breitbart shortly before his death, the film depicts a battle for the "soul" of America. Before moving to the Occupy Wall Street protests in New York's Zuccotti Park, the film begins with clips of legislators and news commentators discussing whether to raise the federal debt ceiling. Calls for fiscal discipline become old news, however, when leftist organizers change the conversation to the responsibility of government to help people. When the government gets involved, disciplined restraint gives way to undisciplined indulgence. According to the film, there were two especially scandalous features of Occupy Wall Street. First, it was organized. Second, it was fun. On the first point, the film argues that rather than a spontaneous movement, the protests were carefully coordinated by organized labor, media outlets, and the hacker group Anonymous. Ironically, the purpose of this organization was to create disorganization. As explained by ex-leftist David Horowitz, the political left was engaged in a century-long pursuit of "structured chaos." Visual chaos structured the film as images of Occupy protests across the United States were interspersed with clips from Vietnam, Hurricane Katrina, Fidel Castro, Code Pink, Black Panthers, Bill Ayers, Joseph Stalin, Saul Alinsky disciples Hillary Clinton and Barack Obama, ecoterrorism, and more. Horowitz warned that the left only pretended to be interested in issues in order to conceal its central goal: to destroy America.

Young protesters were largely unaware of this organized plot to murder America because they were busy having fun. The activists in the Occupy Wall Street movement were privileged economic parasites who lacked the manners of civilized people.[28] Breitbart asked protesters: "Capitalism: Thumbs up or thumbs down?" and suggested that the young people who gave the thumbs down were in reality the beneficiaries of trust funds.

Rather than reinvest their resources, however, the protesters engaged in a bacchanal of what Breitbart described as "raping, pillaging, and pooping." In some ways, the film pushed the definitional limits of the word *documentary*. Unlike most documentaries, *Occupy Unmasked* did not attempt to make its subject matter intelligible. One critic described the film as "a deranged hodgepodge of bizarre memes, wild dot-connecting, and unadulterated fury."[29] As a sustained warning against threats accompanied by menacing images of impending doom, the film had far more in common with propaganda.

The overtly political quality of Bannon's films might suggest a comparison to the agitprop work of Michael Moore. Moore appeared in *Occupy Unmasked* as an example of a Hollywood elite who profits from the frustrations of young people. The film juxtaposes images of Moore's luxurious vacation home with his calls for class warfare. The contrast with Moore is instructive in ways that Bannon did not intend, however. While Moore's documentaries have political agendas, the antagonists in his stories, whether corporations or lobbyists, are motivated by rational interests like money and power. The activists in Operation Wall Street, however, are bestial creatures who lack basic decency and hygiene. While Moore is able to take perverse pleasure in stunts that shame corporate bad guys confronted by their misdeeds, Breitbart is reduced to angry shouting matches with young people. The Occupy activists had no discernible motivation apart from their irrational desire to take down capitalism and were therefore immune to reason.

Another difference was that Moore personalized human suffering at the hand of impersonal institutions to build sympathy with his protagonists' stories. *Occupy Unmasked* could have taken this approach. One narrative path not taken would have been to affirm the economic populism of the young activists but to lament their cultural politics gone awry.[30] One reason why the indecency of the Occupy activists was such a preoccupation for Bannon is that cultural politics are the basis for his economics. This is evident in his 2011 documentary *Generation Zero*, which offers a metahistorical account of the 2008 financial crisis.[31] At times the film echoes the Occupy Wall Street movement. The commentary repeatedly states that the crisis was created by a corrupt system epitomized by the slogan "Socialism for the rich, and capitalism for the poor." In the film's analysis, however, the problem is not structural inequalities created by capitalism but the moral failure of human beings. Capitalism for the poor is fine. Socialism for the rich is the problem.

Generation Zero finds the roots of elite socialism in the timeless story of kids who fail to respect their elders. Kids today are coddled, except that in this narrative the sheltered narcissists are baby boomers instead of millennials in Zuccotti Park. The experience of the Great Depression and World War II forged a generation with a tragic view of the world that taught the importance of hard work and self-sacrifice. Ironically, the desire of the Greatest Generation to provide for their children produced the spoiled and entitled cohort that partied at Woodstock.[32] The film's generational analysis teaches that the world advances through cycles of generation, degeneration, crisis, and regeneration.[33] By wasting precious spiritual energy necessary to make society work, hedonistic expenditure leads to social decay. This in turn creates a crisis that requires a regeneration of civilization.

When the baby boomers' selfish, wasteful, and imprudent economic policies bankrupted the economy, boomers were supposed to learn the hard lessons of poverty. Instead of letting financial institutions fail and teaching the lessons of moral hazard, however, the government bailed out reckless corporations. Like a coddling parent, the government protected citizens from developing the ability to suffer that they need to face a harsh world. *Generation Zero* repeatedly asserts that this inability to hand down moral lessons is a failure to sustain civilization. A generation that did not learn civilized habits of restraint and self-sacrifice created a wasteful form of capitalism that led to economic and cultural failure. According to American religious historian Michael Graziano, Bannon's version of populist critique is not a rejection of capitalist inequality but a search for a properly organized system that makes use of the "spiritual resources" of capitalism. These resources are essential to protect against economic, military, and religious threats. The pervasive sense of threat constructs a common enemy that runs together establishment elites, spoiled millennials, immigrants, refugees, and Muslim terrorists. As Graziano explains, "In this view, the populist revolt against establishment figures (whether Republican or Democrat) is because these leaders have so poorly managed the spiritual resources of capitalism. As a result, Americans have been left economically and militarily defenseless against 'jihadist Islamic fascism.'"[34] According to Bannon, the spiritual resources of capitalism have to be reinvested in the sacred cause of defending civilization. Instead, these resources have been wasted by irreverent, hedonistic elites. A civilization in crisis requires shocking speech and decisive action to take back the culture from these elitist enemies and to reinvigorate its defenses against violent others.

Protecting spiritual resources is one response to the ambivalence about capitalism in populist protests against economic or cultural instability. Bannon's populism makes no distinction between economy and culture as discreet spheres of social life. Rather than see market forces as abstractions governed by numbers, Bannon views economic life as dependent on the private moral habits of people. The freedom of capitalism requires bodies restrained by family, religion, nation, and civilization.[35] As political theorist Wendy Brown explains, "Enthusiasm for the market is typically animated by its promise of innovation, freedom, novelty, and wealth, while a politics centered in family, religion, and patriotism is authorized by tradition, authority, and restraint. The former innovates and disrupts; the latter secures and sustains."[36] For Bannon, the freedom sought by Occupy Wall Street activists was exactly backward because they wanted to restrain markets while liberating bodies from tradition, authority, and restraint. Defending the spiritual resources of capitalism is consistent with an illiberal secularist view of the liberal state as spiritually impoverished. Populists on the left had hoped to empower democratic institutions to fight for the people against corporations. Populists on the right, however, did not share the left's embrace of people in countries transformed by immigration and global markets. Bannon wanted to return power to the people, but only a civilized people identified by family, religion, and patriotism. While Bannon was an ardent capitalist, he had nationalist commitments that meant that he did not entirely share the faith in global markets espoused by his former colleagues at Goldman Sachs. Bannon's populist view of the marketplace emphasized economic nationalism along with an illiberal hostility to the state.

CLASH OF CIVILIZATIONS

According to Bannon, then, economic crisis, civilizational crisis, and national crisis are part of the same story. Civilization is threatened by global markets that cause both economic and cultural displacement. Therefore, globalist elites are insidious enemies of civilization. Unlike working class Americans or

Europeans, globalists benefit from global flows of labor and capital. In Bannon's mind, this creates an alliance between elite globalists (who benefit from immigration for economic reasons) and ethnic and religious minorities (who benefit from multicultural attempts to redefine citizenship in a way that erodes Western civilization).[37]

The globalist threat requires emergency measures of incivility that challenge the values of inclusion and sensitivity to others. This would seem to run counter to the idea that the civilizing process inculcates habits of polite restraint. According to the classical social theorist Norbert Elias, for example, to be civilized is to be able to contain bodily desires in a way that would be the antithesis of a honey badger's unrestrained incivility. Civilized people give a shit about what others think. To be civilized is to have a well-developed capacity for shame. Bannon is not civil in this sense because his defense of civilization rejects globalist prohibitions against insulting the culture and religion of others. Indeed, the purpose of civilizational war is to affirm the cultural, economic, religious, and scientific accomplishments that make Western civilization superior to the rest of the world. This sense of superiority conforms to Elias's observation that civilization "sums up everything in which Western society of the last two or three centuries believes itself superior to earlier societies of 'more primitive' contemporary ones. By this term Western society seeks to describe what constitutes its special character and what it is proud of: the level of *its* technology, the nature of *its* manners, the development of *its* scientific knowledge or view of the world, and much more."[38] Civilization is an imaginary project that defines civilized people over and against what they are not. For this reason, historian of religion Charles Long argues that the concept of Western civilization is itself a modern, colonial invention. The self-identification of

Europe as civilized developed in tandem with the colonial projects to govern the "primitive." As Long explains, "The self-conscious realization of the Western European rise to the level of civilization must be seen simultaneously in its relationship to the discovery of a new world which must necessarily be perceived as inhabited by savages and primitives who constitute the lowest rung on the ladder of cultural reality."[39] Defenses of civilization make sense only in relation to the need to defend against an uncivilized other.

In its opposition to globalism and its advocacy for an America-first policy, Bannon's defense of Western civilization is part of a movement that is both nationalist and transnational at the same time. The United States and European nation-states have a collective interest in protecting their own interests. As Bannon told an audience composed of members of the French National Front, "What I've learned is that you're part of a worldwide movement, that is bigger than France, bigger than Italy, bigger than Hungary—bigger than all of it. And history is on our side."[40] Bannon conflated the defense of civilization with the need to strengthen national sovereignty. About European populist movements, he explained: "They believe their countries will be looked at as administrative units. They don't want to be South Carolina and North Carolina. They want to be Hungary, the Czech Republic, and Austria."[41] This rhetoric unapologetically advanced nationalism for nationalism's sake, sometimes at the expense of coherently articulated economic or political positions.[42]

Rather than coherent economic interests, the most consistent point of agreement among the populist movements that Bannon championed is that sovereignty is threatened by porous borders. Bannon's anti-immigrant views are evident in the Trump administration's proposal for a blanket travel ban from a number of countries with Muslim majorities. Pleading for President Trump to call a state of emergency to address the crisis at the border, longtime nativist Patrick Buchanan identified a common peril facing the Western world and the nation-state: "The whole Western world is worried about its borders as issues of immigration and identity convulse every country. . . . America's southern border is eventually going to be militarized and defended or the United States, as we have known it, is going to cease to exist."[43] Buchanan contends that within the United States, increasing immigration is a strategy of Democrats engaged in a zero-sum demographic game based on their own calculus of friends and enemies. According to theories about the imminent threat of a "Great Replacement," diversity is less a principle of inclusion than an attempt to stack the electoral deck against white men.[44] As Buchanan argues, "The Democratic Party is hostile to white men, because the smaller the share of the U.S. population that white men become, the sooner that Democrats inherit the national estate. The only way to greater 'diversify,' the golden calf of the Democratic Party, is to increase the number of women, African-Americans, Asians and Hispanics, and thereby decrease the number of white men."[45] By identifying diversity as a "golden calf," Buchanan paints liberal efforts at inclusion as a form of idolatry, a profanation of the American nation.

Sociologist Rogers Brubaker has labeled this movement "civilizationalism." As he argues, "This partial shift from nationalism to what I will call 'civilizationalism' has been driven by a striking convergence in the last fifteen years around the notion of a civilizational threat from Islam. The preoccupation with Islam has given rise to an identitarian 'Christianism,' a secularist posture, a philosemitic stance, and an ostensibly liberal defence of gender equality, gay rights, and freedom of speech."[46] Brubaker is describing European movements, and one might object that the American variant is hardly philosemitic or that it supports gender equality and gay rights.[47] Conservative activists do, however, like to score points against an imagined Muslim world that supposedly restricts religious and sexual freedom.[48] The cast of characters in the Breitbart world might not themselves give a shit about the religious and sexual rules that preoccupy many white evangelicals, but they see the need to bond together against common enemies.[49] Illiberal secularism unifies a group whose only shared purpose is to take down secular liberalism.

The vogue for civilizations means that, rather than any postmodernist, the most influential academic of the post-truth era might have been a dead Harvard professor named Samuel Huntington.[50] Huntington was the rare professor who exerted the kind of public influence that Dennett attributes to postmodernists. In the wake of the collapse of the Soviet Union, Huntington warned that the waning of a bipolar world split between capitalism and communism would release new forms of civilizational identity. This thesis is the subject of a widely cited 1992 essay titled "A Clash of Civilizations?"[51] In the wake of the September 11 attacks, the book based upon this article became a bestseller as it prophesied an inevitable clash between Islam and the West. Huntington's argument drew vociferous criticism from academics. According to literary critic Edward Said, civilizations are irresponsibly broad and simplistic explanations of complex social and historical forces: "The personification of enormous entities called 'the West' and 'Islam' is recklessly affirmed, as if hugely complicated matters like identity and culture existed in a cartoonlike world where Popeye and Bluto bash each other mercilessly, with one always more virtuous pugilist getting the upper hand over his adversary."[52]

While Said's critiques resonate in academia, the breadth and simplicity of Huntington's theory make it attractive to wider audiences. Indeed, the point of thinking in terms of civilizations is to imagine culture and history from the broadest perspective possible. According to Huntington, "A civilization is . . . the highest cultural grouping of people and the broadest level of cultural identity people have short of that which distinguishes humans from other species. It is defined both by common objective elements, such as language, history, religion, customs, institutions, and by the subjective self-identification of people."[53] As thinking in terms of civilizations makes sweeping claims about human history, concepts like civilizations are attractive to people looking for a grand theory that explains everything. Huntington also provides a ready explanation of conflict that follows a friend and enemy distinction. As he explains, "Civilizations are the biggest 'we' within which we feel culturally at home as distinguished from all of the other 'thems' out there."[54]

Something so grand and encompassing would seem to be resilient. However, Huntington insists that civilizations face both internal and external challenges. The internal challenges stem from a failure to maintain the cultural and political institutions of civilization while the external challenges come from migration and violence. For this reason, Huntington argues that Westerners need to protect their own cultural resources: "The survival of the West depends upon Americans reaffirming their Western identity and Westerners accepting their civilization as unique and not universal and uniting to renew and preserve it against challenges from non-Western societies. Avoidance of a global war of civilizations depends on world leaders accepting and cooperating to maintain the multicivilizational character of global politics."[55] One important qualification is that Huntington does not call for Western civilization to take over the world. He argues that one problem with Western liberalism is its pretense to universalism. Instead of recognizing that ideals like human rights and individual freedom are distinctly Western, liberals believe that they are universal goods that can be exported to the rest of the world. Huntington's defense of the West anticipates the Bannonist branding of "globalist" as an insult. In an ironic convergence of relativism and ethnocentrism, it is imperative that the West recognize its own provincialism if it can survive in a multicivilizational globe. By asserting that Western civilization is not universal, Huntington could call for Westerners to recover their civilizational roots.

It is unclear whether Huntington's ideas are themselves the basis for Bannon's view of a clash of civilizations.[56] One significant point of convergence is that Huntington and Bannon are both people who liked to think big.[57] The broad scope of civilizations portrays the battle between the Christian West and Islam as a constant theme in the *longue durée* of European history.[58] The big picture of the West produces an eclectic set of grand historical narratives at odds with the careful historical and political analysis practiced by professional scholars.[59] For example, few academic historians would endorse the sweeping claims made by Iowa representative and unabashed white nationalist Steven King when he told a Polish audience: "You have two major heroes. King Jan Sobieski; whose cavalry and with the armies of three German Kings, turned back the Muslim hordes, and Saint John Paul II; who teamed with Margaret Thatcher and Ronald Reagan to turn back the Communists of the Soviet Union. Yes, we have common heroes as well, that tie together our modern Western Civilization."[60] Couched within King's sweeping history is an illiberal idea of personhood that pervades civilizationalism. Rather than celebrate the rights of autonomous individuals, arguments like King's unapologetically cite ancestry in their defense of strong borders. Supporters of Trump's anti-immigration policies, for example, often answered charges of hypocrisy about their own immigrant roots by asserting that their ancestors "immigrated legally."[61] According to this logic, white Americans justly inherited the privileges and protections entitled to them by their bloodline. These privileges should be enjoyed regardless of individual merit or achievement.

King's comments are typical of an autodidactic style found among a cohort of anti-academic intellectuals who have found a home on the internet. As Joshua Green notes, Bannon prided himself on self-directed, systematic studies of everything: "While he was still in the Navy, Bannon, a voracious autodidact, embarked upon what he described as 'a systematic study of the world's religions' that he carried on for more than a decade. Taking up the Roman Catholic history first instilled in him at Benedictine, his Catholic military high school, he moved on to Christian mysticism and from there to Eastern metaphysics."[62] In its appeal to some essential core principle that tied together culture, history, and language across vast expanses of time and space, civilizations had a mystical logic. It is not surprising, then, that Bannon took the sort of interest in world religions that led him to the mystical psychology of Carl Jung.[63] Trump's advisers cite Bannon when they discuss the president's purported facility with Jungian archetypes. As they explain, "Donald Trump has more than a fundamental grasp on a surprising number of fields, including Jungian psychology. One of his favorite books is *Memory, Dreams, Reflections*, Jung's autobiography. Steve Bannon insists that Trump came up with the idea for the names Lyin' Ted, Little Marco, Low-Energy Jeb, and, later, Crooked Hillary, from his knowledge of Jungian archetypes."[64] It is unclear exactly how much of Jung's elliptical prose the president has read, but grand theorizing about the human condition fit with Bannon's own intellectual persona.[65]

The contrast between Bannonism and academic history reflects an underlying disagreement about what scholars do. To learn a discipline is to follow rules. Academic disciplines prescribe painstaking methods for gathering and evaluating evidence, and they tend to foster suspicion of sweeping generalizations. This is why it is not quite right to blame postmodernism for the post-truth era. Unlike post-truth, various academic posts—whether postmodern, post-structural, or postcolonial—consider the epistemic conditions under which knowledge is produced. Furthermore, the "post" disciplines are self-critical projects that provide little ammunition for battle against enemies. Forever complicating and problematizing, postmodern theorists subject truth claims to critical scrutiny. They eschew grand, universal claims about the human condition in favor of placing knowledge within historical and social contexts. Civilizational thinking says nonsense to all of that. According to Bannon, the philosophy, political science, and history produced within academic disciplines is constrained by liberal groupthink that refuses to offend threatening others. With an autodidactic training in great books, Bannon could sweep aside so-called experts as globalist elites. He does not challenge facts as much as he questions the authority of people who see it as their job to interpret facts. As Stanley Fish points out, historical claims hold up if they pass the vetting process of the historical profession. These academic processes still exist, but they are unenforceable in public discourse. The condition of post-truth then, is one in which there is no stable ground upon which everyone stands. As he explains, "A post-truth world does not lack standards; it just lacks standards that can be securely traced back to deity or a universal principle or a brute material reality."[66] Truth in a profane age is plagued by a proliferation of facts immune to the criticism of experts who have been stripped of their halos.

As Ethan Kleinberg argues, the counter-academic intellectuals of the post-truth era are appealing because they promise a form of certainty ruled out of bounds by the academic post disciplines. As he explained, "Revisionists, negationists, climate-change deniers, anti-vaxxers, white nationalists, and authoritarians are not and do not want to be considered postmodernists, constructionists, or deconstructionists. They want to be considered 'realists.'"[67] Shock politics tells the truth that waffling liberals refuse to acknowledge. Civilization, then, is an antihistorical concept that is perfect for a post-truth mindset. The idea of Western civilization evacuates the complexities and nuances of ordinary European or North American history and replaces it with a sacred institution that requires protection.

Civilization, then, is an imaginary project that retrospectively produces boundaries that then appear to be under threat. Without the threat of profanation from transgressed boundaries, there is no civilization to protect. According to Sara Ahmed, anxieties about borders are the product of an "affective economy" that uses emotions like shock and fear to produce the sensation of invasion by others. This affective work produces a civilization that feels true. As she explains, "Through designating something as already under threat in the present, that very thing becomes installed as 'the truth,' which we must fight for in the future, a fight that is retrospectively understood to be a matter of life and death."[68] The retrospective quality of civilization is fostered by a sweeping ahistorical history that produces identity through imagined attachments like lineage and ancestry rather than explaining events within complex historical contexts.

A TALE OF TWO CONFERENCES

The bothsidesism of shock politics exposes a tension between an ideal that civil speech produces the truth and a celebration of speech that wins contests and scores points.[69] When the defense of civilization is an existential battle between friend and enemy, political actors reject polite consideration of diverse points of view in order to do whatever it takes to defeat their opponents. This combative style challenges the liberal precept that truth is the result of debate and deliberation among rational actors. Bannon puts liberals in a double bind when he calls on them to honor their own principles of tolerance and civility, and his invocation of civil discourse plays a prominent role in discussions over whether to engage figures like him in debate. On one hand, refusing to debate Bannon betrays liberal principles of inclusion. On the other hand, agreeing to debate Bannon betrays liberal principles of reason. The latter concern informs a leftist critique of liberalism. As Kate Maltby opines, "Perhaps it illustrates the problem of inviting the likes of Bannon to your event. For better or worse, only the nonconformists are prepared to share a billing. But in the raging culture war between the over-offended left and the out-and-out racist right, our guardians of free speech would do a better job of defending the right to offend if they didn't quite so obviously revel in exercising it."[70]

The debate about debate came to a head in 2018 when the *New Yorker* magazine canceled a scheduled interview with Bannon in its "New Yorker Festival" after a number of scheduled speakers backed out of the event (a move that Bannon described as "gutless"). Across the pond, the classically liberal *Economist* magazine stuck to its guns and kept Bannon in the program for its Open Future Festival. Laurie Penny, one invited participant to the *Economist* conference who refused to share billing with

Bannon, questioned the wisdom of debating a man who had elevated winning to its own ideological end. As Penny explains,

> Bannon is that rare thing: a true Gordon Gekko in the attention economy, a man who is both troll and true believer, a man whose lack of integrity is part of the ideology: win at all costs and screw the other guy, because fools and their morals are easily parted. There is no deeper truth to be divined from "holding him to account," no point at which his racism and xenophobia will somehow become unacceptable to a public that has already bought its penny stocks in neo-nationalism.[71]

According to Penny, liberal principles of free speech are naive in the face of a movement that refuses to play by any rules for evaluating truth claims. From this perspective, taking Bannon seriously is the political equivalent of debating challenges to scientific authority advanced by global warming deniers or advocates for intelligent design. Rather than advance scientific inquiry by considering diverse ideas, these debates make everyone stupider.

Nesrine Malik suggests that, rather than vex liberal defenders of free speech, debating Bannon fulfills what she calls liberal narcissism. Inviting Bannon allows liberals to have a civil debate that, in their view, exposes racism. According to Malik, however, doing so in a polite salon environment produces a veneer of civility that normalizes Bannon's racist views. As she argues, "Just as Bannon baits liberal media for his own propaganda purposes, so liberals benefit from engaging with him because he is really quite an easy person to engage. . . . They can come away from a polite joust with him having challenged racism and also having stood up to the horde by protecting freedom of speech. To use a favourite phrase of Bannon himself, interviewing him is a perverse form of virtue signaling."[72] The image of a polite, witty, and civil salon pervades critiques of the decision to debate Bannon. Aleksandar Hemon conjures images of a cosmopolitan environment in which "Bannon would be mingling with edgy hedge-fund managers, high-end literati and risqué fashion photographers, where all differences in opinion would be temporarily subsumed in celebrity solidarity and washed away with champagne."[73] There is something profane about a civil discussion that debates people's humanity.

Assessments like Penny's, Malik's, and Hemon's raise the question of whether contemporary liberalism itself faces a state of emergency that requires a suspension of its own rules and forms of governance. While Bannon's supporters and critics have different political aims, one ironic point of convergence is that both groups are convinced that liberal norms of tolerance, inclusion, and civility are too weak in the face of crisis. Proposals to return to an imagined pre-post-truth appear to have a naive faith in the power of reason in an age where people will say anything to win. Acknowledging this state of war, critics of liberalism from the left argue that the friend and enemy distinction is an unavoidable feature of a fight against fascism. In this view, fascists cannot be debated. They must be punched. Leftist responses to the honey badger pose the question of whether civility and the truth can survive the violence latent in a prophesied clash of civilizations.

3

CARTOONS AND GUNS

After gunmen killed twelve people in the offices of the French satirical magazine *Charlie Hebdo* in January 2015, outraged citizens around the world demonstrated solidarity with the victims by tweeting the hashtag #JeSuisCharlie. Initially circulated by the French art director Joachim Roncin, the slogan expressed support through identification.[1] To be Charlie was to make a defiant statement that went beyond a commitment to abstract legal principles of free speech. Proclamations of support for murdered cartoonists took sides in an imagined global conflict between freedom and submission. Not just protests against murder, defenses of *Charlie Hebdo* affirmed free speech as a civic value.

A dissenting minority expressed reservations about identifying with a publication known for racist and Islamophobic images. These critics adopted the counter hashtag #JeNeSuisPasCharlie. *Charlie Hebdo*'s supporters lamented that the critics failed to understand satire. The cartoons were not drawn by people who were themselves racists or Islamophobes but by satirists making fun of French nationalist bigotry. As Olivier Tonneau explains in a letter to the anglophone world: "It is only by reading or seeing it out of context that some cartoons appear as racist or

Islamophobic. *Charlie Hebdo* also continuously denounced the [plight] of minorities and campaigned relentlessly for all illegal immigrants to be given permanent right of stay. I hope this helps you understand that if you belong to the radical left, you have lost precious friends and allies."[2] According to this logic, leftist cartoonists were not laughing at racist images; they were laughing at other people's racism. Illiberal racism was funny. In asking his anglophone audience to consider this context, Tonneau asserts that offensiveness is found in an author's intent rather than the sensibilities of whoever takes offense.[3]

None of this would really matter in any case, as iconoclastic satire censors nothing regardless of bad intentions or hurt feelings. In another explanation of French context to American readers, Adam Gopnik describes a satirical ethos that includes a radical secular commitment to profaning everything sacred: "The staff of the French magazine *Charlie Hebdo*, massacred in an act that shocked the world last week, were not the gentle daily satirists of American editorial cartooning. . . . They worked instead in a peculiarly French and savage tradition, forged in a long nineteenth-century guerrilla war between republicans and the Church and the monarchy. The cartoonists lived by the noble motto 'nothing sacred.'"[4] In his characterization of French satire as a "savage tradition" at war with the church, Gopnik captures an ambiguity in the relationship between civilization and secularism. On one hand, Gopnik's use of the word *savage* describes a modern secular project that defies traditional taboos. On the other hand, *Charlie Hebdo*'s unrestrained libidinal expression is not entirely distinguishable from a premodern reversion to savagery unconstrained by the norms of civility. While Gopnik does not intend to use *savage* in the premodern sense of the word, the specter of savagery plays an unacknowledged role within liberal defenses of free speech. It is the unintended consequences of Gopnik's invocation of a savage tradition that interest me here. While *Charlie Hebdo* ridiculed the church that Steve Bannon hoped to defend, their shared commitment to not giving a shit means that it was not always so easy to tell the difference between liberal and illiberal forms of incivility.

SECULAR HEROES

Secular freedom, as opposed to religious submission, requires civil toleration of incivility. As equal opportunity offenders, the cartoonists epitomize what Talal Asad has called secular heroism. As Asad explains, "For the worldly critic, there can be no acceptable taboos. When limits are critiqued, taboos disappear and freedom is expanded. This criticism doesn't merely liberate ideas from taboos, however; it also reinforces the existing distinction between the paradigmatically human and candidates for inclusion in true humanity who do not as yet own their bodies, emotions, and thoughts."[5] Lacking ownership of their bodies, emotions, and thoughts, Muslims who take offense at Islamophobic images do not have a point of view. They lack the basic capacity to understand satire.[6] As Rafia Zakaria notes in her account of public reaction to her criticism of *Charlie Hebdo*, "The non-Muslim white majority is deemed the rational and proper judge of the content of the cartoons; the objections of the subject others dismissed as instances of their general irrational and intolerant blathering."[7] A "savage tradition" is an exciting brand for those whose membership in the civilized world is not in question. For many others, the label savage is no laughing matter.

With their credo of "nothing sacred," the cartoonists were profane martyrs. Across the Atlantic, the PEN America association celebrated secular heroes by giving an award to the surviving cartoonists. When six PEN members protested the award, the novelist Salman Rushdie dismissed them as "Just 6 pussies."[8] Rushdie's condemnation is interesting for what it does not say. He does not accuse the six PEN dissenters of endorsing violence. Instead, Rushdie attacks them as cowards who backed down from a fight. This was not the first time that fearless speech was a test of virility. When asked to apologize for an anti-Semitic cartoon in 2009, *Charlie Hebdo* cartoonist Siné refused and protested: "I would rather cut my balls off."[9] According to secular principles, those who give offense are heroic (but not threatening) while those who take offense are cowards (but threaten civil peace). The masculinist character of heroic secularism, however, means that free speech is often couched in the rhetoric of battle. Secular heroes insist that that their use of nonviolent speech is contingent on the willingness of others to honor the social contract, and that they can and will use violence if necessary.

This masculinist posturing asks us to reconsider the peaceful quality of free speech. Free speech is supposed to address peacefully what otherwise might escalate into violent confrontation. One way of putting this is that free speech is how rational actors settle disagreements. Reasonable arguments win.[10] Another sense of free speech has less to do with the rationality of the content of speech and more to do with habits of restraint where speech substitutes for action. To be reasonable is to agree not to follow through on threats or respond violently to insults. Practitioners of free speech learn to discipline themselves to receive insults in the proper way, to understand that speech is not to be "taken personally." Such discipline is not always easy. In Saba Mahmood's analysis of a 2006 Danish controversy over cartoons featuring Muhammad, for example, she notes that several of her interlocutors registered blasphemous images as personal insults. In the words of one aggrieved person: "I would have felt less wounded if the object of ridicule were my own parents."[11] This wounding raises the question of what would happen if, instead of thinking about religious violence as something distinctive, we thought about insults in the ordinary sense. It would not be difficult to imagine that violence might be the consequence, say, of someone approaching a large man in a bar and insulting his mother. While secular liberals might not condone this violence, it would not be unintelligible. No one would worry about an existential threat to civilization. Furthermore, the referential truth of the insult would be beside the point. Both insulter and insulted would likely concede that the insult is not a true statement. Violence would result not from intellectual disagreement but from testing someone's honor by way of insult.

There are a variety of social contexts in which violent response to insult would be expected—even required—for someone to save face. Someone who backed down, who insufficiently answered an insult could suffer dishonor and loss of social status.[12] Secular liberalism has an ambivalent relationship to these codes of honor. On one hand, secular heroes insist they are ready to fight when threatened. On the other hand, threats made by the wrong people promise a reversion to barbarism. A secular liberal subject should fight only in response to physical threats and not to insulting words or images. In this way, secular liberalism promotes the proposition that no physical response to dishonor is necessary. It also constructs a curious kind of honor for those willing to insult everyone. Equal opportunity offenders put themselves at risk for retribution from those who lack proper restraint. Continued offense-giving in the face of this constant risk constitutes secular heroism. These offenses win awards.

This is not to say that secular liberal views about satirical speech are uniform. In debates about offense, liberals are divided about whether to draw a distinction between satire that "punches up" and "punches down." As *Doonesbury* cartoonist Garry Trudeau explains, "Traditionally, satire has comforted the afflicted while afflicting the comfortable. Satire punches up, against authority of all kinds, the little guy against the powerful. Great French satirists like Molière and Daumier always punched up, holding up the self-satisfied and hypocritical to ridicule. Ridiculing the non-privileged is almost never funny— it's just mean."[13] This distinction begs the question about what criteria determine up or down, but consideration of the social location of satire's targets acknowledges that insults produce winners and losers.[14] Although the state prevents citizens from addressing social inequality through violence, satire gives people the right to insult their superiors. When someone punches down, however, it reinforces the helplessness of those unable to retaliate as social equals. This adds insult to injury.

Liberals who worry about punching down believe that offense can produce dignitary harm that undercuts equality. The threshold for equality in this case is higher than mere legal tolerance; equality requires equal treatment. As Asad suggests, the expectation of equal treatment is itself a secular liberal precept: "In a secularizing world, dignity—treating others respectfully and the feeling that one is entitled to respectful behavior from others—is said to apply equally to all."[15] As Asad points out, however, equal treatment is difficult to calculate, as the concept of dignity has its roots in unequal societies. In the older sense of the word, dignity was a form of special treatment due to members of higher social classes. If everyone is entitled to dignity, then dignity is no longer a mark of distinction. The liberal critique of punching down inverts this traditional sense of dignity by saying that indignity should be reserved for people of higher social status. This economy of offense levels the playing field by insulting relatively powerful people who have a surplus of dignity, honor, and respect that they can afford to lose.

Not everyone agrees, however, about whether to consider social location when evaluating offensive speech. For an unapologetic secular hero, any distinction between punching up and down is a symptom of politically correct cowardice. The equal opportunity offender suggests that a better solution is to subject everyone to indignity so that social distinctions no longer exist. Secular heroes in this vein do not see themselves as illiberal. Rather, the satirists for whom nothing is sacred identify as liberal allies in the fight against racism and Islamophobia. They hope to expose hatred as bad ideas. In the 1950s and 1960s, for example, the comedian Lenny Bruce told offensive jokes because he wanted to undo the "suppression of the word." The best offense against racism is to get it out in the open, to laugh at bigotry and to show its absurdity. Bruce has influenced generations of comedians who adopt a metaracist or ironically racist style akin to *Charlie Hebdo*.[16] By abandoning the safety of liberal taboos, metaracist comedians imagine themselves as the true warriors for equality. But the line between racism and metaracism, or liberalism and illiberalism, is not always so clear.

DON'T MESS WITH TEXAS

Not all offensive speech hopes to produce liberal equality. Illiberal critics of Muslims attempted to replay the *Charlie Hebdo* confrontation by sponsoring Muhammad-drawing contests in the United States. Hardly peaceful celebrations of free speech, these contests were pretexts for displaying private arsenals. One cartoon contest in May 2015 anticipated a confrontation like the *Charlie Hebdo* shooting, but this time, instead of being bound by the constraints and rules of civilization, it would take place in Texas. Unlike France, Texas is a defiantly semicivilized society with lots and lots of guns. Taking pride in the popular injunction not to "mess with" their state, many Texans adhere to codes of personal honor upheld through the implicit threat of violence.

The Texas contest was sponsored by the American Freedom Defense Initiative.[17] Led by Pamela Geller, the organization was founded to prevent the Islamization of America. As she has explained, "In the war between the savage and the civilized man, you side with the civilized man."[18] Geller's statement underscores the ambiguity between savage and civilized within defenses of free speech. On one hand, she sides with civilization against its enemies. On the other hand, deliberate acts of incivility and a willingness to use savage violence are necessary for security. This incivility is perceived as especially necessary in an age where liberal multiculturalism has enervated Western civilization. Indeed, Geller represents herself as the true defender of liberal ideals of anti-Semitism, gender equality, and sexual freedom. As Rogers Brubaker notes, the urgent need to develop a united front has characterized recourse to a rhetoric of civilizational crisis among European populist movements. He explains:

> The argument is that Jews, women, and gays are all threatened—physically as well as culturally—by the "Islamization" of Western societies; that mainstream parties, fearful of being censored as "Islamophobic," remain silent about this threat; that Jews, women, and gays with leftist or multiculturalist sympathies therefore suffer from a kind of false consciousness; and that their interests are in fact best represented by populist parties, who are unafraid to "tell it like it is."[19]

According to many conservative and some liberal critics, multicultural inclusion produces a tolerance for intolerance that makes contemporary liberalism internally inconsistent.[20]

When the Texas contest was indeed attacked, armed security and police were able to kill the attackers. All of this was expected and intelligible. Rather than avoid violence, the contest organizers sought to dramatize an intractable conflict between friend and enemy. This binary view is consistent with Donald Trump's statement: "I think Islam hates us."[21] Pitting "Islam" against "us" means violence is the predictable behavior of enemies. As Nadia Marzouki has noted, this warfare model has been the preferred discourse of anti-Sharia activists who warn of a creeping religious takeover of the American legal system: "While most Muslim organizations and liberal groups are still motivated by the ideal of rational deliberation founded on rule-governed exchange of arguments, the anti-Sharia camp has a warfare mentality where each side adjusts its strategy according to the moves of the opponent, and one speaks of spilling blood on behalf of the good cause."[22]

Spilling blood for a good cause is an illiberal reasoning that differs from secular liberal explanations for religious violence. The Texas cartoonists were not worried about people who were insufficiently disciplined by habits of liberal restraint. These amateur cartoonists wanted to fight. Deliberately profaning what Muslims held sacred was a provocation. In other words, violent responses to religious offenses are incommensurable only to liberals who look to the state's legitimate monopoly of violence to ensure public safety. In a world in which you are expected to protect yourself, shooting people is an expected, even reasonable, response to insult or blasphemy. The answer was not to embrace liberal restraint in the face of threats, but to be a good guy with a gun. Illiberal secularism, which calls Christian nationalists to defend themselves from an enemy that the state is too weak to confront, replaces public safety with private security. Unlike liberal prescriptions for protecting the public through gun control, illiberal security calls for strengthening the armed capacity of the private household.

The recourse to private security provides an apt illustration of how illiberal secularism is the result of processes of privatization. Rather than shrink the power of religion, illiberal secularism consigns the government to a shrinking public and instead expands the private freedom of faith, family, property, and guns. Liberals often scoff at the equation of guns and God as an illustration of the hypocrisy of self-proclaimed biblical literalists who skipped over the Sermon on the Mount. But clinging to guns and God makes sense as defenses of the sanctity of the private household, as ways of protecting family honor.

In the ethos of gun culture, state violence must be supplemented by private security. Participants in the Texas contest were convinced that the law is not powerful enough to police domestic crime or to confront the global threat posed by Islam. Citizens must protect themselves from harm when the state's hold on violence is tenuous. Guns rights advocates are wary of any attempt by the state to consolidate its monopoly of violence by taking away any of the over 300 million firearms owned by American citizens. This wariness only increases after each of the mass shootings that have become a recurring spectacle in American life. Rather than a sign that guns are too numerous, mass shootings further illustrate the need for private protection in the face of public lawlessness. Groups like the National Rifle Association have convinced many Americans that security is best achieved through a well-armed populace who can respond to domestic and international threats. Indeed, advocates for increased gun ownership assert that a country like France is perpetually vulnerable because of its lack of guns. In the wake of a November 2015 attack in Paris that killed 130 people including several Americans, Trump commented: "You can say what you want, but if they had guns—if our people had guns, if they were allowed to carry—it would have been a much, much different situation."[23] Parisians would have been safer if they had equipped themselves like Texans. Leaving security to the state is a weak and naive response to the emergency threat posed by the violence of nonstate actors.

STATE OF WAR

My goal in considering the violence latent in speech is not to show that free speech apologists are inconsistent. Rather, I want to think about the relationship between insult and injury when the state's legitimate hold on violence is insecure. It is easier not to take insults personally when you feel safe, when you are confident that the state will protect you. When people who lose confidence in the state turn instead to private security, they use speech to express what they will do to protect their property and honor. While contemporary liberalism has a lot to say about speech and property, it sidelines the relationship between speech and honor.[24] Violent responses to dishonor are symptomatic of a social instability that habits of liberal citizenship are supposed to resolve.

One case that might illustrate how personal honor haunts the liberal tradition, however, is John Locke's defense of slavery. This might seem like a non sequitur as slaves had no free speech, and honor was not the primary focus of Locke's thinking, but his view of slavery provides a window into an alternate and less obvious strain of liberal understandings of honor and self-defense.[25]

According to Locke, slavery was a result of winning and losing. Enslaved people lost disputes in a state of war before the establishment of civil peace. The winner of a battle could have killed the loser. Instead, the victor decided to preserve the captive's life as property. As people cannot voluntarily enslave themselves, by losing the fight the enslaved becomes virtually dead and forfeits his freedom. Enslaved persons gave up; they accepted the dishonor of captivity instead of fighting to the death. As Locke explains, "Indeed having, by his fault, forfeited his own Life, by some Act that deserves Death; he, to whom he has forfeited it, may (when he has him in his Power) delay to take it, and make use of him to his own Service, and he does him no injury by it. For, whenever he finds the hardship of his Slavery out-weigh the value of his Life, 'tis in his Power, by resisting the Will of his Master, to draw on himself the Death he desires."[26] A free person would prefer death to the dishonor of enslavement. Lacking honor, the enslaved person consents to become someone else's property. In Locke's view, enslaved people were taken captive because they failed to protect themselves.

One apparent inconsistency in Locke's understanding of freedom and slavery is that the establishment of civil peace did nothing to redress the enslavement that resulted from personal disputes in the state of war. The magistrate's monopoly on violence protects the winners of private disputes in a way that ignores the freedom of some human beings, and this protection of property extends to subsequent generations who play no role in their own enslavement. In Locke's account, then, the establishment of civil society does not address past injuries from the state of war by restoring natural equality. On the contrary, it calls a truce that freezes in place whatever forms of inequality exist. Once civil peace is established, that is it. Enslaved people have no recourse to violence in their own defense.

Enslaved people do not have freedom of speech, but Locke's defense of slavery mirrors free speech arguments in that civil peace protects against physical retribution for prior injury. While liberal democratic institutions do not sustain Locke's defense of an institution as hostile to personal freedom as slavery, his logic is employed in a whole host of historical circumstances. Liberals often apologize for the violence accompanying histories of enslavement and colonization. This violence is in the past, however, so disputes must now be resolved peacefully and without too much redistribution of expropriated property. In other words, civil peace does not so much prevent violence as much as it prohibits retribution for past violence that produced the unequal social order that made civilization possible.[27] Insisting that past violence can be redressed only through speech protects the winners. Free speech allows people to express grievances about the violence that produced existing social inequalities as long as everyone rules out the possibility of reopening the state of war that produced these inequities in the first place. Giving awards to religious offenses on the grounds that they neither pick pockets nor break legs guards against retribution for the many picked pockets and broken legs that supposedly civilized people inflicted on what they deemed to be the savage parts of the globe. The main difference between liberalism and illiberalism on this point is that secular liberals are willing to offer apologies whereas illiberal secularists see this contrition as a symptom of politically correct weakness.

CONTEXTS

One possible context for *Charlie Hebdo*'s award, then, is the ongoing legacy of the division of the world into savage and civilized.[28]

The cartoons illustrate Walter Benjamin's suggestion that documents of civilization bear the taint of barbarism. As he proclaims, "There is no document of culture which is not at the same time a document of barbarism. And just as such a document is never free of barbarism, so barbarism taints also the manner in which it was transmitted from one hand to another."[29] By drawing images to provoke violence from intemperate enemies, cartoon contests dramatize the need to protect civilization. Civilization is threatened by the violence of nonstate actors who promise a reversion to savagery, a reemergent state of war in which no sovereign is powerful enough to guarantee property or safety.

Private security protects against this potential volatility, but the nonviolence of speech holds only if the state can guarantee civil peace. Constant vigilance is required to guard against the possibility of exceptional threats that the sovereign cannot contain. Such threats are never entirely removed from the reality of political life in civilized states. When Locke describes the state of war where people were enslaved, for example, he does not refer to events in in the mists of prehistory. People were enslaved in Locke's day and by his own countrymen. Enslavement was legitimate because the civil rules did not apply to places in a state of war. In practice, then, civilized life is often worth a great deal more than life in politically unstable places. The specter of transnational terror, however, threatens to import savage violence into the civilized world. Sara Ahmed notes that the rhetoric of terror produces a crisis in security that calls for new measures of violence at the same time that it marks an urgent need to recover lost values: "It is through announcing a crisis in security that new forms of security, border policing, and surveillance become justified. We have only to think about how narratives of crisis are used within politics to justify a 'return' to values and traditions that are perceived to be under threat."[30]

Achille Mbembe suggests that democratic states fear the eruption of the suppressed violence of colonization that he calls the "nocturnal face of democracy," the masked work that made civilization possible. As he explains, "The great fear of democracies is that this violence, latent on the interior and exteriorized in the colonies and other third places, suddenly resurfaces."[31] The sudden resurfacing of violence within secular states engaged in projects of including diverse peoples might be a better way of contextualizing what is at stake in an imagined clash of civilizations. Rather than contact between civilizations with fundamentally different values, the perceived clash of civilizations is better described as a latent tension interior to societies that have not resolved unequal histories. This internal tension haunts homeland security. As Mbembe states, "Owing to the structural proximity, there is no longer any 'outside' that might be opposed to an 'inside,' no 'elsewhere' that might be opposed to a 'here,' no 'closeness' that might be opposed to a 'remoteness.' One cannot 'sanctuarize' *one's own home* by fomenting chaos and death far away *in the homes of others*. Sooner or later, one will reap at home what one has sown abroad. Sanctuarization can only ever be mutual."[32] In the illiberal secular imagination, the *Charlie Hebdo* controversy dramatizes the need for guns because they seek to protect the sanctity of their own homes in a refusal of any mutual project of sanctuarization. Illiberal secularism ups the ante in its defense of civilization.

The state of crisis means that self-owning persons are continuously threatened if they are not careful. As personal freedom requires constant vigilance, preparing for violence through private forms of security is a reasonable (although not equally distributed) response of persons who seek to protect themselves in cases where personal harm could result in the loss of property or freedom. A cartoon contest designed to provoke a violent confrontation demonstrates its participants' willingness to fight when necessary.

To be clear, the legacies of civilization and barbarism are not the context for every debate about free speech. I would suggest, however, that this context does frame the discourse about cartoons and guns in the United States. It comes down to how broad you want the context to be. *Charlie Hebdo*'s supporters, along with their American imitators, insist that the context begins and ends with the intent of the cartoonists. This context works well for secular heroes who seek the freedom to express themselves however they wish, but it pointedly excludes other explanations.[33] In his thoughts on responses to the *Charlie Hebdo* shooting, Russell T. McCutcheon observes that the choice of context serves to make some explanations of events into self-evident truths: "When we do and do not choose to dip into the background on the story, provide the context that we think is necessary to understand what might be going on, is therefore telling, I think; for it creates a situation where only certain explanations are even possible to conceive, where only certain plans of action can be seen as credible or desirable."[34] Choosing some contexts over others makes it obvious that the civilized world is a peaceful place apart from threats from outside.[35] This choice of context deflects from the diverse forms of state violence perpetrated by Europe or the United States.[36]

One irony in the call to understand cartoons in context is that free speech absolutists often insist that context is irrelevant as long as no one is directly harmed. Those who call for balancing speech with concerns about discrimination want attention to context. As legal scholar john a. powell has argued, "It seems obvious that the mere assertion of one narrative perspective, with no attendant concern for competing world views, does little to promote social and political dialogue. Yet our free speech

jurisprudence analyzes each individual speech act indepen-
dently, with little regard for how that expression fits into the
complex web of social discourse."[37] This minimal context follows from an emphasis on free speech as a legal principle. *Charlie Hebdo*'s supporters and critics in the United States largely
agree that it would be unwise to give the state the punitive
power to censor images because they profane someone's sense
of the sacred.[38] Conflating legal principles with civic virtues,
however, means that equal opportunity offense is not merely
legally tolerated, it is celebrated and rewarded within both liberal and illiberal contexts. Celebrating offensive speech without
reflection upon the role that honor plays in private security
avoids discussion about winners and losers within the free
speech economy. As with all private freedoms, access to private
security is selectively distributed and reinforces existing distributions of cultural and political power that have been produced
by the violence that taints the past acquisition of property and
the establishment of civil peace.[39] To ensure this peace, private
institutions like corporations, churches, and families need to be
protected from threats posed by savage violence and state regulation. While the former poses a direct threat, the latter threatens the forms of private security necessary for self-defense.[40]

Liberal codes of free speech repress the violence latent in private inequity. The rules that govern insult, personal honor, self-
defense, and the sanctity of the household do not have a clear
place within secular liberal theories of free speech because these
are forms of governance that reduce public goods to illiberal contests between friends and enemies. This is not to say that the
friend and enemy distinction plays no role in liberal defenses of
free speech. While there are differences between the level of violence in liberal and illiberal responses to threats, one notable
unifying feature of the discourse on cartoons and guns is the

ubiquity of the rhetoric of identification in response to a perceived state of emergency.[41] Following a friend and enemy binary, identifying with the slogan #JeSuisCharlie asked everyone to choose sides. As Gavan Titley has suggested, this free speech binary is consistent with the war on terror: "Anti-Muslim racism—across a range of political tendencies—frames 'the Muslim' as a figure of implacable cultural difference, gendered threat and value-based incompatibility. Respect for freedom of speech has emerged as a primary marker of *integratability*. In a corollary of the logic of the 'war on terror,' it is increasingly presented in absolutist terms: you are either for freedom of speech, or you are not."[42]

The demand to choose sides is notable because liberal principles of free speech are supposed to make identification irrelevant. However, when many Americans feel that their families, their schools, their churches, and their borders are threatened by enemies, they call for emergency measures to defend the civilized world. Unlike liberals, illiberal secularists offer no apologies. They reject the liberal economy of punching up and down because they do not feel like they have any surplus honor to give away. Illiberal cartoonists see themselves as the targets of disrespect from liberals who punch down, and they worry that the people punching up might hurt them.

4

CHRISTIAN VALUES AND THE
WHITE EVANGELICAL

Amid his failed run for an Alabama Senate seat in 2017, the former judge Roy Moore picked a Twitter fight with a late-night talk show host. Jimmy Kimmel had previously dispatched a writer with the fake name of Jake Byrd to pose as a supporter wearing a T-shirt with the slogan "Gimme Moore." Standing up in an Alabama church, Byrd shouted in the direction of the candidate: "That's a man's man! Does that look like the face of a molester?"[1] In his guise as surreal super-fan, Byrd made light of accusations that the candidate had sexually assaulted children he met in a mall several decades earlier.[2] When Moore learned that Kimmel's show was behind the disruption, the offended candidate charged the host with disparaging "Christian values" and invited him to come to Alabama and settle things "man to man." In response, Kimmel tweeted: "Sounds great Roy—let me know when you get some Christian values and I'll be there!"[3]

Kimmel's response was an "own." Kimmel not only trivialized his opponent's pugilistic challenge, he poked fun at the hypocrisy of the Alabama judge's professed Christian values. Kimmel compounded the ownage when he responded to a follow-up invitation from Moore by tweeting: "OK Roy, but I'm leaving my daughters at home! P.S.—wear that cute little leather vest."[4] Calling attention to the cute little leather vest was a dig at the cowboy attire Moore donned to show off his country bona fides by riding a horse named Sassy to vote.[5] Within a few tweets, Kimmel insulted the judge's piety, regional posturing, and masculinity.

Kimmel upped the ante during his show by discussing his own Catholicism. Ceding no ground to his opponent's religiosity, the television host explained that his Christian values required habits of repentance that the Alabama judge lacked. As Kimmel lectured, "At my church, forcing yourself on underage girls is a no-no. Some even consider it to be a sin. Not that you did that, of course. Allegedly. But when you commit a sin at our church, we're encouraged to confess and ask forgiveness for the sin. Not to call the women you allegedly victimized liars and damage them even more. But maybe your church is different."[6] Moore's church, of course, did not endorse attacks on women in place of repentance.[7] Kimmel's mockery was directed at the gap between the judge's private behavior and his public persona. The joke was on a Christian hypocrite. For Moore, however, this brief exchange was only further evidence of what he called "D.C. and Hollywood elites' bigotry toward southerners."[8] By recasting a critique of Moore's person as an attack on Moore's people, the judge stoked a feud between Hollywood and the South. Poking fun at alleged sexual indiscretions rallied evangelicals angry at a smug Hollywood liberal who was mocking a Christian man.

Liberals like Kimmel wanted to know how Christian voters made peace with hypocrisy. Not everyone excused Moore's behavior. He did lose a senate race in a reliably Republican state. Of those who remained loyal, some blamed the media's fabrication of false charges. This was Moore's own explanation. A remarkable number of Alabama Republicans, however, seemed resigned to the idea that the charges were true and instead concocted creative excuses for Moore's actions.[9] In the end, the truth of Moore's predatory behavior was less offensive to Christian values than a talk show host's fixation on talking about lurid details of a good man's private sexual history.

The dispute between Moore and Kimmel demonstrated that hypocrisy and value are two sides of the same coin. Whereas Kimmel presumed that private behavior should be consistent with public convictions, Moore rigorously policed the boundary between public exposure and private activity. What Moore called Christian values were norms tied to an idealized way of life that could be inconsistent with the actual private behavior of persons. Christians can handle sin. Sin is familiar. Sin is a part of life. In her study of political sex scandals, for example, Leslie Dorrough Smith notes that sins can be forgiven as long as otherwise good men admit their sinful behavior. Conservative Christians embroiled in sex scandals affirm their values even when they do not act upon them: "They typically assert that the discourse is still really authoritative, it's just that they screwed up. Simply put, they claim to still 'believe in' monogamy and 'believe' that they have 'sinned.' They reinforce the religious discourse even as they supposedly violate it."[10] While Moore did not himself admit to any wrongdoing, the stories of his indiscretions did not register as a profanation to his supporters because he respected the sanctity of the moral code he transgressed.

What Moore could not tolerate were insults from outsiders who belittled the norms that governed sin. What outsiders saw as hypocrisy served to protect a way of life. As this way of life was integrally tied to sexual, racial, and religious order, it was less threatened by sinful behavior than by attacks on the sources of authority that govern a social world aligned with Christian values. Such visible Christian commitments would seem to be a clear example of antisecularism, but I do not think so. While secular liberals and illiberal secularists have disagreed about the value of Moore's values, they have largely agreed about what values were. Values, understood to be sacred and fundamental, work differently from ordinary political interests. While political views are subject to public debate and criticism, criticizing matters of value is offensive because values are core features of identity that should be treated differently from ordinary political interests. This division between values and interests fits with secular divisions between religion and politics. Values are deeply held commitments that are inscrutable private matters. For secular liberals, Moore is free to have whatever values he wishes as long as he keeps them out of political life. For illiberal secularists, the liberal exclusion of Christian values devalues politics. Moore's charge that he has been the target of "bigotry" illustrates that the public arena is hostile to Christians. Tying values to religious identity renders critics like Kimmel as bigoted and offensive. By invoking bigotry, Moore depicts Kimmel as punching down. While liberals might not like Moore's ideas, they do not want to be seen as discriminating against his religion. Complaints of bigotry play on secular liberal principles of inclusion by insisting that conservative Christians are excluded. Feeling that they have lost the ability to shape the public, Christian activists like Moore shore up the private spaces in which they can exercise some power. The value of values, in this illiberal usage, is that they are an effective tool to protect the sanctity of the private sphere from a profane government.

81 PERCENT

Moore's supporters also excused indiscretions when they turned out for Donald Trump a year earlier. Polls record that Trump received the votes of 81 percent of white evangelicals.[11] This was a remarkably precise number for an imprecise label. Like all poll numbers that measure religious affiliation, 81 percent is a deceptively simple summary of a diverse set of motives and identities. Few people self-identify with the label "white evangelical," and the category is in many ways an interpretive fiction invented by polls.[12] With or without a racial qualification, *evangelical* is notoriously hard to define.[13] The term is sometimes used interchangeably with *fundamentalist*, but *evangelical* has a more inclusive and less combative connotation.[14] It is not obvious to label Moore an evangelical as he would be a perfect example of a fundamentalist. Moore certainly would fit with historian George Marsden's definition: "An American fundamentalist is an evangelical who is militant in opposition to liberal theology in the churches or to changes in cultural values or mores, such as those associated with 'secular humanism.'"[15]

Scholars have often followed a four-part definition of evangelicalism developed by David Bebbington. In his history of evangelicalism in Britain, Bebbington lists the core evangelical tenets as an emphasis on conversion (an insistence that to be a Christian is to be born again), activism (an active commitment to evangelize others), biblicism (an investment in the authority of scripture over the church or reason), and crucicentrism (a focus on Christ's sacrifice on the cross).[16] This definition has shaped conventional narratives of evangelicalism in the United States. According to this history, in the early republic the term *evangelical* could be used interchangeably with Protestant.[17] In the late nineteenth century, new intellectual currents within liberal thought challenged traditional evangelical authority.[18] New ideas led to disputes between modernist and fundamentalist factions in major Protestant denominations in the 1920s.[19] As modernist forces won elite institutional battles, fundamentalists retreated into a subculture of Bible schools and nondenominational churches that were often publicly apolitical.[20] Political disengagement appeared to make sense for fundamentalists who believed that politics was a profane engagement with a world that faced an imminent end. In the 1950s, however, some conservative Protestants like the revivalist Billy Graham forged a neo-evangelical movement that aspired to reengage the culture.[21] Evangelicals gained further confidence in the 1970s and 1980s when they rejected their separatist past to gain national prominence under the banner of the New Christian Right. According to Jerry Falwell, leader of the Moral Majority, evangelicals were reluctantly dragged back into the political sphere by an expanding federal government that threatened the sanctity of the Christian family.[22] Conservative Christian activists responded to the threat of an encroaching liberal state with a vigorous defense of "family values."

In conventional evangelical narratives, conflict over religious doctrine is at the center of the story. Evangelicalism is a coherent belief system that is challenged by liberalism, modernism, and secularism. Reducing evangelicalism to a system of beliefs and practices, however, cannot explain why 81 percent voted for someone who did not appear to share evangelical beliefs and practices. Indeed, the apparent gap between evangelicals' religiosity and their voting preferences has provided fuel for liberals who scold white evangelicals for betraying their own values. Scolding has also come from within the evangelical fold. The election brought anguished hand-wringing from among the 19 percent of self-identified white evangelicals who did not support Trump.[23] *Christianity Today*, a magazine founded by the evangelist Billy Graham, warned that turning a blind eye to Trump's moral indiscretions undermines Christian witness. Addressing evangelicals who supported Trump in the wake of impeachment, a widely circulated editorial warned: "Consider what an unbelieving world will say if you continue to brush off Mr. Trump's immoral words and behavior in the cause of political expediency."[24] Jim Wallis, the head of the Sojourners organization and someone who has long complained that the Christian right has hijacked the gospel, lamented: "When a president, as a moral role model, would make serial adultery, constant philandering, and pornography normal in America . . . it is a hypocrisy that puts the integrity of Christian faith at stake."[25] Rejecting the equation of evangelicalism and whiteness, Sojourners hope to build a coalition that includes African American, Asian American, and Latinx conservative Protestants. Trump support, according to Wallis, demonstrates that white evangelicals are more loyal to race than to Christian morality. David Gushee, then president of the American Academy of Religion, took the election of Trump as the final straw that broke the back of his own evangelical allegiance. In his view, evangelicalism is a noble tradition that has been sacrificed to an idol in the form of a New York real estate mogul: "We are certainly witnessing the self-immolation of U.S. white evangelicalism, as it sacrifices its remaining credibility on the altar of Donald Trump. Even after this disaster, many millions will remain attracted to U.S. white tribalist religion of this type."[26] Disaffected evangelicals think that evangelical politics should have moral and theological content. For the 19 percenters, voting for Trump was a profane sacrifice to a false tribalist religion.

Gushee's use of the word *tribalist* appears repeatedly in descriptions of evangelical voting habits. These accounts warn that tribalism excited collective sentiments, but not ones that advance rational political interests. Tribal loyalties explain the irrational commitments of evangelicals who vote against their own economic interests and Christian values. Tribalism is loyalty for the sake of loyalty. It connotes something primal, a set

of irrational and emotional attachments that abandon civilization as well as the Christian virtue of love for one's neighbor. A
flurry of essays on tribalism interpret Trumpism's incivility as a
reversion to savagery. As former George W. Bush speechwriter
and evangelical Never Trumper Michael Gerson describes the
president, "His tribalism and hatred for 'the other' stand in direct
opposition to Jesus's radical ethic of neighbor love. Trump's
strength-worship and contempt for 'losers' smack more of
Nietzsche than Christ."[27] Depending on who is writing, evangelical tribalism is either a contradiction in terms or the natural
fulfillment of American Christian traditions of white supremacy.

In drawing an opposition between Christian ethics and tribalism's contempt for losers, Gerson suggests the embrace of
Trump is the desperate response of people who would do anything to win.[28] The will to win led prominent evangelical leaders to fawn obsequiously over their vain leader in the hope that
he would reward their loyalty. The spectacle of shameless power
grubbing led evangelical scholar John Fea to dub these lackeys
"court evangelicals."[29] In Fea's account, evangelical leaders have
abandoned their sacred calling to gain temporal power in the
profane world of politics. As fellow 19 percenter Thomas S. Kidd
laments, the focus on political engagement distracts from the
spiritual essence of a movement: "Perhaps I am naïve to hope
that there remains a core of practicing, orthodox evangelicals
who really do care more about salvation and spiritual matters
than access to Republican power."[30]

Another explanation for the rise of evangelical tribalism is
that conservative Christians have taken up identity politics.
Francis Fukuyama argues that the combination of tribalism
with complaints of victimization is a sign that evangelicals "had
adopted language and framing from the left."[31] While Fukuyama's diagnosis resonates with think pieces that warn against

identity politics on college campuses, it does not account for the long legacy of advocacy for a Christian nation. As settler colonialists who developed an extensive regulatory apparatus tied to race, white Christians had long privileged their own identities as the source for American nationalism. What Fukuyama identifies as leftist identity politics are political movements developed in response to white Christian nationalism. Identity politics on the left, however, is more visible because of the relative invisibility of an unmarked whiteness.

While tribalism seems new, Christian political activism is not. It is more commonly described, however, as "culture wars." The analysis of culture wars works differently from the analysis of tribalism. Although "wars" conjure up images of winning and losing, culture is not quite like tribe. Unlike tribalists who have abandoned reason, culture warriors are engaged in an understandable battle to defend deeply held values.[32] Rather than focus on irrational loyalty, cultural analysis of Christian values steer clear of media portrayals of extremism in favor of attention to what sociologist James Davison Hunter described in the 1990s as "the honest concerns of different communities engaged in a deeply rooted cultural conflict."[33] In Hunter's influential account, Americans are divided between citizens with an impulse toward orthodoxy and those with an impulse toward progressivism. These impulses cut across religious denominations and are not reducible to doctrinal or institutional conflict. Cultural conflicts are rooted in world views. Arising from religious values, the impulse toward orthodoxy is motivated by "the commitment on the part of adherents to an external, definable, and transcendent authority."[34]

According to analysts who prefer "culture wars" to "tribalism," white evangelicals are protecting traditional values against progressive elites. This narrative dovetails with empathetic portrayals of white evangelicals as people who live in the parts of the country that are left behind by the rapid cultural changes and economic prosperity enjoyed by coastal America. In these accounts, conservative Christians in flyover states are victims of cultural and economic forces beyond their control. During the 2016 presidential campaign, a number of commentators took these self-identifications of white victimhood at face value. This resulted in an array of stories that portrayed Trump supporters as fueled by "economic anxiety."[35]

While many evangelicals undoubtedly face economic hardship, the anxiety analysis cannot explain why most Americans facing economic insecurity did not vote for Trump. This is not to say that economics is irrelevant. A more precise formulation is that Trumpism appeals to people who understand economic interests in racial, religious, and regional terms. For his part, a lawyer and judge like Moore is hardly poor or powerless.[36] Like many vociferous Trump supporters, Moore is aptly described as a local elite.[37] Elites like Moore hold a great deal of civic sway in the communities in which they live, and they are committed to protecting what they imagine to be a threatened way of life. This life is located in the idealized rural, small-town, and suburban worlds inhabited by family and neighbors who attend the same churches, patronize the same small businesses, and cheer for kids in the same little league and high school football teams.[38] All of this makes Moore feel safe.[39] He prefers social arrangements defined by consistency and familiarity among people who know each other. This works differently from liberal ideals of public goods, which require thinking in abstract terms about competing interests in a diverse public inhabited by strangers.[40]

Moore's defense of his way of life could look like tribalism because maintaining these relatively homogeneous social spaces depends upon tightly shared norms and a commitment to racial and sexual hierarchies in which everyone "knows their place."

This in turn requires submission to the forms of authority that produce and govern these norms. Moore's supporters' refusal to repudiate his hypocrisy stems from his commitment to the proper forms of authority, while recognizing that personal behavior will often fall short.[41] Moore is committed to displays of submission to visible representations of sacred authority like the flag, the police, the military, and the Ten Commandments inscribed on a big rock.[42] Learning to respect these forms of authority is essential to becoming a good person.

AUTHORITY AND CHAOS

The fixation on authority confused liberal commentators who read the Ten Commandments for their moral or theological content. For critics like Kimmel, rules are reasonable propositions that people agree to follow. Liberals see hypocrisy among Christians who cherish monuments of the Ten Commandments but cannot themselves list them, or who engage in sexual behavior at odds with their professed morality. One reason that Kimmel's jokes failed to sway Moore's ardent supporters, however, is that for them it is more important to have the rules than to follow them. What Moore finds so offensive about contemporary liberalism is that he believes liberals want to redraw rules to accommodate diverse forms of behavior in ways that eliminate sin. Changing the rules challenges the way of life that makes local elites like Moore feel safe and powerful, especially when the rules are replaced with regulations produced by a government accountable to religiously, ethnically, and sexually diverse publics in an increasingly urban nation. The specter of diversity poses an existential threat to Moore's way of life as well as the Christian character of the nation. As he asserted, "We were not founded on the faith of Buddha or the Hindu faith or the faith of Islam, but on the faith of Jesus Christ."[43] While Moore does not believe that the state should force Buddhists, Hindus, or Muslims to convert to Christianity, he does feel that the nation's failure to acknowledge the sovereignty of God has created a breakdown of authority and order. Casting diversity as disorder is a feature of what Leslie Dorrough Smith describes as "chaos rhetoric."[44] As with shock politics, chaos rhetoric requires emergency measures to counter the moral decadence of liberal elites. While Moore would have preferred to live in a nation with a shared commitment to godly principles, secular liberals had so undermined the political order that illiberal secularism welcomed a profane man like Donald Trump as a necessary emergency response.

It is telling that tribalism emerged as the term to describe this alliance between Moore and Trump. Tribalism was liberalism's word for illiberalism. Explaining Trumpism as a reversion to tribalism, then, says less about the rationale behind Trump support than it does about the inability of liberal commentators to make sense of what was going on. Amy Chua suggests that confusion plagues naive liberals who fail to understand primal drives within human nature. As she asserts, "Human beings aren't just a little tribal. We're *very* tribal, and it distorts the way we think and feel."[45] While Chua hoped to show the limits of liberalism, she instead flipped it on its head. Rather than a peculiar feature of Trumpism, tribalism is now everywhere. It is unclear, however, what empirical measure would distinguish between a "little" tribal and "very" tribal. Saying people are very tribal says less about why people find themselves in the tribes that they do, or why some forms of identity seem to lend themselves to tribalism more than others. Instead of explaining political interests, the rhetoric of tribalism asserts that people act out of an instinctive sense of loyalty that is pre-political. Insisting that everyone is equally tribal deflects attention from the historical legacies and sociological conditions that produce unequal relationships among groups.

The problem with viewing an apparent rise of tribalism as a reversion to universal human instincts is that the rhetoric identified as tribal arose in response to a particular historical reckoning with inequality. Fashioning liberal projects of inclusion as bigotry that excluded Christian values was a practical response to threats to Christian authority. According to the sociologist Gerardo Martí, confronting perceived threats led white evangelicals to make pragmatic compromises. As he explains, "It is entirely plausible to suggest that *the greater the threat of religious decline, the greater the expansion of acceptable orthodoxy*—as long as those actions are perceived to protect and enhance orthodoxy rather than further diminish it."[46] This practical concession to political reality shows a flexibility that does not quite fit with the image of mindless tribalism. Casting white evangelicals like Moore as strategic actors who selectively use the rhetoric of Christian values to seek power suggests that tribalism might not be the best way to think about white identity politics. For that matter, it is not clear that tribal is a helpful analytic term at all. The use of tribalism drew critics like journalist Christine Mungai, herself a member of a Kenyan tribe. She argues that American usages of the term have racist connotations that have more to do with colonial stereotypes than with the actual behavior of tribal peoples.[47] The groups that have been labeled tribes throughout the colonized world are complex and fluid forms of social organization that are not driven by the impassioned blind loyalties that appeared to have consumed American politics.

Also focusing on colonial legacies, Charles McCrary notes that the discourse of tribalism rests on an opposition to an imagined individual liberal secular subject: "The tribal subject, conversely, is owned by the collective. In the modern world, that's no way to do politics *or* religion. Secularism is a political ideology that defines the modern as nonsectarian, public, and above all rational."[48] While I agree with McCrary, for the purpose of my analysis the political ideology is a specific feature of secular liberalism. The illiberal secularism of Trumpism does not require nonsectarianism, rationality, or a commitment to public goods. Such commitments are the sign of an encroaching liberal state. The trouble with the rhetoric of tribalism is that its emphasis on primal instincts obscures how illiberalism is the product of modern, secular institutions.

The conceptual limits of tribalism might also pose a problem for theories that explain culture wars as fundamental disagreements over values.[49] While white evangelicals want to win, losing culture wars is useful to a movement that requires threats to survive.[50] Rather than tied together by any central belief system that rests on shared values, white evangelicalism is best defined by what it is against.[51] Collecting diverse groups of conservative Protestants into an evangelical movement is part of a political project to produce Christian values in response to a diversifying social environment. The reason that Moore's brand of white identity politics needs the Kimmels of the world is that much of Moore's performances are not necessarily indigenous to Alabama or to conservative Protestantism. Alabamians do not routinely attend formal political events dressed in cowboy costumes while waving a gun.[52] Rather, Moore is a coastal liberal's caricature of Alabama. He imagined all the things that liberals hated, and then crafted a political persona in this image. This negative identification gave Moore's political performances their hyperbolic, over-the-top quality. The more he offended liberal civility, the more he triggered the condescension that validated his image of a spokesman for victimized white southern Christians railing against a shadowy establishment comprised of economic, political, media, and educational elites.[53] He performed this victimization while living the life of a racially and economically privileged person who held a great deal of local power.

GODLY STATUS

Rather than an organic whole, evangelicalism in the United States seeks to unite people with different and often conflicting beliefs, sentiments, and practices into a single movement. This is not to say that all of the diverse practices, beliefs, and institutions that fall under the evangelical umbrella are reducible to this project. It is to say that the formation of a transdenominational movement that took the name evangelicalism only makes sense as a response to the perceived growth of modernism, liberalism, and secularism.[54]

This means that secularism is interior to evangelicalism rather than a threat from outside.[55] There is no church of the white evangelical. It is a secular category produced by pollsters that has been embraced by secular liberals and illiberal secularists who have investments in the existence of white evangelicalism.[56] For different reasons, both separate values from ordinary politics. Rather than political ideas to be criticized and debated, values are sacred beliefs that lay beyond scientific, economic, political, and even theological reason. The problem with the culture wars analysis, then, is that it takes values at face value. According to theories of culture wars, values are sui generis principles that exist prior to political engagement. Therefore, values either shape politics, or are distorted by politics, or are ignored altogether by hypocritical political actors. This analysis neglects how values are themselves the products of political contests.[57] Within these contests, it is useful to define values as different from ordinary political interests. Unlike interests, values invest sacred matters with an aura of depth and profundity. To attack someone's Christian values, then, is to attack core features of their identity. This allows Moore to dismiss Kimmel's satire as elitist bigotry and places Christian values beyond criticism.

Placing values beyond critique also protects interlocking features of white evangelical identity like family and nation. Christian values, family values, and American values are synonymous commitments under attack by liberal elites. As Smith explains, "If the 'religious' quality of religious speech is its ability to claim authority beyond human critique, it seems entirely possible to assert that there is no distinction between God and nation, for both are positioned as equally unquestionable, and mutually reinforcing entities. Sexual regulation is the vehicle by which the nation proves is exceptional, godly status."[58] But while the nation has a godly status, the government is a profane institution beholden to godless liberals. Rather than Washington, D.C., the true location for the nation is in private institutions like the church and the family. The American nation, like Christian values, is an exception to ordinary political interests. All of this is consistent with secular divisions between religion and the state.

This is not to say that Moore is pleased with the secular bargain. Moore longs for a government based on Christian principles, but bigoted liberals have made this impossible. By casting attacks on Christian values as bigotry, white evangelicals have portrayed themselves as victims of attacks designed to limit their public influence. As Christian psychologist and spanking enthusiast James Dobson has complained, "Certain powerful groups and organizations seek to weaken the church of Jesus Christ and limit what pastors and ministers can say and do publicly. They believe some of our teachings represent 'hate speech' and must be stifled."[59] If the public witness of Christian teachings is labeled as offensive hate speech, then it makes sense to shore up private institutions to protect the sanctity of Christian values.

Refuting charges of hate speech gets to the heart of the sexual and racial projects that have gone hand in hand in the formation of white evangelical identity. As Randall Balmer notes, family values activism in the 1970s was the rhetorical strategy of Christian right activists who recognized that they had lost the public battle for overt racial segregation: "Although abortion had emerged as a rallying cry by 1980, the real roots of the religious right lie not the defense of a fetus but in the defense of racial segregation."[60] Fighting a culture war was more palatable than fighting a race war.[61] Stressing religion over race framed Christians as victims of bigotry rather than the beneficiaries of white supremacy.[62] In her study of persistent racism among white evangelicals, Anthea Butler argues that this persecution complex also serves to excuse the transgressive behavior of white men like Moore: "Because conservative evangelicalism embraces patriarchal culture imbued with a persecution complex, its leaders will always have an excuse for their excesses, transgressions, and sins. And sin for evangelicals is always personal, not corporate, and God is always available to forgive deserving individuals, especially, it seems, if the sinner is a white man."[63]

The point here is not that Christian values are really about race instead of sex or religion.[64] Rather, these are all part of an imagined way of life tied to the defense of the white, heteronormative Christian family.[65] Advocacy for family values fits within a broader political project to shore up the power of private institutions like families, churches, and corporations to govern civic life.[66] Trump support becomes less hypocritical and mysterious once white evangelicalism is recognized not as some cultural or religious force that influences politics but as a political movement.

Rather than examples of irrational tribalism, appeals to Christian values are an effective political strategy.[67] It is useful to be offended. This strategy allows a demographic minority to help elect a president who would vigorously fight for them. The persistence of chaos rhetoric, however, depends upon the danger of losing. As is often the case in cases of minority rule, the people identified as white evangelicals manifest the particular intensity of groups who see themselves as outnumbered. Taking a page out of the Jim Crow playbook, the Republican Party views demographic threats as the justification to undercut democratic institutions in order to survive. Strategies like gerrymandering, voter suppression, immigration restrictions, and cooperation with fellow ethnonationalist movements abroad are existential necessities for a minority who seeks to do whatever it takes to win.

5

MASTERPIECE CAKESHOP
AND THE ART OF
RELIGIOUS FREEDOM

n an interview that appeared in the *Advocate* in 2000, Donald Trump discussed a potential run for the presidency as a candidate of the Reform Party. Consistent with his habit of tailoring his message to whomever he is speaking, Trump expressed support for gay rights. As he explained, "I like the idea of amending the 1964 Civil Rights Act to include a ban of discrimination based on sexual orientation."[1] During the 2016 presidential campaign Trump insisted that he was a closer friend to the LGBTQ community than Hillary Clinton was. As he proclaimed, "I'm much better for the gays."[2] While Trump's sincerity would be called into question by his later nominations of antigay crusaders for judicial and cabinet appointments, amending the Civil Rights Act would have amounted to more assertive protections than existed in American law. While same-sex marriage was legalized in the landmark 2015 *Obergefell v. Hodges* decision, explicit protections against discrimination based on sexual orientation existed in a patchwork of local and state statutes.[3]

One such statute became the subject of *Masterpiece Cakeshop v. Colorado Civil Rights Commission*, in which a baker named Jack C. Phillips violated Colorado's public accommodations law when he refused to bake a cake for the wedding of Charlie Craig and David Mullins. The Colorado Civil Rights Commission ruled that Phillips discriminated against Craig and Mullins on the basis of sexual orientation. The U.S. Supreme Court, however, ruled in favor of Phillips because some members of the commission demonstrated "hostility to religion." As Justice Anthony Kennedy stated, "The official expressions of hostility to religion in some of the commissioners' comments—comments that were not disavowed at the Commission or by the State at any point in the proceedings that led to affirmance of the order— were inconsistent with what the Free Exercise Clause requires."[4] Hostility impeded the commission's ability to make a "neutral and respectful consideration" of the baker's religious freedom claim. Respect played a central role in *Masterpiece Cakeshop*. Phillips claimed that his religious convictions were disrespected by the commission, while Mullins and Craig felt disrespected by Phillips.

THE ART OF RELIGIOUS FREEDOM

Deciding that Colorado was hostile to religion was a boon to conservative Christians who argued that antidiscrimination laws discriminated against them. Phillips's defense team insisted that forcing a baker to bake a cake for a same-sex wedding means that the state of Colorado was "ordering him to sketch, sculpt, and hand-paint cakes that celebrate a view of marriage in violation of his religious convictions."[5] The baker's religious convictions held that same-sex unions profane the sanctity of marriage. According to Phillips, forcing him to bake same-sex wedding cakes amounted to an unconstitutional form of "compelled speech." By highlighting speech, Phillips's lawyers focused less on selling cakes than on the expressive work of designing them.

Phillips did not refuse to sell premade cakes to same-sex couples. His willingness to sell existing cakes was a part of his defense. According to Phillips, he did not discriminate against persons because of their sexual identities. Such discrimination would have violated Colorado civil rights law. His refusal was limited to customized cakes with messages that he considered offensive or that violated his conscience. Phillips argued that he was not singling out any group of people because he had a consistent policy against offensive cakes. For example, he refused to bake cakes for divorces or Halloween (on the grounds that it is a pagan holiday). Compelling him to bake a cake for a same-sex wedding violated his rights as a religious person as well as a cake artist. Doubling down on the First Amendment, this strategy coupled religious freedom with free speech in attempt to beat secular liberals at their own game.[6] Phillips's lawyers portrayed the baker as the victim of intolerant hostility toward sincere religious convictions.

Arguing over hair-splitting distinctions between premade and customized cakes is the kind of thing that lawyers do. Indeed, Phillips's artistic integrity appears to be invented for the purpose of making a legal argument. It was unclear why a sincere artist would make a distinction between baking two cakes that look the same except for different gendered names on them. If the consumption of his art in an immoral ceremony is such a moral quandary, why would it not bother a baker if he is aware that one of his already-made artistic creations is indeed bought and used to celebrate a same-sex marriage? When does his artistic intent begin and end? A remarkable portion of the case's oral arguments turned on whether Phillips is really an artist, and this in turn raised hypothetical questions about who else could make such a claim. Is a florist who produces custom-made flower arrangements an artist? Phillips's lawyer answered yes. A floral arrangement has the kind of expressiveness that makes it count as art. How about the designer of a wedding invitation? The answer was yes as well. How about a jeweler? A jeweler could possibly be an artist, but it would depend on how much customization. What about a hairdresser? No, hairdressers are not artists according to Phillips's defense team. This puzzled Justice Elena Kagan, who asked: "Why is there no speech in creating a wonderful hairdo?"[7] Why should hair and makeup not count as art? After all, she protested, a makeup artist is the only category that actually has *artist* in its name. Kagan's objection drew a laugh, but she had a serious point. If what matters is whether people feel like they are making art when they do their jobs, then objective standards for who counts as an artist become less significant. Who is to tell makeup artists that they are not artists?

Tailors and architects also did not count as artists. The architect exclusion puzzled Justice Stephen Breyer, who asked: "So in other words, Mies or Michelangelo would not be protected when he creates the Laurentian steps, but this cake baker is protected when he creates without any message on it for a wedding?"[8] Justices objected that all of these occupations have expressive qualities. Remarkably, the defense did not claim that chefs produce art. This raised the question of what distinguishes a baker from a chef. Both occupations involve harnessing heat to produce things to be eaten. Was it the icing? Was it because a cake has words and pictures, but people do not customarily write things on steak?

The Court's metaphysical discussion of the definition of art arose because of the legal strategy articulated by Kristen Waggoner of the Alliance Defending Freedom. The progressive magazine *The Nation* christened Waggoner's organization "an army of Christian lawyers."[9] The specter of a Christian army manipulating the language of religious freedom frightened liberals not only because of the threat to roll back gains in LGBTQ rights but also because the recent appointment of Justice Neil

Gorsuch meant that the Christian legal warriors might win.[10] Deciding to make the case about artistry instead of focusing strictly on religious objections was a curveball that showed legal savvy.

The novelty of the conceptual questions posed by legal definitions of cake artistry demonstrates that the law does not merely protect religious freedom; it produces religion. In the process of trying to win legal or moral arguments, bakers and lawyers invent ideas and practices. New sets of questions arise in response to practical situations, such as competing interpretations of state civil rights statutes by interested parties. The American adversarial system expects that lawyers use all legal means at their disposal to win cases, and strategic uses of religious freedom shape what people identify as sincere convictions. In this process, things become religious that people would not necessarily have recognized as religious until there was a legal need to do so.[11] In this case, the legal production of religion was a consequence of *Masterpiece Cakeshop*'s overlapping defenses of religious freedom and free speech.

Phillips's defense of his rights as both a Christian and cake artist asserted that religious and artistic sentiments should be sincere, and that the way one expresses oneself should emanate from interior convictions free from outside coercion. This is consistent with secular models of religious privacy. The logic implicit in Phillips's argument is that Colorado asked him to be a hypocrite who outwardly expressed views with which he did not really agree (in violation of his rights to free speech), and which did not conform to his conscience (in violation of his free exercise of religion). If cakes are art and artistic sincerity is religious sincerity, then baking becomes religion.

Beyond the courtroom, there was popular confusion about gay cakes. On the internet, Facebook and Twitter feeds were full of posts and tweets that asked whether Jewish bakers would be forced to bake Nazi cakes. Such hyperbolic arguments diverted attention from the legal issues at stake in *Masterpiece Cakeshop*. The government was not seeking a general right to compel speech that would force bakers to bake things for anyone and everyone who happened to walk into their shop. The controversy in *Masterpiece Cakeshop* arose because of Colorado law that prohibited discrimination against certain specified categories, and sexual orientation was one of those. There were no statutes in Colorado that made Nazis a protected class.[12] The law in question states: "It is a discriminatory practice and unlawful for a person, directly or indirectly, to refuse, withhold from, or deny to an individual or a group, because of disability, race, creed, color, sex, sexual orientation, marital status, national origin, or ancestry, the full and equal enjoyment of the goods, services, facilities, privileges, advantages, or accommodations of a place of public accommodation."[13] The people of Colorado, through their democratic institutions, decided to regulate public accommodations to prevent discrimination. That Phillips's business serves the public while discriminating in violation of Colorado law is why cake artistry ended up in court. Part of what was at stake was drawing the lines between public and private. The state insisted that Phillips does business with the public and therefore has to accommodate everyone equally. Phillips's argument stressed his private right to run his business in accordance with his conscience.

To gain protection under Colorado's civil rights law, hypothetical Nazis would have to argue that their beliefs are a creed of some sort (and there is some discussion in oral arguments about whether an African American baker would be forced to bake a cake for a Klansman on the ground that this could be a creed). However, courts have addressed racism-as-creed arguments before. In *Newman v. Piggie Park*, Maurice Bessinger, an owner of several barbecue restaurants, argued that he has the right to refuse service to African Americans on the grounds that he has a religious belief that God intends the races to be separate.[14] The ruling does not necessarily challenge Bessinger's sincerity. Indeed, the courts rarely challenge the sincerity of belief as it would require them to provide an objective definition of religion as well as look into people's hearts to determine whether they are sincere.[15] In the *Piggie Park* case, the ruling held: "Undoubtedly defendant Bessinger has a constitutional right to espouse the religious beliefs of his own choosing, however, he does not have the absolute right to exercise and practice such beliefs in utter disregard of the clear constitutional rights of other citizens."[16]

The fluidity of creeds highlights a recurring theme in legal debates about religion. As with art, what counts as religion can be arbitrary. Lots of things have been labeled religious for a variety of reasons, and not all the reasons cohere with each other. In *Masterpiece Cakeshop*, seeking protections from commerce with offensive messages invented forms of religious sincerity to be protected by secular law. To be clear, the purpose of this chapter is not to make an argument for how this or any case should be decided. For that matter, the decision does not technically settle the question of whether Phillips could claim a religious exemption from baking a cake for a same-sex marriage. The decision holds only that government officials should not demonstrate hostility to religion. It does not address what would happen if the officials in charge of enforcing an antidiscrimination statute do not express antireligious animus.[17] Rather than resolve these legal questions, my analysis focuses on the political implications of arguments that secular institutions should protect the rights of its citizens to avoid complicity with the offensive actions of others.[18] I suggest that complicity claims are part of a legal strategy advanced by people who feel like they have lost the power to regulate public morality. Refusing to be complicit in immoral behavior does not advance any public moral argument but instead dramatizes the impossibility of public moral arguments. Complicity claims are therefore a useful vehicle to advance an illiberal secularist project to privatize public goods, but this requires an acceptance of secular models of religious tolerance.

COMPLICITY

So what does complicity mean? Complicity claims, such as in the refusal by the craft store Hobby Lobby to provide some forms of contraceptive coverage for their employees (or at least their refusal to do so with their own money), insist that to do business with immoral practices is to tacitly endorse them.[19] There is no discussion of complicity in the *Masterpiece Cakeshop* decision. This is because the Court offered no analysis of the religious practice Phillips sought to exercise. As Winnifred Fallers Sullivan observes, "As with the owners of *Hobby Lobby*, Mr. Phillips believes that he will be complicit with evil, in the words of moral theology, if he takes actions to enable what he takes to be sinful activity. The Court does not inquire whether his views are orthodox Christian teaching. There is an easy assumption by the Court here and in the *Hobby Lobby* opinions that conservative views about sex are religious while liberal ones are secular. No explanation need be given."[20] While it offered no explanation, the Court accepted the logic of complicity claims when it agreed that businesses should not have to participate in what their owners consider to be immoral actions.

Anxieties about complicity continue to exist even when there is no financial cost to the corporation or when there is no chance of making any difference in people's behavior. People who seek protection from complicity sometimes concede that they will have no actual effect on the actions of others but that they still need to make symbolic displays of their disapproval of other people's behavior. Hobby Lobby, for example, conceded that its employees would get contraceptive coverage that was mandated under the Affordable Care Act, but it wanted to make clear that the money to pay for this came from a separate fund provided by the insurer. The need to avoid complicity implies that religious actors suffer harm when their commercial activity comes into symbolic contact with a practice that offends them. This objection to taking offense reveals a tension at the heart of both religious freedom and free speech. On one hand, offense is often understood as a necessary by-product of free speech. To live in a free society means that one will have to occasionally endure offense, but you need to shake it off. On the other hand, Phillips insisted that religion posed a special case. One should not have to be complicit in other people's immoral activity if one can show a reasonable fear that the offense causes *religious* profanation.

Phillips's actions met the criteria for the kind of negative freedom ensured by secular liberal views of religious toleration. That is, he was willing to legally tolerate Craig and Mullins even if he did not agree with them. Phillips would not bake for them, but he would not refuse to sell them cakes. Furthermore, Craig and Mullins were able to find a baker who would design a cake for their wedding. Their complaints were not about the material inability to acquire a cake. Rather, they were stung by the harm to their dignity that came from their being the target of discrimination. Recounting how he felt when Phillips refused to bake his cake, Mullins recalled: "I admit we were very emotional. We hadn't gone through anything like this. We were embarrassed, and we felt degraded."[21] They were offended not because Phillips held Christian beliefs but because he acted on those beliefs to harm them. His refusal was directed at them. It hurt them. In addition to their wounded dignity, they lost their civil protections from discrimination. To all of this, the lawyers defending Phillips could protest that such dignitary harm was unfortunate but, in the end, merely symbolic. Yet the same point could be made in the other direction. A same-sex marriage neither picks a baker's pocket nor breaks his leg. In the end, Phillips was engaged in a symbolic grudge match with his rejected customers. So who should have to shake it off?

FREE EXERCISE

The conflict between dignitary harm and religious freedom raises the question of what religious activity Phillips performs when he does not bake a cake. Exactly what kind of religious exercise is noncomplicity? Free exercise tends to be relatively uncomplicated in matters of obvious religious worship. Any law designed to target the rituals or beliefs of a particular group is illegal. The tricky part is how far the law can go to accommodate people who break neutral laws that apply to everyone. Another complication is that in addition to worship, religious exercise also covers the right to make moral claims based on conscience. Phillips could have objected to baking the cake on the grounds of religious worship. He could have argued that he did not want to participate in a religious ritual that was not his own. Less attention has been paid to marriage as a sacred ceremony, however, as arguments have focused on moral objections to same-sex marriage.[22] This raises the question of why some moral arguments are religious. Are religious moral arguments different from other moral arguments because they originate in teachings understood to be religious?[23] This distinction is significant because Phillips was insisting not only on his right to be a Christian but also to make moral rules that govern the behavior of people who do not share his religious convictions.

Before further investigating Phillips's desire to make rules for everyone, it might be helpful to briefly review the conditions under which people can ask for religious exemptions from following the law. A classic example would be the refusal of Quakers to fight in war. It has been less clear what exemptions exist apart from conscientious objection to military service. One view is almost none. In the 1879 case *Reynolds v. United States*, a member of the Church of Jesus Christ of Latter Day Saints argued that he should have the ability to enter into multiple marriages.[24] The Court ruled that while Reynolds was free to believe in polygamy, he was not free to do it.[25] Religious freedom extends only to beliefs. Actions that violate the law are actions that violate the law and could be treated no differently because of their religious intent. Laws that ban polygamy do not violate Mormon religious freedom because they are not discriminating against Mormons. Everyone has to follow them.

A couple of cases in the 1940s changed this. These cases involve Jehovah's Witnesses who did not salute the flag in school. The *Minersville School District v. Gobitis* case in 1940 followed *Reynolds* by stating that Jehovah's Witness children still have to follow the law and could be compelled to say the Pledge of Allegiance.[26] But in the 1943 decision *West Virginia Board of Education v. Barnette*, the Court reversed itself.[27] Much of this was in response to events in Europe where Jehovah's Witnesses were persecuted by Nazis for a similar failure to salute. This helped to create a precedent for allowing some students to have exemptions from an otherwise neutral law.[28]

The 1963 case *Sherbert v. Verner* helped to specify a legal standard for exemptions.[29] In this case a Seventh-day Adventist woman lost her job because she did not want to work on Saturday, when she observed the Sabbath. The state insisted that she was ineligible for unemployment benefits because she quit voluntarily. The Court ruled that it is not hard to make an exemption that respects Sabbath observance as it requires little more than giving unemployed benefits to an unemployed person. This ruling produced the Sherbert Test, which suggests that state can refuse to grant a free exercise exemption only if it possesses some compelling state interest to do so and no alternative form of regulation can be found.

However, in a 1990 ruling, *Employment Division v. Smith*, another unemployment benefits case reached a different conclusion.[30] Drug counselors were fired and then denied unemployment benefits for ingesting peyote, a banned substance that was part of ritual practice within the Native American Church. However, this time the Court held that because drug laws apply to everyone, there was no religious discrimination. This rejection of the Sherbert Test alarmed many who saw an erosion of religious liberty. This alarm led to the 1993 Religious Freedom Restoration Act (RFRA), in which Congress told the Supreme Court to go back to the Sherbert Test. In 1997, however, the Court struck this down as Congress cannot tell the Court how to interpret the Constitution.[31] However, there was a loophole. While Congress cannot tell the Court how to interpret the Constitution, it can tell the Court how to interpret its own statutes. This means that RFRA still holds for federal statutory law but does not hold for state laws that would require a Fourteenth Amendment ruling.

In response to the ruling that RFRA does not cover state law, some states passed their own RFRAs. These state efforts became closely tied to discrimination on the basis of sexual orientation, and they faced a great deal of high-profile opposition. Colorado does not have a RFRA. Therefore, *Masterpiece Cakeshop* was decided on First/Fourteenth Amendment grounds. In that sense, the legal questions are different from the *Hobby Lobby* case. But one thing that *Masterpiece Cakeshop* and *Hobby Lobby* have in common is that, as complicity claims, they concern themselves with other people's behavior. This was not really the case for Jehovah's Witnesses who refused to salute the flag, or the Seventh-day Adventist who wanted to observe the Sabbath, or members of the Native American Church who ingested peyote. These were freedoms sought by people who understood themselves to be religious minorities and who hoped to govern their own actions while also affirming their equal participation in American public life. To this end, they hoped to benefit by tying legal protections of religious freedom to secular liberal ideals of diversity and inclusion.

THE TYRANNY OF THE MINORITY

People who register complicity complaints are acting as groups who at least *should* be in the majority, and who should be able to make the rules for everyone's behavior. Christians like Phillips insist that the heteronormative family is necessary to inculcate the habits of moral discipline that govern the behavior of future citizens but that the state has abandoned its responsibility to protect the family. Christians who recognize that they have lost the power to regulate everyone's behavior, however, settle for religious freedom. The reason that same-sex marriage is a profanation is not that it broke the sexual rules of marriage. Conservative Christians break marital rules all the time. Private behavior does not always live up to public norms. The problem is that same-sex couples are not penitent. Rather than apologize for breaking the rules, Craig and Mullins sought to redraw the rules. Furthermore, they insisted that Phillips respect their marriage. This is why a marriage between consenting adults is more of a threat than a predatory attorney harassing teenagers in a mall.

Phillips's anxieties about complicity, then, did not require intolerance of personal behavior. His customers were free to do what they wished in their own private lives, but Phillips believed their state-sanctioned marriage should be illegal. His refusal to bake a cake stemmed from his insistence that his norms should be legal rules because he should be acting as the voice of the majority. As legal scholars Douglas NeJaime and Reva B. Siegel argue, this is a crucial feature of arguments that hinge on complicity: "Without a change in numbers or belief, religious actors can shift from *speaking as a majority* seeking to enforce traditional morality to *speaking as a minority* seeking exemptions from laws that offend traditional morality."[32] The view that a Christian majority should have the authority to make rules is often coupled with a nostalgic vision that this was how it was in the past. In this narrative, there was a time when everyone understood that America was a Christian nation and that this national identity was right and just. While much of this national narrative is nostalgia, it was not long ago that same-sex marriage was universally illegal in the United States. Even the decision in Phillips's favor still made clear that the majority of the Court supported civil rights protections for gay couples. As Justice Kennedy insisted, "Our society has come to the recognition that gay persons and gay couples cannot be treated as social outcasts or as inferior in dignity and worth. For that reason the laws and the Constitution can, and in some instances must, protect them in the exercise of their civil rights."[33] The quickness with which American law and culture has shifted on this question has left the conservative Christian bakers of the world deeply confused about their power. From a Christian majoritarian perspective, it might be okay for religious or sexual minorities to ask for toleration. It upsets the order of things, however, when religious or sexual minorities begin to make the rules.

With their newfound perceptions of themselves as religious minorities, conservative Christians have expanded the language of religious freedom to describe a broad range of objections. It is because of perceived losses in authority and power that conservative Christians have resorted to complicity claims. Fueling these claims is the complaint that those who should be in the majority are unable to rule because democratic institutions have been co-opted by a coalition of religious, sexual, racial, and ethnic groups in collusion with morally and spiritually impoverished liberal elites. All of this is felt as a profanation of an otherwise holy and Christian American nation, and this profanation is registered as religious offense. The rise of complicity claims marks a protest over this perceived loss of Christian authority to govern other people's actions.[34]

While *Masterpiece Cakeshop* affirms the civil rights of same-sex couples, there are significant gains for Alliance Defending Freedom beyond winning the case. In addition to establishing that Colorado is hostile to religion, the decision equates state discrimination against Phillips with Phillips's discrimination against Craig and Mullins. Justice Kennedy's majority decision as well as concurring opinions by Justice Clarence Thomas and Justice Gorsuch focus on the commission's decision to allow other bakers to refuse to bake homophobic cakes requested by Christian customers. According to the Court, such a distinction is a problem because it favors sexual freedom over religious freedom. Homophobia and antihomophobia should be given equal consideration when deciding a case where citizens decide to opt out of compliance with a law. Everyone who is offended must be treated the same way. As Justice Kennedy explains, "A principled rationale for the difference in treatment of these two instances cannot be based on the government's own assessment of offensiveness."[35] In drawing this equivalence, however, the Court sidestepped an important difference between the legal goals of Phillips and his customers. If Phillips had his way, the marriage of Craig and Mullins would be illegal. Craig and Mullins, however, were not seeking a legal prohibition of Christian marriage. Rather than restrict sexual relationships, the rulebook proposed by Craig and Mullins accommodates diverse practices.

For conservative critics, the mandate to accommodate other people is an enforced regime of political correctness. To adhere to the norms of this politically correct world means that they have to revise their own speech and practices in light of new information about diverse sensibilities. This is felt as an acute loss of freedom for people who did not previously have to consider sensibilities apart from their own. It is only in response to this perceived loss of freedom that conservative Christians have decided that views about same-sex marriage should be protected by the free exercise of religion. It was not self-evident that marriage fell under the institutional governance of religion rather than the state. Of course, Phillips is a Christian who identifies his motives as religious. For this reason, the Court did not bother to analyze the religious logic of noncomplicity claims. Phillips, however, did not object to the religious practices of his customers. Indeed, religious discrimination could violate Colorado law. For that matter, Craig and Mullins did not see themselves as doing anything profane or irreligious. They wanted to buy a cake without facing discrimination. Similarly, the *Hobby Lobby* case involved employees who wanted access to a government-mandated health benefit without interference from their employer's religion. One point of agreement among

all parties is that the actions of Masterpiece Cakeshop's customers and Hobby Lobby's employees were not religious.

In other words, the conflict between Phillips and his customers was not a disagreement about religion but a disagreement
about law. Nevertheless, complicity claims still treat religious
motives for legal disagreements differently from other legal disagreements. Classifying motives as religious, much like classifying a baker's cakes as art, is a process that draws arbitrary lines
around some forms of human behavior. This is not to say that
arbitrary classifications of what counts as religion are new.
Scholarship in religious studies has noted that while practices,
institutions, and beliefs that are currently conventionally classified as religious have existed for a long time, the idea that all of
these are part of complex, internally bounded systems called
religions is relatively modern.[36] In the process of this category
formation, some things were called religion and some things
were not. Religious law often overlaps with civil law. The things
that we call religions have rules against murder or stealing that
are not usually identified as distinctly religious rules. Rules are
identifiably religious when they contradict civil law or create
legal or ritual regulations that exceed the law.

In the American case, much of what has been labeled religion or nonreligion can be traced to practical strategies to win
legal arguments. These legal arguments invoke the wisdom of
secular separations between ecclesiastical and civil institutions,
or the separation or church and state. Within the logic of this
separation, civil laws govern everyone whereas church laws govern those people who voluntarily join churches. The decision to
join a church is voluntary because it is driven by interior commitments dictated by one's conscience. However, Christian conservatives had not previously argued that marriage is a matter
to be resolved by conscience without interference from the state.

Rather, they believe that same-sex marriage should be prohibited by civil law for *everyone* without regard to religious convictions. There should be no religious exemptions for Craig and Mullins. A similar point could be made about *Hobby Lobby*. The owners of Hobby Lobby thought that no one should have access to some forms of birth control because these amount to murder. Religious freedom is irrelevant, and this is not a matter to be left to people's consciences. Marriage and murder fall on the civil side of the ledger. While Christians might have seen marriage as a religious sacrament or murder as a religious prohibition, they also thought these matters should be regulated by civil law without regard for people's consciences.

The specific issue in *Masterpiece Cakeshop* was that Phillips had a religious obligation to make a symbolic display of noncomplicity with a law that failed to outlaw someone else's behavior, and that the ability to express his symbolic objection through commerce required a religious exemption from civil law. The purpose of complicity claims, then, is to allow dispossessed majorities to argue that issues they previously insisted were civil matters were now distinctly ecclesiastical. They conceded that they had lost the power to shape civil laws about marriage, but their private religious rights should be protected. Therefore, the Alliance Defending Freedom was making a more rigorously secular argument than conservative Christians had made in the past.

The arbitrary line between civil and ecclesiastical law is evident in how circumstances changed during the time between Phillips's refusal of service and when the case ended up in the Supreme Court. When Craig and Mullins walked into Masterpiece Cakeshop in 2012, same-sex marriage was against the law in Colorado. Justice Samuel Alito raised this issue in oral arguments as a defense of Phillips, and the illegality of same-sex marriage informed Justice Kennedy's decision. After all, how could a baker be punished for complying with state law? The civil prohibition of same-sex marriage, however, created problems that the Court did not think through. It would not be the Court's position that it created a novel right in the 2015 *Obergefell* decision. That is not how constitutional rights are supposed to work. Rather, the Court recognized a right in 2015 that should have been protected before but was not because of the discriminatory blind spots in previous interpretations of the law. This meant that Colorado law in 2012, with the support of people like Phillips, denied the rights of same-sex couples like Craig and Mullins. For this reason, they had to fly to Massachusetts to get married. Only later would they hold a celebration in their home state. This is more than dignitary harm. Colorado's violation of their rights did, in a very practical sense, pick the pocket of Craig and Mullins. When Phillips refused service, he was not expressing his own personal religious convictions; he was speaking for laws that discriminated against same-sex couples. Complicity claims often amount to such indirect forms of pocket picking. Those who point to the harmlessness of noncomplicity assert that citizens who are denied services or entitlements are still free to purchase them by using their own money. This gets back to the question of who should have to shake off offense. Many Americans might respond that the same-sex couple should have to deal with offense because owners should be able to do what they want with their businesses, but this makes freedom dependent on property.[37] A business owner could opt out of the rules that govern how people live together, but this freedom is distributed unequally. As Wendy Brown argues, the *Masterpiece Cakeshop*'s combination of commercial and religious freedom "sets free exercise loose in the public and commercial sphere and generates the scene of its entitlement to discriminate, indeed, to abridge the laws of equality. This is more than constitutional constructivism. This is the U.S. Supreme Court empowering a revolutionary antidemocratic force through a novel joining together of ownership, religion, and speech."[38] Phillips's free exercise of religion fits with broader trends toward privatization in which businesses seek freedom from government regulation.

If businesses could refuse to comply with rules governing what they previously believed to be civil matters, then large chunks of civil society would be relocated to the private sphere.[39] Those who advance complicity claims invoke religious tolerance to protect themselves from demands for civil equality.[40] This is why discrimination statutes hit so close to home. The Alliance Defending Freedom objected to an active engagement with difference among equal citizens rather than an ability to tolerate people from a position of power. The lost ability to tolerate a less powerful person is at the heart of complicity claims. Noncomplicity is a protest against a public order in which antidiscrimination has become a feature of learning to live with people in a sexually and religious diverse world. Phillips's defense of his artistic sincerity and religious freedom is consistent with how appeals to free speech deflect from practical attempts to address dignitary, economic, and physical harm.

IS ANYONE LISTENING TO
MASTERPIECE CAKESHOP?

There is a price for legal victories. The owners of Hobby Lobby and Masterpiece Cakeshop protected their businesses but conceded that they could not govern other people's behavior. By settling for the protection of property, the logic of religious freedom made Phillips's moral and theological views irrelevant

to Colorado law. Acknowledging that their employees or customers are free to sin, Christians who make complicity claims
hunker down with private liberty. As Brown suggests, render-
ing religion as private property sets free exercise loose in the
commercial sphere. But what does this mean for Phillips's religious beliefs? In her study of corporate religious freedom, Sullivan objects that focusing exclusively on the commercial logic of
complicity claims reflects an "impoverished understanding of
christian theology."[41] According to Sullivan, scholars of religion should push back against the flat secular categories used
by courts to decide religious freedom cases. Scholarly analysis
should dig deeper to recover the complexity of the moral and
theological views that give rise to concerns about complicity.
Addressing scholarly treatments of the *Hobby Lobby* case,
Sullivan argues the failure to take theology and ecclesiology
seriously has led to superficial interpretations in which "the religious lives and claims of the plaintiffs in *Hobby Lobby* are simply dismissed as the inauthentic products of late capitalism run
amok."[42]

Rather than accept flat, secular categories that make moral
debates between Phillips and his customers impossible, Sullivan offers a counternarrative that aspires to speak theologically
to the law. She imagines a richer moral and theological conversation that would engage Phillips about his own professed religious convictions. To this end, she imagines a scenario in which
Phillips and his customers could meet for a civil dialogue. This
conversation would address not only Phillips's legal claims but
his theological rationale. As Sullivan asks, "Could we then say
back to Phillips that Jesus ate with sinners? Or that all are sinners? Or 'judge not that ye be judged?' Or that hospitality and
table fellowship have been virtues in many traditions? *And then
listen to his response.* Is all that can be done is, first, to isolate and

segregate devout religious people, and then, either vilify them or treat them with kid gloves?"[43] Sullivan laments how the impoverishment of legal discourse makes moral discussions impossible. In her account, secular liberals are as responsible for this impossibility as supposedly intolerant religious believers.

The question is whether this secular impasse is the fault of liberal refusals to engage with Phillips or the legal strategy pursued by the Alliance Defending Freedom (or some combination of both). The purpose of complicity claims is to isolate and segregate. The legal strategy of the Alliance Defending Freedom could be summarized as a vigorous effort to preempt the conversation that Sullivan imagines. And this strategy has won. The price of this victory is that Phillips and his lawyers accepted the secular terms laid out by the law that make theological discussion impossible. As far as the law is concerned, Phillips sincerely believed that same-sex marriage is wrong and that was that. Once registered as a religious objection, it was immune to political, legal, economic, scientific, and even theological discussion. Secular liberal assumptions that religion is unreasonable worked to the advantage of complicity claims. These assumptions are part of an illiberal legal strategy that uses tolerance to beat secular liberals at their own game. But legal victories come with a price. As M. Cathleen Kaveny notes, "Most religious conservatives believe that their moral judgments are supported by reason; they strive to refurbish the broader Christian view of flourishing that would make those judgments intelligible. But their litigation strategy undercuts their ultimate aims."[44] By gaining secular rights, Christian conservatives sacrifice theological and moral persuasion.[45]

Ironically, Phillips welcomes the theological conversation that Sullivan describes. He laments that his interaction with Craig and Mullins lasted only twenty seconds and that he was unable to communicate the reasons for his refusal. As he explained, "On other occasions when I'd been asked to create something I could not in good conscience provide, I had at least been given the opportunity to talk it over with the customer, and we had always resolved the difference of opinion amicably."[46] In his autobiography, he is careful not to disparage Craig and Mullins. Phillips agrees that Jesus ate with sinners and that Christians have a duty to be hospitable. To this end, he welcomes non-Christians into his shop: "If you want to reject Jesus and purchase a cupcake, go ahead. I'll gladly sell you that cupcake and a cup of coffee to go with it, maybe even engage you in a conversation about our differences."[47]

According to Phillips, it is intolerant liberals who are unwilling to engage in conversation. They are also hypocrites in their defense of free speech. The hypocrisy of American Civil Liberties Union, for example, is demonstrated by its support for April Anderson, a lesbian baker in Detroit who was asked to bake a cake with the message: "Homosexual acts are gravely evil. (Catholic Catechism 2357)."[48] The cake was requested by a self-described "Retrograde Catholic" who hoped to demonstrate that antidiscrimination statutes amount to bigotry against Christians.[49] The ACLU sided with the baker's refusal to bake an offensive cake on the grounds that this would violate her First Amendment rights. As an ACLU attorney stated, "When you are asked to do a particular message, you might be crossing the line of what could be compelled speech, especially if it's offensive."[50] Phillips notes that the ACLU used similar language as his own legal defense and that both bakers have an equal right not to be forced to bake cakes that offend them. As Phillips protests, the ACLU lawyer "cannot see why that truth applies to me as well as the baker in Detroit."[51] This is an imperfect analogy. Catholics do not hold sacred ceremonies with homophobic cakes. Anderson notes that the purpose of ordering the cake was "to troll us."[52] This was not the motive of Phillips's rejected customers. For that matter, the baker baked the cake but never wrote messages on cakes, so there was no discrimination.[53] Regardless of the legal merits of this analogy, in supporting the baker's right of refusal, Phillips wanted to show the sincerity of his commitment to consistency and fair play. But the basis for this consistency is telling. The cakes themselves were not morally and theologically consistent. They were moral opposites. Rather, Phillips was consistent in his respect for secular privacy. This sort of reasoning is why it is helpful to understand the legal strategy that defended Phillips as a form of secularism employed by Christians rather than an attempt to Christianize the public.

The willingness to play by secular rules might also help to explain why so many people who share the theological views of Phillips so eagerly voted for Donald Trump. Trump is late capitalism run amok. While Trump supporters' complex private lives might not be reducible to late capitalism, their politics are. Illiberal secularism produces a separation of private virtue from public goods that creates a vacuum filled by Trumpism. It is possible that listening to *Masterpiece Cakeshop* offers some explanation for this. Trump listened to Phillips. Rather than dismissing Christians as ignorant bigots, Trump takes them seriously. What Trump heard was people who are tired of losing and want to win. Christian support for Trumpism makes perfect sense within the framework of illiberal secularism, which abandons moral persuasion in favor of a no-holds barred late capitalist identitarian slugfest.

One person who thought Trump was listening is Jeff Sessions, the first senator to publicly endorse the Trump presidential campaign. In a 2017 speech to members of the Alliance Defending Freedom, Attorney General Sessions underscored the importance of their work by citing a Facebook post by a law professor who claims that conservatives have lost the culture war. As Sessions warned, "Many Americans have felt that their freedom to practice their faith has been under attack. This feeling is understandable. Just last year, a Harvard Law professor publicly urged judges to 'take aggressively liberal positions. . . . The culture wars are over. They lost; we won. . . . Taking a hard line is better than trying to accommodate the losers.'"[54] It is telling that Sessions rallied his audience with his fear of losing to a Harvard professor. With war metaphors, debates about sexual norms can be reduced to contests between winners and losers. When supporters of the Alliance Defending Freedom throw their support behind Trump, they accept that this is what complicity claims are all about. You recognize that you do not have the legal power to outlaw someone else's behavior, but you are not ready to admit defeat. I am not convinced, however, that Craig and Mullins saw themselves as victors in a culture war. Culture wars in the United States have tended to be fought by one side. Phillips might have been fighting a culture war, but his customers were not. They took no pleasure in profaning what Phillips held sacred. Craig and Mullins did not see marriage as a zero-sum game where some people have to win and others have to lose. They walked into a bakery not because they intended to score cultural victories but because they wanted to share a cake with their friends.

6

NFL PROTESTS AND THE
PROFANE RITES OF SOMETHING

In a raucous Alabama speech in the fall of 2017, President Trump elicited cheers when he called on National Football League owners to discipline players who knelt during the American national anthem. In what would have been a remarkable use of profanity coming from any other president, Trump asked the crowd: "Wouldn't you love to see one of these NFL owners, when somebody disrespects our flag, to say, 'Get that son of a bitch off the field right now. Out. He's fired. He's fired!'"[1] Colin Kaepernick, who played quarterback for the San Francisco 49ers, had begun the practice in 2016 to show support for Black Lives Matter protests. Trump welcomed the opportunity to rail against both Black activism and unpatriotic dissent. Kaepernick initially sat during the national anthem, but he changed to kneeling to clarify that the players who knelt meant no disrespect for veterans. As he explained, "We came up with taking a knee because there are issues that still need to be addressed and there was also a way to show more respect for the men and women that fight for this country."[2] While taking a knee often signifies reverence, Trump supporters saw the players' protest as a profane gesture that disrespected the flag and the nation it symbolized.

One feature that NFL protests share with the legacy of 1960s civil rights activism is that they are models of civility. Silently kneeling is a disciplined and reverent action that threatens no one's safety. Tattooed with biblical verses, Kaepernick is to many a model of virtue with one of the most impressive records of charitable giving of any professional athlete.[3] Furthermore, the protests broke no laws. Taking a knee was nevertheless framed as uncivil disrespect that caused a crisis for civil unity.

Trump's use of uncivil language to denounce the lack of civic respect made the NFL protests an example of what sociologist Ruth Braunstein calls "civility contests." Not just debates between people with different political views, these contests are about the rules for civil discourse. What gets labeled civil or uncivil often has less to do with the content of words and actions than in who has the power to define civility: "The fact that large numbers of Americans interpreted this peaceful protest by a handful of black players as shocking, threatening, and beyond the pale reveals clearly how attributions of incivility are informed by entrenched social biases, especially when those biases are stoked by those in power."[4] Trump's denunciation was a deliberately offensive response that clarified who should be in charge and who was unworthy of civil treatment. By crossing a taboo line, the players invited the president's profanity. But Trump's counter-incivility left unclear what norms of civility held at all. According to journalist William C. Rhoden, the president's endorsement of incivility threatened to become a norm in its own right. Trump granted white football fans a license to treat African American players with disrespect: "He's in Huntsville, Ala., and he whips up this crowd of white supporters. And this is during the whole—you know, when players were protesting, and that then translates into in-stadium behavior. I think we're in this period of time where being uncivil has become the new norm."[5] NFL protests and counterprotests so inverted civil discourse that incivility became the normal language of American patriotism.

The controversy over the national anthem raises the question of whether the NFL protests registered as uncivil because they profaned the rituals of American civil religion. I am interested here in the multiple, overlapping senses of *civil*. The term *civil* describes civic principles of citizenship (such as in civil rights) as well as speech that conforms to the norms of civility or politeness. These senses of civility are often in tension with each other. Polite civility can be threatened by protest movements that make people uncomfortable by drawing attention to injustice. Civil rights activists have long faced criticism that their methods were too confrontational and divisive. This was no less true when activists demonstrated a disciplined commitment to nonviolence. In the 1963 statement that prompted Martin Luther King Jr.'s "Letter from a Birmingham Jail," for example, eight Alabama clergymen called on African Americans to work through legal means to unite locally as well as "to observe the principles of law and order and common sense."[6] According to King, law and order maintain a negative peace that mask the violence that enforces legal inequality. Through direct action that uses "creative tension" to force citizens to confront injustice, civil rights activists unmask illusory peacefulness.[7]

Producing unity is a central task for civil religion. According to the eighteenth-century philosopher Jean-Jacques Rousseau, civil religion has religious features but lacks the divisiveness of Christianity. As a generic religiosity that includes all citizens, civil religion is "a purely civil profession of faith of which the Sovereign should fix the articles, not exactly as religious dogmas, but as social sentiments without which a man cannot be a good citizen or a faithful subject."[8] Civil religion is something like religion but distinct from it, and similar to nationalism but not exactly like it either. Ideally, civic sentiments are not imposed by the state. According to Rousseau, shared sentiments reflect a "general will" that animates a common commitment to civic life. Respect for the law grows out of the organic free will of the people. In cases where an individual's will does not align with the general will, a citizen could be forced to conform. This compulsion does not make citizens less free, however.[9] As Rousseau asserts, "Whoever refuses to obey the general will shall be compelled to do so by the whole body. This means nothing less than he will be forced to be free."[10] While Rousseau's statement seems like a paradox, the apparent necessity of forcing people to be free might capture the spirit of the opposition to NFL protests. Players should be forced to salute the flag to show proper gratitude for their own freedom.

In Robert Bellah's application of civil religion to the United States, collective rituals of civic life produce national cohesion. Symbols like the flag or documents like the Declaration of Independence are revered by all citizens regardless of their personal religious commitments. Civil religion provides a common religious sensibility that fills a vacuum created by the separation of church and state. Shared rites and symbols teach citizens to respect the sanctity of national institutions.[11] Civil religion's cohesive character is particularly important in a pluralist society as it brings together people from diverse backgrounds to participate as equals in civic life. Writing in the 1960s, Bellah identifies the civil rights movement as a central test for the American creed of the equality of all citizens. In his view, racism is foreign to civil religion. Although noting that the rhetoric of God and country has often been used to attack ideals of inclusion, he insists that this is an anomaly: "It has been difficult to use the words of Jefferson and Lincoln to support special interests and undermine personal freedom. The defenders of slavery before the

Civil War came to reject the Declaration of Independence. Some of the most consistent of them turned against not only Jeffersonian democracy but Reformation religion; they dreamed of a South dominated by medieval chivalry and divine-right monarchy."[12] Southern racism was written out of civil religion as an anachronistic aberration, as a departure from the principle that all men are created equal.[13] By identifying patriotism with exclusive forms of Christianity and whiteness, Trump's bellicose rhetoric does not live up to Bellah's expectation that civil religion provides "a transcendent goal for the political process."[14] Indeed, it is not clear that Trump's habit of literally embracing the flag meets any criteria for sacred reverence.[15] For him, "our flag" is a symbol of power that marks some groups as more American than others rather than an ideal of equal treatment under the law.[16]

In later reflections on his 1967 essay, Bellah acknowledges the limitations of the civil religion concept. One problem is that transcendent language could be used for anything: "Every movement to make America more fully realize its professed values has grown out of some form of public theology, from the abolitionists to the social gospel and the early socialist party to the civil rights movement under Martin Luther King and the farm workers movement under Cesar Chavez. But so has every expansionist war and every form of oppression of racial minorities and immigrant groups."[17] By transcending any particular movement, American ideals of freedom and equality are so malleable than they risk becoming meaningless. Ironically, civil religion's aspirations to inclusivity dulls its critical edge. Some have argued, then, that civil religion has no explanatory efficacy at all.[18] Rather, it is merely another name for nationalism with some references to God thrown in.[19]

Critics argue that by teaching that racism is un-American, civil religion obscures the divisiveness and exclusivity of nationalism.[20] It is possible, however, that this aversion to divisive rhetoric might make civil religion a useful category to understand the civility contests surrounding the NFL protests. Rather than clearly distinguishing between civil religion and nationalism or throwing out the distinction altogether, this chapter stipulates that it can be useful to evaluate civil religion as a prescriptive form of nationalism that hopes to include all citizens under the law. Civil religion is an aspirational project, a liberal ideal of a perfected nationalism defined by civic principles instead of divisive markers of identification like race, ethnicity, or sectarian religion.[21] Positioning itself against nationalism, it is an idealized form of civic life with no need for friends and enemies.

Civil religion offers an idealized model of equality in two senses. First, it suggests that the nation is a polity without division. Second, it contends that citizens voluntarily follow the law in a way that makes police power necessary only when people fail to recognize their own freedom. This means that the violence of the state is imagined as an organic reflection of the will of the people rather than as police power applied unequally. By unmasking the divisive nature of the polity and the use of police power in the service of the safety of some citizens at the expense of others, Black Lives Matter protesters criticize two sacred tenets of American civil religion. The profane rites of protest reject false ideals of civic life in favor of a realistic appraisal of the distribution of power and money.

The reality that this profanation reveals is an underlying illiberalism masked by the rituals of civil religion. In illiberal civil religion, civic duty is reduced to loyalty to the police and the military. Respect for the flag is synonymous with respect for the troops. There are no civic virtues or public goods apart from policing crime or protecting borders. Consistent with illiberal secularism, it has no moral or theological content. Illiberal civil religion replaces civic belief with winning. Furthermore, many Americans insist on the value of religious and racial unity all the more strenuously in the face of critics who assert that no such unity exists. The founding creed "All men are created equal," while never a description of American reality, fits within a rhetoric of racial and religious neutrality that simultaneously maintains visceral identifications between whiteness, Christianity, and American citizenship. In other words, civil religion is liberal piety that, once profaned, reveals underlying inequalities. This profanation produces negative energy that can be appropriated for protests against injustice or for illiberal defenses of American nationalism.

SHAMEFUL PUBLICITY

It is worth noting that Kaepernick has resisted the characterization of his activism as religious.[22] Regardless of the players' motives, however, the offense to civil religion was felt in the reception of the protests rather than their intent. The public flare-up shows that, if nothing else, many fans registered the protests as a profanation regardless of what the players said. Indeed, Trump's reduction of the protests to an attack on American patriotism was a way of ignoring political content. Focusing on disrespect to sacred symbols like the flag, the anthem, and the troops turned a complaint about police violence into an existential attack on the nation. Civility contests drew lines between offended football fans who asserted that protesters insulted America and players who sought to make a political statement.

The NFL protesters dissented from American civil religion by rejecting the idea that police violence is a problem to be solved through an appeal to unity and transcendence. Rather, the Black Lives Matter movement insists on the racial particularity of injustice. Rather than unify Americans behind a supposedly shared transcendent goal, the profane rites of NFL protests drew attention to national divisions. These divisions were not invented by the protests as much as they revealed divided responses to violence present in American life. Taking a knee is a profane gesture not so much because it is deliberately offensive but because it refuses to participate in the cohesive rites of civil religion. This refusal displays what Nicolas Howe has described as an "aversive affect" that he finds in secular opposition to public displays of religiosity. In his examination of battles over public displays of the Ten Commandments, for example, Howe notes that the arguments have less to do with the wisdom of the commandments themselves than with the question of whether such displays represent the will of all Americans. Criticism of religious symbols, civil or otherwise, can animate divisive sentiments. This division becomes especially intense when dissenters assert that civil religion does not include them. As Howe explains, "Secularism need not be rationalistic and dispassionate. On the contrary, it can thrive on 'aversive affect,' on feelings of shame, outrage, and revulsion. By this means, it produces a kind of negative, agonistic solidarity against the positive, integrating solidarity of civil religion."[23]

If there is one small point of unity between Trump and the NFL protesters, it is that they both sought to create negative, agonistic solidarity. The Black Lives Matter movement provokes feelings that philosopher Christopher Lebron describes as "shameful publicity." In some sense, the belief that Americans can be shamed bears some resemblance to the principle that America is based on ideals of equality. There is a significant difference, however, in foregrounding shame rather than transcendence. As Lebron explains, shameful publicity seeks to go on the offensive to compel white Americans to reflect on whether they live up to their own ideals: "The idea of shameful publicity is something distinct from post-hoc protest. It is an offensive rather than defensive strategy that mobilizes the ideal of America as we seem to endorse it against the failure of America as it actually is. Its goal is to shed light on institutions whose mandates are carried out unfairly with impunity, to the great detriment of black lives."[24]

Taking a knee creates a crisis for civil religion not only because of perceived insults to national symbols but because this gesture of visible dissent challenges the belief that the foundation of American civil discourse is a reasonable center that avoids extremes in favor of an inclusive consensus. The NFL protests disrupted civil religion's embrace of civility as a cornerstone of American political discourse. One of the tenets of civil religion is that everyone, regardless of political or religious affiliation, shares an underlying commitment to national unity and inclusion. In addition to challenging Trumpism, Black Lives Matter activists question this inclusiveness by asserting that racism is not an extreme deviation from the normal principles of civil republicanism. As Barbara Ransby explains, "The powerful phrase resonated as a moral challenge, and as a slap in the face, to the distorting and deceptive language of colorblindness and postracialism that gained traction in the United States after voters elected the country's first African American president in November 2008."[25] Refusing to salute the flag insists that racial violence is a normal and familiar feature of American life, and that Trumpism is an exaggerated and unapologetic articulation of that norm rather than a deviation from American history.

The NFL controversies are especially dissonant because, like civil religion, sports are packaged as post-racial, unifying events.[26] The socially cohesive rituals of sporting events have led some scholars to study sports as their own form of implicit religion.[27] Like civil religion, sports are extolled as unifying features of American life that reward merit without regard to race or religion. Theologian Michael Novak insists that sports have a particular genius for fostering unity out of diversity: "Sports are an almost universal language binding our diverse nation, especially its men, together. Not all our citizens have the gift of faith. The religion, even so, is an ample one, and it allows great freedom for diverse experiences, diverse interpretations, and mutual dissents."[28] Novak's connection between civil religion and sports helps to explain the intensity of the counterprotests outrage.[29] Taking a knee during the anthem disrespects two models of idealized social cohesion at once.

Faith in the universal language of sports holds that football unifies while politics divides.[30] Political protests about racial injustice seem out of place in a social space designed to celebrate teamwork among officially racially unmarked equals.[31] In his study of the 1968 Olympics protests in which two African American athletes raised their hands in a Black Power salute during the national anthem, historian Douglas Hartman notes this ceremonial dissonance: "The enduring intrigue of the image Smith and Carlos produced can be traced to the way these athletes were able to interject 'blackness'—in the form of their own black bodies—into a ceremonial system that quite literally had no place for nonnational identities such as race, class, religion, or (in a more complicated case) gender."[32] By dramatizing their exclusion from the nation, the NFL protesters fit within this tradition of African American athletes who challenge American inclusiveness. Taking a knee during the national anthem hearkens back to Jackie Robinson's refusal to salute the flag. As Robinson recounts in his autobiography: "I cannot stand and sing the anthem. I cannot salute the flag; I know that I am a black man in a white world. In 1972, in 1947, at my birth in 1919, I know that I never had it made."[33]

Tellingly, opponents of the protests rebuke the slogan Black Lives Matter not with an explicit appeal to white racial solidarity but with official race neutrality. The counter slogan "All Lives Matter" articulates the simultaneous assertion of race neutrality and white supremacy that is at the heart of American civil religion. By stripping the veil of sacrality from national symbols like the flag and the anthem, the NFL protests did what acts of profanation do. By provoking an angry assertion that all lives matter in a way that is pointedly exclusive, the protests demonstrate the tension between this sacrosanct ideal of American equality and the ordinary political reality of inequality. In other words, when you profane civil religion, you get illiberal nationalism. This is somewhat different, however, from saying that civil religion and nationalism are two words for the same thing.

AMERICA'S GOD

Divisive nationalism is one response to racial division, but it is not necessarily the preferred reaction of multinational corporations. Football fans have ambivalent feelings about the connection between athletics and money. The anger aroused by the protests is an extension of the familiar complaint that professional athletes have obscenely large salaries.[34] Some fans feel that protesting athletes are ungrateful for the financial rewards of their profession.[35] Ironically, the undiscriminating power of money might have helped to integrate professional sports in the first place. Robinson suggests that the financial power of African American ticket buyers played no small role in his playing for the Brooklyn Dodgers: "Money is America's God, and business people can dig black power if it coincides with green power, so theses fans were important to the success of

Mr. Rickey's 'Noble Experiment.'"[36] The suggestion that green power tempered the nobility of integration plays on the sense that there is something profane about money.[37]

Trump's assertion that the proper response to the protests is to fire the protesters raises the question of what role for-profit corporations play in enforcing national obedience. Trump's speech was directed to a dereliction of duty on the part of NFL owners, who should have forced their players to obey. When he lamented that owners had failed to discipline Black players, he invoked a racialized threat to corporate and national authority. Far from sacred rites that exist outside of the logic of markets, NFL flag waving is a corporate spectacle. Corporate-funded nationalism calls for a consideration of what rituals do. Rituals are often imagined as a physical expression of belief, as an external performance of some interior conviction. Following this logic, standing during the *Star-Spangled Banner* would be a physical sign of support for America. But Trump did not call for a patriotic conversion of the interior lives of Black athletes. He did not care what athletes believe. In his lack of concern for the sincerity of displays of national loyalty, Trump welcomed the prospect of forced hypocrisy. Noting the irony of forcing people to be free, NFL player Michael Bennett stated: "That's crazy to me: saying we'll celebrate freedom by forcing people to stand."[38] Rather than an outward expression of interior conviction, the rites of corporate nationalism are supposed to produce patriotic citizens by compelling Americans to follow rules. The principles themselves are less important than deference to national unity.

Explaining the rituals of civil religion calls for a theory of how rituals mediate between interior belief and exterior performance. According to historian of religion Jonathan Z. Smith, rituals help to mediate the gap between the ideal and the real, but they do not exactly close it. While rituals can dramatize ideal visions of society, these visions are at odds with reality.

In an essay on bear hunting rituals among indigenous people in Siberia, for example, Smith notes that hunters describe an idealized hunt that is nothing like the way bears are hunted in practice. Hunters claim that they follow detailed ritual prescriptions in which hunters ask bears for their permission to kill, that they kill bears only while facing directly, and that they eat the meat of a bear only when properly killed. In reality, hunters do none of these things. Rather than see these rituals as hypocritical, Smith argues that the idealized models of bear hunts help people to come to terms with a reality that does not conform to ideals. As Smith suggests, "Ritual is a means of performing the way things ought to be in conscious tension with the way things are in such a way that this ritualized perfection is recollected in the ordinary, uncontrolled, course of things."[39] Ritual has a socially conservative function of helping people to come to terms with social imperfection.

When this gap between the real and ideal is applied to civil religion's principles of equality and freedom, however, it is a vivid reminder that these values do not hold in the ordinary, uncontrolled course of things but are artificial ideals enacted in civic ceremonies.[40] Civic rituals serve to reinforce what Eddie S. Glaude Jr. has called the "value gap" that values white lives over Black lives. According to Glaude, "We laud our democratic virtues to others and we represent ourselves to the world as a place of freedom and equality, all while our way of life makes possible choices that reproduce so much evil, and we don't see it happening—or, worse, we don't want to know about it."[41] The conservative work of civic rituals receives less attention in liberal models of civil religion. Rituals like the national anthem do not just express a commitment to uncoerced national unity and equality; they articulate these ideals in tension with reality. Civic rituals help people to make peace with the reality of disunity and inequality. This is one reason why these rituals are especially appealing to those who benefit from existing inequalities. In other words, civil religion is a tool to make people adjust to the impossibility of achieving civic ideals. Equality is always an unrealized aspiration. When protesters profane civic rituals, they refuse to make peace with the gap between civic ideals and real life.

BELIEVE IN SOMETHING

The gap between the ideal and the real is a space in which consumer markets flourish. After NFL teams refused to sign Kaepernick, he starred in a Nike advertising campaign featuring a photograph with the slogan: "Believe in something. Even if it means sacrificing everything."[42] The Nike ads claim to endorse what Kaepernick really believes. If nothing else, money is at least honest. A check from Nike requires no hypocritical lip-service to phony ideals. In contrast to Trump's calls for NFL players to be forced to stand during the national anthem, Nike encouraged its spokesperson to express himself however he wished.

Does Nike's endorsement of the profane rites of protest suggest that the shoe company opposes American civil religion? It is not clear that Nike's advertisement committed the company to support the Black Lives Matter movement. As Nathaniel Friedman states, "It's just as instructive to look at what the ad *didn't* say. It cosigns the Nike brand to Kaepernick's determination and integrity, not the substance of his 'something.' . . . Nike pointedly does *not* decry white supremacy, police violence, the carceral state, or environmental racism—all themes Kaepernick has touched on via his public statements and charitable work."[43] The ad campaign celebrates sincerity for the sake of sincerity. While you might disagree with Kaepernick's politics, you cannot

not doubt his passion. According to journalist David Zirin, this focus on the affect of political activism is part of a long-established pattern that recognizes the abstract appeal of "rebellion" to a youth market that might otherwise be apolitical. As he argues, "When it comes to marketing, for three decades—from Spike Lee's famous Air Jordan ads and John McEnroe's 'Rebel With a Cause' campaign to its current campaigns featuring LeBron James and Serena Williams—Nike has used the image of rebellion to sell its gear, while stripping that rebellion of all its content."[44] This is not to equate the protests themselves with Nike's attempt to appropriate the protests for its brand. Rather, Nike's ads demonstrate the power of brands to attach themselves to a variety of social causes. To this end, Robinson's observation that money is America's God helps to explain why an advertising campaign sought to harness the affect of the protests. Nike's framing of the civility contest over the NFL protests emphasizes a shared nonconflictual commitment to the values of belief and sacrifice in a way that attempts to reintegrate the protests within an American religion of buying and selling.[45]

One could interpret the Nike campaign as another example of hypocrisy or cooptation. Another possible interpretation is that Kaepernick seized the means of consumerist production. The NFL owners attempted to deprive a player of his livelihood, but he won. By signing a lucrative advertising deal and winning a legal battle that made the NFL pay him, Kaepernick beat the owners both in the marketplace and in the courts. As journalist Jemele Hill succinctly stated, "Kaepernick won. The NFL lost."[46] The victory was compounded by the futility of conservative boycotts of Nike products.[47] In the face of this evidence that the boycotts failed, Trump insisted that they had succeeded. He could not concede that his opponent was winning in the marketplace. As Trump tweeted, "Just like the NFL, whose ratings have gone WAY DOWN, Nike is getting absolutely killed with anger and boycotts. I wonder if they had any idea that it would be this way? As far as the NFL is concerned, I just find it hard to watch, and always will, until they stand for the FLAG!"[48] Not only did Trump fail to prevent players from kneeling for the anthem, by the summer of 2020 kneeling had become normal in professional baseball and basketball games during the COVID-shortened season. The phrase "Black Lives Matter" was painted in large letters on streets blocks from Trump's White House.

By appropriating the language of belief and self-sacrifice in order to score a financial victory over Trump and the NFL owners, Kaepernick inverted the ideals of civil religion in favor of a realistic appraisal of the distribution of political and economic power. In the end, civil religion might be most potent when profaned because it releases negative energy that can be channeled to diverse political and financial ends. The aversive affect elicited by the protests expressed opposition to police violence, solidified Trump's political support, and sold sneakers. Kaepernick's profane belief in something simultaneously offended and redeemed.

7

FEAR AND SAFETY ON CAMPUS

While Trumpism was building momentum throughout 2015, pundits were busy warning against the threat of political correctness on college campuses. A barrage of think pieces lamented that sensitive snowflakes, retreating to the protection of safe spaces, were holding colleges captive.[1] Students did not know how to take offense. Thin-skinned undergrads refused to allow controversial speakers on campus, and they demanded measures like trigger warnings on course syllabi that would identify potentially traumatizing material. From across the political spectrum, commentators asserted that young people's resistance to confronting offensive ideas posed a crisis for liberal education.

To combat intellectual cowardice, Dean John Ellison of the University of Chicago wrote a letter warning incoming students that their demands are unreasonable. As he explained, "You will find that we expect members of our community to be engaged in rigorous debate, discussion, and even disagreement. At times this may challenge you and even cause discomfort."[2] Pronouncements like Ellison's have an aura of wisdom and maturity. Whether coming from university administrators or pundits, warnings against trigger warnings give older, wiser generations an opportunity to admonish fragile youth. For their part, administrators and pundits welcome all speech regardless of what makes them uncomfortable.

Although student fragility is an apparently new trend, the portrayal of toughened elders lecturing young people sounds like a familiar nostalgic lament about "kids today." Critics of contemporary students, however, insist that there is a difference from radical student activism in the past. According to *Atlantic* columnist Caitlin Flanagan, the difference is that the left has won the culture war. Whereas 1960s radicals used free speech to challenge cultural norms, students now have the power to enforce their views on others. One example of this newfound power is that students now refuse to allow irreverent and politically incorrect comedians to perform on campus. As Flanagan opined, "O, Utopia. Why must your sweet governance always turn so quickly from the Edenic to the Stalinist? The college revolutions of the 1960s—the ones that gave rise to the social-justice warriors of today's campuses—were fueled by free speech. But once you've won a culture war, free speech is a nuisance, and 'eliminating' language becomes a necessity."[3] This assessment employs rhetorical excess for dramatic effect. On one hand, turning so quickly from Edenic to Stalinist would indeed be an irrational escalation. Imprisoning and executing enemies is hardly consistent with social justice. On the other hand, students in the United States have not done this. The escalation, then, is not in student conduct but in Flanagan's own hyperbolic rhetoric. Hyperbolic projections about authoritarian students are common among warnings against what have come to be known as "cancel culture." Cancellation has its origins in leftist critique but quickly has become a talking point mobilized by liberal and illiberal critics who invented the specter of authoritarianism they then confronted.

To be fair, the pundits do not claim that Stalinist purges have happened yet but that students would adopt these tactics if they could because they lack any sense of proportion or sense of humor. Like the critics of *Charlie Hebdo*, censorious students do not get satire.[4] Several prominent comedians have refused to perform at college campuses.[5] Chris Rock asserts that college students have become too "conservative" not so much in their voting habits but "in their social views and their willingness not to offend anybody. Kids raised on a culture of 'We're not going to keep score in the game because we don't want anybody to lose.'"[6] Rock's connection between not giving offense and not keeping score recognizes that an offended person does lose something, but coming to terms with the harsh realities of winning and losing is part of growing up. Giving and taking offense teaches important life lessons that elude a generation raised on participation trophies.

At times, discussions of trigger warnings have become preemptive fantasies of politically correct persecution. One professor posted on his syllabus a trigger warning for liberals in which he warned that classes would include favorable discussions of capitalism, patriotism, heterosexuality, and Christianity: "Please drop the class immediately if you are triggered by recurring encounters with heterosexuality, traditional gender identities, sympathetic representations of Christianity (or religion in general), positive examples of free markets or capitalism, or unapologetic encounters with patriotism, hierarchies, or meritocracy-based institutions or attitudes."[7] While bracing students for "recurring encounters with heterosexuality" does sound pretty threatening, such trigger warnings probably say as much about a conservative Christian professor's own zeal for martyrdom as anything else.

A widely circulated *Atlantic* essay by Greg Lukianoff and Jonathan Haidt, however, offers a more reasoned account.[8] Unlike conservative professors with an ax to grind, they are left-of-centrists who are in sympathy with advocates for social justice. Advancing an argument supported by empirical data, they worry that coddled students cannot handle negative information in the real world. Young people's desire for safety is the result of protective parenting practices that had shielded children from danger to such an extent that students are powerless to deal with threats on their own. Safety culture is so pervasive that it merits its own "ism." As a quasi-religious set of values, "safetyism" is a novel belief system that treats safe spaces as sacred spaces. As Lukianoff and Haidt explain in a later book, " 'Safetyism' refers to a culture or belief system in which safety has become a sacred value, which means that people become unwilling to make trade-offs demanded by other practical and moral concerns."[9] Safety cannot handle discomfort for the same reasons that the sacred cannot handle profanation. Attempting to protect themselves from harm, students turn negative information into a desecration.

A psychological explanation of the sacred is consistent with the work of evolutionary psychologists of religion who have found divisions between sacred and profane within human cognitive architecture. In her work on the cognition of special things, for example, Ann Taves suggests the possibility that "the value of things people set apart in this way is derived directly or indirectly from relationships that humans as a species need to survive and which, for that reason, people viewed as inviolable."[10] The cognitive association between sacrality and safety explains why profanation stimulates feelings of anxiety along with a sense that the order of the world is in peril. According to evolutionary psychologists, organizing space and cognition by classifying some things as sacred excites the part of the mind that protects against hazards.[11] The ritual and intellectual work that protects the sacred makes people feel safe.

According to Lukianoff and Haidt, safetyism subscribes to three great untruths: "fragility," "emotional reasoning," and "us versus them."[12] As sacred beliefs, these axioms go unquestioned by young people. Fragility is epitomized by the slogan: "What doesn't kill us makes us weaker." In this first untruth, fragile students protect themselves from contact with what makes them uncomfortable. In the second untruth, emotional reasoning invests a false confidence in feelings that imperil rational analysis of prospective threats. In the third untruth, divisions between us and them excite tribal passions that cast people who are different as threats. Taken together, the three untruths provide a false sense of security that renders students unable to distinguish between reasonable and unreasonable threats.

While I am not competent to evaluate the merits of evolutionary psychology, I am interested in the rhetoric that frames some people (in this case, students) as pathologically concerned with offense, profanation, and safety while others (in this case, wizened elders) are able to shake it off. Rather than accept that some people are preoccupied with safety and others are not, however, I suggest that what is at stake in debates about free speech in higher education are attempts to privilege some forms of safety over others. Lukianoff and Haidt's effort to cast political arguments as unreasonable responses to threats makes student protests into symptoms of psychological fragility. But these psychological diagnoses are not politically neutral. Rather, they seek to pathologize and depoliticize critiques of higher education that make some liberal academics feel unsafe. As in other chapters, I show that arguments about profane speech are tied to the production and maintenance of inequality. Complaints about coddled kids dodge critiques of institutional inequalities by asserting that unreasonable protesters cannot handle the real world. In the real world that the students supposedly seek to avoid, there could be no escape from the division between winners and losers. This means, then, that one unacknowledged threat is the possibility that the students might win. The coddling thesis is itself a product of frightened professors, administrators, and pundits who want to feel safe.

FIRE

In addition to warning about the dangers of coddling, Lukianoff is president of an organization called Freedom of Individual Rights in Education (FIRE). FIRE advocates for free speech rights on college campuses. As part of this effort, FIRE has developed a color-coded rating system that assesses school policies. A "red light" school clearly infringes on free speech. A "yellow light" school either restricts some aspects of expression or has vaguely worded policies that do not offer clear protections. A "green light" school either actively supports free expression or at least does not cause any public harm.

While all institutions can receive any color, public institutions have a legal obligation to protect free speech. This means that many of the red light schools are private institutions with elite admissions criteria. FIRE has been especially disappointed that students at the "best" schools are so intellectually fragile:

> Even America's best private, secular, and liberal arts colleges and universities are becoming centers of censorship and repression on behalf of campus orthodoxies. Speech codes, sweeping "anti-harassment" regulations, and broad and vague anti-discrimination

policies increasingly have stifled discourse. More and more, vaunted Ivy League and similar universities are becoming places where a vast number of religious traditions and ideas are simply not welcome.[13]

After noting the correlation between high academic standards and low intellectual tolerance, the FIRE statement complains that this is manifested in a secular intolerance of religion as well: "Many secular, private schools appear as committed to their anti-religious orthodoxy as Bob Jones University is to its fundamentalist Christianity and anti-secularism."[14] Interestingly, Bob Jones University is not listed as a red light school. Indeed, as of 2021 Bob Jones appears to have no rating at all. If Bob Jones were to receive a rating, it would probably fall in the additional "blue light" category for schools that do not actively protect free speech but do not receive a red light because they do not promise this freedom. Exemptions from the tricolor warning system have been granted mostly to schools with religious affiliations. In 2021 seven schools received an exemption: Baylor University (Baptist), Brigham Young University (Church of Jesus Christ of Latter-day Saints), Pepperdine University (Churches of Christ), Saint Louis University (Roman Catholic), United States Military Academy, United States Naval Academy, and Yeshiva University (Jewish). FIRE acknowledges that these schools have a reasonable (albeit regrettable) restriction of free speech for the purposes of military or religious discipline.[15]

Unlike religious schools, public institutions (except military academies) have to assess harm based on a "reasonable person" standard. In their defense of free speech on campus, law professors Erwin Chemerinsky and Howard Gillman explain that reports of personal harm could not be merely subjective: "The assessment is based on a 'reasonable person' standard, not on the subjective view of any concerned person, because otherwise campuses will be back in the position of having to censor or punish speech merely because an especially sensitive or fearful person claims to feel threatened by the expression of ideas he or she does not like."[16] A reasonable person is a curious legal fiction: a hypothetical rational being who possesses the correct amount of the affective responses common among persons who live in the real world. Under this standard, to be sensitive is to be unreasonable. It goes without saying that someone who is especially sensitive is not especially perceptive or especially insightful. Following this logic, sensitive people could not make the dispassionate rational calculations of a reasonable person.

Free speech absolutists warn that the mandates of politically correct discourse would render everyone vulnerable to a variety of complaints, and this in turn would require constantly revising norms in the face of new concerns. To be fair, Chemerinsky and Gillman are aware of the practical difficulty of identifying a reasonable person. The antagonism between sensitivity and reason raises the question, however, of what threats make a reasonable person feel unsafe, and what measures are justified to protect against reasonable threats. At the heart of civility contests on college campuses, then, is the question of who sets the criteria for legitimate forms of offense and how these criteria produce institutional definitions of intellectual freedom.

VINDICTIVE PROTECTIVENESS

While students have been faulted for their inability to endure threats, there seems to be something threatening about the students.[17] Many who deride millennial snowflakes are cowed by the students' power. Professors and administrators report feeling vulnerable and offended by charges that they are racist, sexist, ablest, and homophobic.[18] Lukianoff and Haidt warn against "vindictive protectiveness" in which the desire for protection turns into aggression. Instead of safety, this creates a climate of fear: "The ultimate aim, it seems, is to turn campuses into 'safe spaces' where young adults are shielded from words and ideas that make some uncomfortable. And more than the last, this movement seeks to punish anyone who interferes with that aim, even accidentally. You might call this impulse *vindictive protectiveness*. It is creating a culture in which everyone must think twice before speaking up, lest they face charges of insensitivity, aggression, or worse."[19] Lukianoff and Haidt are correct that critics of insensitive speech are indeed asking people to think twice before speaking up. The question is whether this amounts to an unreasonable restriction on speech.

There is, then, a notable exception to the precept that enduring uncomfortable feelings builds psychological health. Discomfort caused by public shame does not build character.[20] There are no positive therapeutic possibilities in shame. Instead, reasonable people self-censor because they worry about facing criticism for giving offense within a "call-out culture." According to Lukianoff and Haidt, a call-out culture animates the us-versus-them sentiments native to tribalism. Tribalism hearkens back to evolutionary roots when people learned to band together in groups to protect themselves: "The bottom line is that the human mind is prepared for tribalism. Human evolution is not just the story of individuals competing with other individuals within each group; it's also the story of groups competing with other groups—sometimes violently. We are all descended from people who belonged to groups that were consistently better at winning that competition."[21] A tolerant, liberal citizen learns to discipline tribal instincts. This discipline is tenuous, however. Calling people out on digital media like Twitter activates a "tribe switch" that excites a primal mob mentality.

The tribe switch resembled what Haidt previously described as a "hive switch." The word *hive* refers to the instincts in bees who gained evolutionary benefits by acting in concert. According to Haidt, the hive switch is not all bad. Hive instincts are sources of altruism, cooperation, and sympathy for others. One function of the hive switch is to instill a shared respect for the sacred. On this point, Haidt harmonizes Darwinian theories of human origins with the sociology of Émile Durkheim. As he explains, "Durkheim believed that these collective emotions pull humans fully but temporarily into the higher of the two realms, the realm of the sacred, where the self disappears and collective instincts predominate. The realm of the profane, in contrast, is the ordinary day-to-day world where we live most of our lives, concerned about wealth, health, and reputation, but nagged by the sense that there is, somewhere, something higher and nobler."[22] While the hive instinct allows appreciation of the higher realm, it also means that people can be triggered by threats to the sacred. By this logic, safetyism animates tribal instincts to protect against profanation. When offensive speech threatens safetyism, it flips on the tribe switch to create a recurring spectacle that Lukianoff and Haidt describe as "witch hunts."

Witch hunts on college campuses hit home. Yale's Erika Christakis was called out for psychological arguments that resembled Lukianoff and Haidt's. In an email questioning guidelines against offensive Halloween costumes, she suggested that overly protective university administrators lack confidence in the "strength and judgment" of young adults.[23] As Christakis asks, "Is there no room anymore for a child or young person to be a little bit obnoxious . . . a little bit inappropriate or provocative or, yes, offensive?"[24] Christakis was fine if students registered her email as obnoxious, inappropriate, provocative, and offensive, but it was out of line to see her words as more than mere speech.[25] Her critics, however, argue that to suggest minority students lack the intellectual and emotional maturity of adults does more than express a provocative idea. They see Christakis's arguments as contributing to institutional racism that denigrates the students she is supposed to educate. But in the wake of calls for sanction, Christakis insists that she is the victim of the intolerance of unpopular ideas. As she concludes, "Certain ideas are too dangerous to be heard at Yale."[26]

One problem with alarms about Ivy League censorship, however, is that ideas like Christakis's are heard all the time. Far from absent from university discussions, these arguments are found in the subject matter of college classes. Indeed, Christakis's critics had spent more time thinking about Christakis's ideas than Christakis had. This is not to say that her critics know more about her academic field of childhood psychology, but they likely know more about the scholarship about cultural appropriation that Christakis derided. What she lacked was not the ability to be heard but the legitimacy that comes from being treated as a conversation partner with equally valid ideas. In her assessment of Christakis's claim that Yale's culture is not conducive to civil dialogue, Sigal Ben-Porath suggests that the unequal treatment claim has merit: "Erika Christakis was probably right. Civil dialogue is hard to sustain when many feel that they are not equal parties to the dialogue and when the overall atmosphere on campus is not open to dissenting views."[27] Ben-Porath is probably right that Christakis was not treated as an equal party in campus dialogue. This points to a confusion, however, between the legal toleration of free speech and the affirmation of the equality of speech.

In another example, law professors Amy Wax of the University of Pennsylvania and Larry Alexander of the University of San Diego penned an opinion piece suggesting that social problems such as unqualified workers, opioid abuse, homicidal violence, and single-parent families come from the decay of bourgeois culture.[28] They defend the value of bourgeois hegemony by suggesting that all cultures are not equal. According to Lukianoff and Haidt, this drew fire from academics because it "violates a wide-spread taboo in the academic world. One is not supposed to say that a dominant culture is superior to a nondominant one in any way."[29] Violating taboos, however, provides exactly the sort of attention sought by contrarian law professors.[30] A taboo argument has more cachet than a stupid one. But Wax and Alexander were not making edgy and transgressive points that shook the epistemic foundations of academia. Arguments for the superiority of bourgeois culture are old, obvious, and familiar.[31] Cultural historians and critics encounter them time and time again, and scholars document how these arguments harm vulnerable people.[32]

Critics who hoped to cancel dated arguments suggest that there is something like intellectual progress, and that this progress has moved on from basic discussions that rehash the same premises. As novelist Porochista Khakpour argues, "We joke about 'cancel culture' and those who love to misunderstand it classify it as a 'morality policing' but what is it but a brazen acknowledgment, uttered and echoed, that we in our culture in this day and age can agree on certain elements of progress and that we do not accept any steps backwards."[33] The social progress Khakpour describes depends upon establishing basic points to move on to more complex conversations about how to apply these insights to institutional change. In this view, demands that Wax and Alexander receive equal time to speak are the cultural equivalent of giving equal consideration to intelligent design in a biology class or to flat-earthers in geography. There is a difference between censoring all ideas with which you disagree and classifying some ideas as unworthy of serious consideration. In a way, the cancellation of Wax and Alexander draws on a different version of a "reasonable person" standard. In this case, a reasonable person considers the sensibilities of others instead of taking pleasure in offending them.

Liberal ideas of free speech, however, begin with the observation that people do not consistently agree about what is reasonable or progressive. Faith in progress is cold comfort for liberals who worry that whoever determines what counts as progressive potentially wields censorious power. It is not clear, however, what sort of power this is. The body of criticism labeled call-out or cancel culture largely (although not entirely) involves critics without formal institutional power who instead use informal means of social and economic pressure.[34] This raises the question of whether it is the challenge to the proper channels of institutional evaluation of speech that make cancel culture so threatening.

PAID SPEECH

It is possible, then, that the underlying tension has less to do with the liberal embrace of the free exchange of ideas than with anxieties about who wields institutional power. Campus witch hunts are especially frightening to Lukianoff and Haidt because criticism goes beyond intellectual disagreement to threaten the jobs of professors. No one wants to lose their job. The victims of witch hunts are traumatized by the experience in a way that makes them unlikely to speak in public. As Lukianoff and Haidt explain, "Life in a call-out culture requires constant vigilance, fear, and self-censorship."[35] They do not advise the victims of call-out culture to buck up and get a thick skin. Paralyzing fear of criticism is a reasonable response to public shame. Public shame is worse than mere offense because it has professional consequences for professors. In effect, this means that racism is a matter of feelings to be endured, but public harm to reputation has unacceptable material effects. The logic of Lukianoff and Haidt's analysis of witch hunts suggests that unlike a hypersensitive critic of racism, a reasonable person has good cause to be afraid of professional harm. The students were so threatening, then, because they inverted the proper placement of vulnerability on the public/private spectrum. They were causing private harm for what should have been protected public speech. Furthermore, student protesters insisted on publicizing vulnerabilities that should properly have been dealt with in private. Shameful publicity challenged the rules of propriety in institutions of liberal education where many professors and administrators felt safe and powerful. As Kelly J. Baker suggests, at the heart of the coddled student controversy were professors who were anxious about losing: "This isn't really about the hurt feelings of students, but the feelings of professors who bristle at the decline of professional privilege."[36] In short, Lukianoff and Haidt are thick-skinned about things that do not threaten them but thin-skinned about things that do.

This status anxiety was evident in a 2020 letter in *Harper's Magazine* that advanced a vigorous defense of free speech. As the letter lamented, "Editors are fired for running controversial pieces; books are withdrawn for alleged inauthenticity; journalists are barred from writing on certain topics; professors are investigated for quoting works of literature in class; a researcher is fired for circulating a peer-reviewed academic study; and the heads of organizations are ousted for what are sometimes just clumsy mistakes."[37] The usage of passive voice leaves unclear who is enforcing all of this. None of these examples involve free speech censored by the state. There is no First Amendment guarantee of publication. Rather, the letter expresses fears that editors, authors, journalists, professors, researchers, and heads of organizations might be barred from receiving financial compensation for speech. This compensation comes from highly selective gatekeeping institutions that measure excellence by how much speech is kept out. It is not the job of an editor to publish everything. The signatories of the *Harper's* letter are prominent figures who have professionally and financially benefited from this institutional gatekeeping. They want to get paid. In the end, the practical access to compensated speech is the central issue in debates about cancel culture.

Digital natives often see liberal ideals of free speech as beholden to a naive faith in a public discourse shaped by print culture with forms of editorial control that no longer exist. Requests for trigger warnings come from a generation that has unprecedented access to information. People who grew up on Twitter are suspicious of the promise that negative speech will disappear in the face of better ideas. Media savvy young people learn that more exposure does not lead to debunking; it leads to more exposure. When building a media brand is the priority, a wider platform to recruit is just that. In the world of social media, platitudes about responding to hate speech with more speech seem like the calls to chat with Steve Bannon in the liberal salon. Instead, students respond to speech with action. Protesters argue that words and images have effects, and that these effects help to make institutions unequal places.

Insisting that words should be measured by social impact advance an implicit theory of language that is in tension with the idea that the classroom is a space for the dispassionate discussion of intellectual abstractions that cause no material harm. For this reason, student activists work to deplatform overtly bigoted speakers on campus. After College Republicans at the University of California, Berkeley invited former *Breitbart* editor and self-described troll Milo Yiannopoulos, intense protests forced administrators to cancel the talk because of the threat to public safety. The protesters who deplatformed Yiannopoulos were not avoiding confrontation with people who made them uncomfortable; they were fighting them in the streets.[38] According to the pundits, however, this fighting ethos made Stalinist students just as bad as the alt-right racists they protested. Equating violent leftists with violent racists made sense to the decidedly illiberal and unprofessorial Donald Trump. In the wake of clashes between the alt-right and counterprotesters at the University of Virginia in 2017, Trump asked, "What about the 'alt-left' that came charging at, as you say, the 'alt-right?' . . . Let me ask you this: What about the fact they came charging—that they came charging with clubs in their hands, swinging clubs?"[39]

PUBLIC SAFETY

While administrators at schools like the University of Chicago protect challenging and uncomfortable speech, they are not unconcerned with safety. After all, the university employs a large private police force. Like many wealthy, cosmopolitan universities in urban spaces, the University of Chicago is a literal safe space within Chicago's South Side. For that matter, the police force is resistant to public transparency and criticism.[40] A large police force sends a message about whose safety is important. Many students have seen a gap between the intellectual ideals and practical realities of college. Higher education includes an uneasy pairing of radical critique with institutional inequality.[41] You could criticize the neoliberal university until the cows came home, and it would be just fine. Threats to private property and physical safety, however, get a response. These threats mobilize resources.

Activists were not persuaded by Flanagan's assertion that the left had won the culture wars. Despite the media portrayal of universities as sites of liberal brainwashing, many students view higher education as elitist, hierarchical, and conservative. This is evident among students expected to diversify the schools they attend. As Wesleyan University president Michael Roth acknowledges, "Students who themselves were counted as evidence that the schools were becoming more diverse asked whether they were mere window dressing for the institution's public relations efforts."[42] In an essay titled "The Year of the Imaginary College Student," Hua Hsu notes that many students recognize the uneven benefits of this institutional conservatism: "An educational system built on legacy admissions and de facto segregation, with traditions of grade inflation that perpetuate privilege, is also a form of coddling."[43] In an essay on campus life at Oberlin College, Nathan Heller observes that teaching radical criticism to students is also meant to serve as a vehicle of economic advancement: "In exchange, they're groomed for old-school entry into the liberal upper middle class. An irony surrounds the whole endeavor, and a lot of students seemed to see it."[44] The irony that students in Heller's essay saw could be termed *hypocrisy*, but the hypocritical divisions between public and private spheres work differently from the divisions between public norms and private behavior that govern the life of Roy Moore. Whereas sex is the subject of Moore's gap between public norms and private behavior, the gap in higher education is between public critiques of neoliberal institutions and the private practices of citizens who sometimes benefit from institutional inequities.

Academia has its own culture of winners and losers. While higher education is tasked with the broad promotion of learning as a civic good, there is little effort to distribute resources equally among people and institutions. Rather, disproportionate rewards go to the "best" schools with a reputation for exclusivity. One conventional measure of educational excellence is how many students are refused admission. The word *competitive* is a synonym for *good*. This selectivity plays a crucial role in reproducing the inequalities that diversity initiatives are supposed to fix. Despite Roth's earnest efforts to diversify a school like Wesleyan, for example, he is still committed to the distinction between the best schools and everywhere else. When he worries that low-income students are underrepresented at Wesleyan, he notes: "But most low-income students in higher education attend institutions with the lowest graduation rates, putting them at a distinct disadvantage in climbing toward or above the median income."[45] Roth's proposal to address this disadvantage is not to distribute resources more equally in order to improve graduation rates at the schools working-class students attend. Rather, his hope is to get them out of these schools and into better ones.

There is, then, a tension that arises from valuing inclusivity and exclusivity at the same time. Academics often recognize these disparities and can document their own complicity, but this can create a tension between public criticism and private life. Jennine Capó Crucet, for example, notes the contradiction between her commitment to critique of educational inequalities and her personal success as a tenure-track professor: "I push my students toward protest, toward using their understandable and justifiable rage to be heard, to literally and metaphorically burn things down. Then I come back to my own campus and sit in my office and listen to the lights buzz overhead while thanking the universe that, for now, I have health insurance. The contradiction makes me sick. And the only thing that eases the nausea is the writing."[46] Soon after she read these words at a public lecture to an unruly and disrespectful audience at Georgia Southern University in 2019, students literally burned her book because they took offense to her discussion of white privilege. On one hand, this fiery protest appears to undermine the pundits' account of universities as havens for political correctness.[47] Hardly leftist thought police, the protesters in south Georgia targeted a Cuban woman who criticized structural racism in a speech reflecting on her own experience as a first-generation college student. On the other hand, as a regional state university with a largely working-class student body in the heart of Trump country, Georgia Southern might not be the kind of school that raises red flags to the pundits concerned about coddled students. In its fixation on progressive activists at elite institutions and lack of attention to actual racism, the discourse about political correctness on college campuses reflects an underlying anxiety about whether the "best" schools are living up to their exclusive reputations.

TOXIC STRESS

One common feature of jeremiads against coddling is that they use politically conscious student protesters as a stand-in for an entire generation. The large swaths of higher education occupied by Greek life or tailgating are largely absent from these accounts. The coddled kids thesis also tends to ignore practical matters like the proliferation of preprofessional majors among students under pressure to find jobs to pay off increasing levels of debt. Practical financial concerns are particularly pressing within community colleges and regional state schools that are rarely profiled in the coddling literature. Unlike the exclusive institutions that draw red lights from FIRE, witch hunts are less likely to occur at these schools because safetyism is reported to be a product of affluence.

Lukianoff and Haidt note that class differences structure psychology. Despite their concerns about fragility, they recognize the practical economic benefits sometimes bestowed by the protections of affluent parents. In a section titled "Class Matters," they observe that poor and working-class children, while possibly stronger in some ways, run the risk of growing up with "toxic stress."[48] Toxic stress causes harm that could result in real material and psychological disadvantages. Lukianoff and Haidt do not see toxicity at work in controversies at elite colleges, however, because these are affluent institutions. But while protesters have a diverse set of backgrounds and motives, a number of the examples Lukianoff and Haidt use to illustrate coddling involve people who describe themselves as working class, minority, and first-generation college students who are alienated within a culture of affluence. As Lukianoff and Haidt recognize, "Working-class kids are therefore more likely to feel like 'fish out of water' in college."[49] Even when recognizing that student activists are protesting affluence, the coddling analysis treats them as affluent anyway. Rather than take stock of the diverse biographies of a politically active students, the coddling literature treats all students at elite schools as rich. The coddling thesis presumes that protests are a product of affluent institutions rather than a protest against different forms of privilege within such institutions.[50]

Competing visions of safety are evident in cases where students are profiled by campus police.[51] In April 2019 a Columbia student was pinned down by campus "public safety" officers after he refused to show an identification card to enter a library on the grounds that the policy was inconsistently enforced.[52] Students at Smith College and Yale University have found themselves subject to police questioning after calls reporting suspicious persons.[53] Lukianoff and Haidt understand why students are upset: "It is understandable that many black students were on edge, felt a generalized sense of threat, and became increasingly active in movements to oppose systemic racism, particularly in the criminal justice system."[54] While they acknowledge the validity of the criticism of the criminal justice system, Lukianoff and Haidt still could not understand why students would direct these same critiques at universities: "But why did college students direct so much of their passion and effort toward changing their universities and to finding enemies *within* their own communities?"[55] According to Lukianoff and Haidt, finding enemies within is a consequence of safetyism's internal purification of safe spaces rather than a result of student protests against unequal institutions. In this way, psychological explanations deflect from political critique. According to Wendy Brown, reducing protests to psychological fragility is typical of rhetoric that prescribes tolerant feelings as the antidote to political inequality. When the recommended resolution for conflict is tolerance of difference, "A justice project is replaced with a therapeutic or behavioral one."[56]

Student protests take aim at the gap between radical public critique and the perceived reality of the professional, material, and physical safety of tenured professors. This is not to say that professors are as safe as many think, but it might be the case that Yiannopoulos posed a smaller threat to Lukianoff and Haidt than student protesters who threaten the jobs of professors. The coddling thesis, then, is a product of competing visions of safety.[57] Elder guardians of free speech laud intellectual courage in environments in which they feel safe while activists argue that the free exchange of ideas without consequences protects the institutional inequalities they criticize.

Efforts to uncoddle kids seek to build character to the point where slights no longer cause discomfort. In some sense, Lukianoff and Haidt's thesis resembles civil rights activists' refusal to allow for the comfort promised by negative peace. However, the political purposes of discomfort are almost diametrically opposite. Black Lives Matter protesters seek to make people uncomfortable so that injustice can no longer be ignored. Lukianoff and Haidt teach people to deal with uncomfortable information so they can learn to live with it. Whereas Black Lives Matter activists seek to politicize discomfort, Haidt and Lukianoff hope to depoliticize it. There is, then, one sense in which the connection between sacred and safetyism might work. Safetyism—in this case, the culture that protects professors and administrators at elite institutions—goes without question and lies beyond critique. It is taken for granted that the physical and material safety of professors is valuable, even if this protects some people at the expense of others. Once professional safety and the norms of higher education are protected, students and professors are free to publicly criticize the many injustices of the real world. Students would learn to analyze inequality while still gaining the economic benefits of a college education. According to Lukianoff and Haidt, this mature ability to adapt to the realities of an unjust world is psychologically and socially necessary. Their problem with social justice warriors is that their unrealistic expectations fail to prepare young people to win in a world that is necessarily unjust. This liberal maturity has to be learned, however, as it is not obvious to students that offensive speech is merely words with no material affects. It takes training and discipline to internalize this liberal theory of language. This is one reason why the failure to learn the rules of free speech poses a crisis for liberal education. The coddling thesis is not a coherent historical or sociological explanation, but it is itself a normative project to discipline prospective liberal subjects to view language in the proper way.

ILLIBERALISM?

Does the leftist critique of liberalism amount to illiberalism? The *Harper's* letter thinks so. Echoing Trump's alert about the alt-left, *Harper's* asserts: "The forces of illiberalism are gaining strength throughout the world and have a powerful ally in Donald Trump, who represents a real threat to democracy. But resistance must not be allowed to harden into its own brand of dogma or coercion—which right-wing demagogues are already exploiting. The democratic inclusion we want can be achieved only if we speak out against the intolerant climate that has set in on all sides."[58] It is possible that some tenets of progressive activism resemble dogma, but this is also why it is not just the flip side of Trumpian illiberalism. Illiberal secularism has no dogma. Trump supporters are not intolerant of ideas; they are trying to defeat their enemies. The body of criticism dubbed "cancel culture" is a response to illiberal rejection of liberal ideals of persuasion. The difference between the liberal pundits and student activists, then, lies in divergent appraisals of the threat that illiberalism poses.

According to Osita Nwanevu, blindness to the real threat of Trumpism is a form of "reactionary liberalism." He argues that the *Harper's* letter narrows the scope of liberal freedom by refusing to consider the practical realities of unequal access to speech. This, in turn, undermines the associative nature of liberal society. As he explains, "The tensions we've seen lately have been internal to liberalism for ages: between those who take the associative nature of liberal society seriously and those who are determined not to. It is the former group, the defenders of progressive identity politics, who in fact are protecting— indeed expanding—the bounds of liberalism. And it is the latter group, the reactionaries, who are most guilty of the illiberalism they claim has overtaken the American Left."[59] While some leftists would not want to be called liberals, debates about free speech on campus have arisen from tensions internal to liberalism. Unlike reactionary liberalism or illiberalism, campus protests aspire to balance freedom with equality. The criticism dubbed as cancel culture does not see illiberalism as a set of ideas to be discussed but as a political force to be defeated.

CONCLUSION

T his book is about the challenge to liberalism posed by going low. It begins with the observation that people did not support Donald J. Trump despite his profane style but because of it. Liberalism is vulnerable to shameless displays of disrespect for liberal norms of speech and behavior. Disrespecting these norms by giving offense disregards the sensibilities of others in a way that underscores a rejection of public goods. One sense of public goods involves faith in democratic institutions. Another sense of the public is a civil society made up of a diverse population of strangers. Participants in illiberal politics reject participation in both these publics in favor of private institutional power as well as loyalty to people with whom they feel some sense of kinship or shared identity.

Devaluing the public in favor of private freedom is consistent with illiberal secularism. This is a counterintuitive label because many opponents of liberalism complain of the loss of a Christian nation. They feel that American values have been profaned by an encroaching state as well as a politically correct liberalism that classifies what Christians hold sacred as hateful and bigoted. In response, they double down. Illiberal politics adopts a deliberately profane style that dramatizes the moral and theological impoverishment of politics. The impoverishment is evident in the shocking rhetoric of Trump, Steve Bannon, and illiberal cartoonists, all of whom sought to gain power by deliberately offending religious and racial others. While Roy Moore and Jack Phillips were not so overtly profane, they worked within a secular framework that privatized religion. Fashioning themselves as offended victims of liberal bigotry and intolerance, Moore and Phillips protected their own private freedom. Liberals who congratulated themselves for taking the high road only reinforced the sense among conservative Christians that someone was looking down on them.

One common theme in the first five chapters is that illiberal political activists hoped to protect a Christian nation from a profane state. Rejecting public goods in favor of private institutions placed antigovernment sentiment in harmony with Christian nationalism. Illiberal secularism detached the nation from democratic institutions as well as from the inclusive public imagined by an American civil religion. One irony is that is that the zeal to combat liberalism on secular grounds could constrain Christian witness. This is not to say that people stopped having moral and theological conversations. *Going Low* is not a study of people's private lives. Rather, it focuses on how illiberal secularism flattens moral and theological complexity within political discourse and on how this profane politics can be especially satisfying to those convinced that liberal democracy threatens them. To be clear, this usage of illiberal secularism is something that I made up rather than a self-identified movement that exists in the world. It is a hermeneutic lens that I hope offers a more pragmatically useful interpretation than seeing illiberalism in terms of hypocritical or extreme religiosity. Hypocrisy is a non-explanation. Behavior that appears hypocritical is an invitation to scholars of religion to investigate why people make the inconsistent choices that they do. Instead of identifying principles that govern free speech and offense, it is more descriptively accurate to accept that they are unprincipled. This inconsistency means that the book offers no single explanation for the relationship between offense and illiberalism. Rather, each chapter makes distinct arguments about speech in different contexts. Furthermore, the contention that offensive speech profanes liberal pieties is a way of making sense of the appeal of illiberal rhetoric to those who deliberately give offense. While proponents of civility might be upset about the violation of liberal norms, the targets of offensive speech are more likely to be offended because it harms them. Illiberal rhetoric, however, is invested in celebrating heroic violations of what are perceived to be other people's taboos. The people with the greatest investment in cancel culture or wokeness are not progressive activists but self-identified "deplorable" or politically incorrect heroes who take pleasure in owning the libs.

The last two chapters consider protest movements that pose a different sort of challenge to liberalism. One limit of the sixth and seventh chapters is that they are not comprehensive studies of the political logic of protest movements themselves but focus on liberal and illiberal reactions to them. While high-minded liberals hoped to debate illiberal opponents without compromising the principles of inclusion and civility, critics from the left warned that the threat posed by illiberalism calls for more assertive measures than liberal tolerance. This debate about the limits of liberalism marks another chapter in a long argument about freedom. Free speech is a right to express oneself without interference from the state. By this logic, a person whose speech is free should be able to offend. This liberal defense of free speech can sometimes equate legal protections with civic principles in a way that conflates of the public with the state. That is, a legal principle that prevents the state's ability to censor speech becomes a public good in and of itself. Granting all speech equal consideration uses private rights as a substitute for producing criteria to evaluate public discussion.

Fear of so-called cancel culture, however, is not a fear of state censorship. Calls for cancellation or something like it are better understood as attempts to imagine a civil sphere with rules and norms governed by informal means of social and institutional pressure. *Going Low* does not offer a normative or prescriptive evaluation of these or any criteria for civil discourse. The more modest goal of the book is to unpack the logic of contemporary arguments about civility and offense in order to think about their implications for democratic institutions.

Free speech advocates might reasonably object that while it might be possible to deplatform hatred in some situations, there are practical limits to canceling the political participation of the 74 million citizens who voted for Trump in 2020. Those who keep faith in democratic persuasion hold out hope that while winning and losing are familiar features of social life, they are not inevitable ones. Whether Trump supporters come around to the pursuit of common goods within a diverse public depends upon whether they accept the view that other people's gains are not necessarily their losses. But whatever the merits of more assertive efforts to combat illiberalism might be, those efforts are driven by the view that the negative freedom of liberal tolerance is inadequate for a more expansive understanding of equality. This understanding of the relationship between freedom and equality holds that offensive speech can discursively reinforce inequality. For this reason, appraisals of what counts as offensive are tied to assessments of relative social power. Following this logic, speech that punches down is judged by objective sociological and historical conditions rather than subjective feelings. The lines between liberals and leftists are not always so clear on this point. Even when people share criteria for identifying offensive speech, they do not necessarily agree about the appropriate response.

For its part, illiberalism embraces freedom but asserts that expanding democratic institutions makes people less free. Illiberal political activists reject the sociology that informs critiques of punching down, arguing instead that they are the targets of repressive political correctness. At times there are points of agreement between liberal and illiberal defenses of free speech. Commentators who decry threats to free speech on campus warn against illiberal threats from the left. For Greg Lukianoff and Jonathan Haidt, coddled students would trade freedom for safety. Lukianoff and Haidt have mixed views of the sociology of punching down. Even when they concede these assessments have merit, they classify offensive speech as a matter of hurt feelings. Their recommendation is to learn to handle psychological harm rather than fix political problems. It is possible that having a thick skin provides psychological benefits to individuals living within an unequal status quo. But the result of this self-protection means that if someone is depressed because of inequality, the solution is to deal with their depression. The advocates for more vigorous responses to offense disagree. They see offensive speech as both symptom and cause of institutional inequity, and they seek political solutions.

Part of the reason for so much attention to Lukianoff and Haidt is that one audience for this book is the sort of liberal who thinks that cancel culture poses a threat. *Going Low* disputes the contention that Trumpism and leftist criticism of offense are comparable forms of illiberalism. Casting a generation as coddled and hypersensitive is not a viable sociological explanation. What has been called cancel culture is better understood as a vigorous response to the threat of illiberalism. It raises the question of whether high-minded liberalism is up to the task of defeating a movement dedicated to so much winning.

Each chapter has used debates about offense as a platform to reconsider conventional narratives about American religion and politics. Rather than a deceptive leader who duped his followers, for example, Trump was appealing because of his honesty. Rather than a symptom of postmodern criticism of facts, a post-truth era was driven by a search for certainty and stable foundations that could withstand the shocks of social change. Rather than preserve peace, the rhetoric of free speech identified who could use violence in defense of their own security. Rather than a hypocritical betrayal of evangelical principles, Christian support for Trump was consistent with family values. Rather that Christianize the public, complicity claims constrained Christian witness in favor of the privacy of religious freedom. Rather than establish equality, the rituals of American civil religion taught how to live with the reality of inequality. Rather than a response to coddled college students, laments about cancel culture on college campuses sought to protect safe spaces for liberal professors. In the end, one theme throughout *Going Low* is that confident projections of so much winning say a lot about what people fear they have to lose.

NOTES

INTRODUCTION

1. Brian L. Ott and Greg Dickinson, *The Twitter Presidency: Donald J. Trump and the Politics of White Rage* (New York: Routledge, 2019), 63.

2. As Twitter explained, "Our public interest framework exists to enable the public to hear from elected officials and world leaders directly." "Permanent Suspension of @RealDonaldTrump," Twitter, January 8, 2021. https://blog.twitter.com/en_us/topics/company/2020/suspension .html.

3. Claire Landsbaum, "Donald Trump Uses Albany Rally to Criticize Delegate System Again," *New York Magazine*, April 12, 2016. http:// nymag.com/daily/intelligencer/2016/04/trump-criticizes-delegate -system-at-albany-rally.html.

4. Donald J. Trump with Tony Schwartz, *Trump: The Art of the Deal* (New York: Ballantine Books, 1987), 59. I am aware that *The Art of the Deal*, like all Trump publications, was largely ghostwritten. However, my interest is not so much in the inner workings of Trump's mind as much as what he represents.

5. On the attractive and repulsive qualities of taboo violation, see Michael Taussig, "Transgression," in *Critical Terms for Religious Studies*, ed. Mark C. Taylor (Chicago: University of Chicago Press, 1998), 349–364.

6. Luvell Anderson and Ernie Lepore argue that rule violation is the primary defining feature of words defined as "slurs," which offend less

because of their content than that they have been deemed offensive. As they explain, "Our positive proposal is that slurs are *prohibited* words *not* on account of any content they get across, but rather because of relevant edicts surrounding their prohibition." Luvell Anderson and Ernie Lepore, "Slurring Words," *Noûs* 47, no. 1 (March 2013): 26.

7. According to secular liberal models of the public sphere, debates require shared principles that allow for the reasoned exchange of ideas. This requirement often excludes religious convictions that are not universally shared and cannot be rationally criticized and defended. The need for shared principles is evident in John Rawls's description of a "well-ordered" society:

> To say that a society is well-ordered conveys three things: first (and implied by the idea of a publicly recognized conception of justice), it is a society in which everyone accepts, and knows that everyone else accepts, the very same principles of justice; and second (implied by the idea of the effective regulation of such a conception), its basic structure—that is, its main political and social institutions and how they fit together as one system of cooperation—is publicly known, or with good reason believed, to satisfy these principles. And third, its citizens have a normally effective sense of justice and so they generally comply with society's basic institutions, which they regard as just.

John Rawls, *Political Liberalism* (New York: Columbia University Press, 1996), 35. This book is about a society that looks nothing like that.

8. Keeanga-Yamahtta Taylor, *How We Get Free: Black Feminism and the Combahee River Collective* (Chicago: Haymarket, 2017), 9.

9. According to Mark Lilla, attempts to expand civil society to include diverse sensibilities amount to illiberal restrictions on speech as well as distractions from more pressing economic concerns. The hope that divisive populism will disappear if liberalism focuses exclusively on the distribution of property, however, takes white Christian identity politics as an aberration in a way that ignores large swaths of American history. Mark Lilla, *The Once and Future Liberal: After Identity Politics* (New York: Harper, 2017).

10. Jonathan Z. Smith, *Imagining Religion: From Babylon to Jonestown* (Chicago: University of Chicago Press, 1982), xi.

11. In my reading, Smith's pronouncement is akin to statements like Donald Davidson's: "Nothing, however, no *thing*, makes sentences and theories true: not experience, not surface irritations, not the world, can make a sentence true." Donald Davidson, *Inquiries into Truth and Interpretation* (New York: Oxford University Press, 1984), 194. Another example would be Jacques Derrida's "There is no outside-text." Jacques Derrida, *Of Grammatology*, trans. Gayatri Chakravorty Spivak (Baltimore: Johns Hopkins University Press, 1997), 158. While Davidson, Derrida, and Smith all have different theoretical frameworks, they are in their own ways scrutinizing common sense connections between words and things.

12. As Richard Callahan points out, "Even if religion is in some sense the creation of the scholar's study, there is no denying that it has entered the world. Scholars are not the only people with a claim to the term or to what it signifies." Richard J. Callahan Jr., "The Study of American Religion: Looming through the Glim," *Religion* 42, no. 3 (2012): 428.

13. On the colonial baggage that comes with the category religion, see Tomoko Masuzawa, *The Invention of World Religions; Or, How European Universalism Was Preserved in the Language of Pluralism* (Chicago: University of Chicago Press, 2005).

14. Émile Durkheim, *The Elementary Forms of Religious Life*, trans. Karen E. Fields (1912; repr., New York: Free Press, 1995), 34–35.

15. Giorgio Agamben, *Profanations*, trans. Jeff Fort (New York: Zone Books, 2007), 73.

16. For his part, Agamben sees this aspect of profanation as politically useful. As he explains,

> *Religio* is not what unites men and gods but what ensures that they remain distinct. It is not disbelief and indifference toward the divine, therefore, that stand in opposition to religion, but "negligence," that is, a behavior that is free and "distracted" (that is to say, released from the *religio* of norms) before things and their use, before forms of separation and their meaning. To profane means to open up the possibility of a special form of negligence, which ignores separation or, rather, puts it to a particular use.

> Agamben, *Profanations*, 75.

17. Karl Marx and Friedrich Engels, *The Communist Manifesto* (1848; repr. New York: Signet Classic, 1998), 54.

18. Marx and Engels, *The Communist Manifesto*, 54.

19. Carlin A. Barton and Daniel Boyarin, *Imagine No Religion: How Modern Abstractions Hide Ancient Realities* (New York: Fordham University Press, 2016), 43.

20. One example of Trump's demonstration of the futility of liberal norms was when he spoke from the White House's South Lawn to accept the Republican nomination in a brazen violation of campaign rules: "Mr. Trump's aides said he enjoyed the frustration and anger he caused by holding a political event on the South Lawn of the White House, shattering conventional norms and raising questions about ethics law violations. He relished the fact that no one could do anything to stop him, said the aides, who spoke anonymously to discuss internal conversations." Katie Glueck, Annie Karni, and Alexander Burns, "Rival Themes Emerge as Race Enters Final Weeks: Covid vs. Law and Order," *New York Times*, August 28, 2020, https://www.nytimes.com/2020/08/28/us/politics/joe-biden-trump-conventions.html.

21. Bruce Lincoln, *Discourse and the Construction of Society: Comparative Studies of Myth, Ritual, and Classification* (New York: Oxford University Press, 1989), 120.

22. The flip side of the power gained from giving offense is the power lost by the targets of offensive speech. In his challenge to free speech absolutism, Jeremy Waldron seeks to understand the tangible harm of speech that undermines the dignity of persons. As he argues, statements and images that defame the character of groups "attack a shared sense of the basic elements of each person's status, dignity, and reputation as a citizen or member of society in good standing." Jeremy Waldron, *The Harm in Hate Speech* (Cambridge: Harvard University Press, 2012), 47.

23. According to Michael Warner, recognizing shared interests with strangers is a key feature of the formation of a public. As he explains, "Publics orient us to strangers in a different way. They are no longer merely people whom one does not know; rather, an environment of strangerhood is the necessary premise of some of our most prized ways of being." Michael Warner, *Publics and Counterpublics* (New York: Zone, 2005), 75.

24. Pankaj Mishra, *Age of Anger: A History of the Present* (New York: Farrar, Straus and Giroux, 2017), 19.

25. According to Jason Stanley, resentment about the redistribution of power promised by liberal ideals of equality is one of the major sources for fascism. As Stanley explains, "Equality, according to the fascist, is the Trojan horse of liberalism. The part of Odysseus can be variously played—by Jews, by homosexuals, by Muslims, by non-whites, by feminists, etc. Anyone spreading the doctrine of liberal equality is either a dupe, 'infected by the idea of freedom,' or an enemy of the nation who is spreading the ideals of liberalism only with devious and indeed illiberal aims." Jason Stanley, *How Fascism Works: The Politics of Us and Them* (New York: Random House, 2018), 88.

26. Nadia Marzouki, *Islam: An American Religion*, trans. C. Jon Delogu (New York: Columbia University Press, 2017), 140.

27. In keeping with the idea that it is possible to register a loss of the people as its own form of profanation, Daniel Nilsson DeHanas and Marat Shterin have proposed a definition of populism as "a political style that sets 'sacred' people against two enemies: elites and others." Daniel Nilsson DeHanas and Marat Shterin, "Religion and the Rise of Populism," *Religion, State, and Society* 46, no. 3 (2018), 180.

28. On this point, this book revisits debates about "political correctness" and "hate speech" that became particularly prominent in the 1990s. For two of the more influential critiques of liberal models of absolute distinctions between speech and action, see Catherine A. MacKinnon, *Only Words* (Cambridge: Harvard University Press, 1996); and Stanley Fish, *There's No Such Thing as Free Speech: And It's a Good Thing Too* (New York: Oxford University Press, 1994).

29. Thomas Jefferson, *Notes on the State of Virginia*, ed. Frank Shuffleton (1785. Reprint, New York: Penguin, 1999), 165.

30. I suggest that religious offenses, the affective appeals of populism, and the role of winning and losing occupy a structural hole in liberal thought. As Chantal Mouffe has noted, the insistence that communal passions are irrelevant to political life renders liberals perpetually surprised by populist movements. As she explains, "The refusal to acknowledge the political in its antagonistic dimension, and the concomitant incapacity to grasp the central role of the passions in the constitution of collective identities, are in my view at the root of political

202   INTRODUCTION

theory's failure to come to terms with the problem of populism." Chantal Mouffe, "The 'End of Politics' and the Challenge of Right-Wing Populism," in *Populism and the Mirror of Democracy*, ed. Francisco Panizza (New York: Verso, 2005), 51.

31. John Locke, "A Letter Concerning Toleration," in *Locke on Toleration*, ed. Richard Vernon (New York: Cambridge University Press, 2010).

32. Saba Mahmood, "Religious Reason and Secular Affect: An Incommensurable Divide?" in *Is Critique Secular? Blasphemy, Injury, and Free Speech*, by Talal Asad, Wendy Brown, Judith Butler, and Saba Mahmood (Berkeley: University of California Press, 2009), 70.

33. Andrew March has objected to Mahmood's suggestion that the conflict over cartoon controversies reflects any fundamental difference over semiotic ideology. March suggests that defenders of free speech understand the injury caused by offensive images but simply value free expression more. As he explains,

> I think the secular resistance to (in this case) Muslim objections is no more attributable to appreciate that Muslims are genuinely wounded by ridicule of the Prophet Muhammad than the Muslim objection to blasphemous speech is attributable to a radical failure on their part to appreciate the value of free speech. The deepest incommensurability, rather, is between the belief that even painful speech about sacred matters may be a legitimate form of self-expression and the contrary belief that certain sacred objects are more valuable than individual self-expression. Fair-minded persons on both sides can understand the other well enough; they just value each side of the equation differently.

Andrew March, "Speech and the Sacred: Does the Defense of Free Speech Rest on a Mistake about Religion?" *Political Theory* 40, no. 3 (2012), 338. March's claim that there is not necessarily an essential epistemic incommensurability between Islam and secularism is convincing, but his formulation still leaves unanswered the question of why Muslims and secularists value speech differently. I would suggest the reason is that they have different stakes in the outcomes of offensive speech. That is, those who feel like their social place is secured by free speech are far less likely to worry about the injury caused by offense than those who feel like they have something to lose.

34. Stanley Fish, *The First: How to Think About Hate Speech, Campus Speech, Religious Speech, Fake News, Post-Truth, and Donald Trump* (New York: One Signal, 2019), 11.

35. According to John Dewey, this tension between freedom and equality precipitated what he called an "inner split" in liberalism. John Dewey, *Liberalism and Social Action* (1935; repr. Amherst, N.Y.: Prometheus, 2000).

36. On the use of the trope of "taking religion seriously" within liberal scholarship, see Elizabeth Pritchard, "Seriously, What Does 'Taking Religion Seriously' Mean?" *Journal of the American Academy of Religion* 78, no. 4 (December 2010): 1087–1110.

37. Donovan Schaefer, "Whiteness and Civilization: Shame, Race, and the Rhetoric of Donald Trump," *Communication and Critical/Cultural Studies* 17, no 1 (2020): 7.

38. In her study of Tea Party conservatives in Louisiana, Arlie Russell Hochschild describes the emotional satisfaction Trump supporters felt from not having to be governed by politically correct rules as a liberation from shame. As she explains, "They yearn to feel pride and instead have felt shame. Their land no longer feels their own. Joined together with others like themselves, they now feel hopeful, joyous, elated." Arlie Russell Hochschild, *Strangers in Their Own Land: Anger and Mourning on the American Right* (New York: New Press, 2018), 225.

39. Schaefer, "Whiteness and Civilization," 8.

40. For histories of agrarian movements that define populism as an economic platform that would exclude Trump, see Lawrence Goodwyn, *The Populist Moment: A Short History of the Agrarian Revolt in America* (New York: Oxford University Press, 1978); and Charles Postel, *The Populist Vision* (New York: Oxford University Press, 2007). For a study that places agrarian populism within a broader rhetorical tradition that could be more politically malleable, see Michael Kazin, *The Populist Persuasion: An American History*, rev. ed. (Ithaca, N.J.: Cornell University Press, 1998). For a study of contemporary populism that includes Trump but has come so far that it would in effect exclude the original

populists, see Jan-Werner Müller, *What Is Populism?* (Philadelphia: University of Pennsylvania Press, 2016).

41. According to Pippa Norris and Ronald Inglehart, populism is a rhetoric project that can show up in a variety of places on the political spectrum but is centrally concerned with returning power to an imagined people. As they explain, "We define populism minimally as a rhetorical style of communication claiming that (i) the only legitimate democratic authority flows directly from the people, and (ii) established power-holders are deeply corrupt, and self-interested, betraying public trust." Pippa Norris and Ronald Inglehart, *Cultural Backlash: Trump, Brexit, and Authoritarian Populism* (New York: Cambridge University Press, 2019), 66.

42. On crossover voters, see John Sides, Michael Tesler, and Lynn Vavreck, "The 2016 U.S. Election: How Trump Lost and Won," *Journal of Democracy* 28, no. 2 (April 2017): 34–44.

43. While I believe that illiberal secularism captures the antigovernment sentiments of the coalition that elected Trump, there are still exceptions in the form of groups like Christian reconstructionists who aim to create a Christian state. For more on the Christian reconstruction movement, see Julie J. Ingersoll, *Building God's Kingdom: Inside the World of Christian Reconstruction* (New York: Oxford University Press, 2015); and Michael J. McVicar, *Christian Reconstruction: R. J. Rushdoony and American Religious Conservatism* (Chapel Hill: University of North Carolina Press, 2015). Saying that Christian reconstructionists are exceptional does not mean to imply that they do not share the goals of other Christian nationalists. They might indeed subscribe to similar vision of an ideal Christian state and society, but illiberal secularism takes a more pragmatic assessment of political reality that accepts the legal division of church and state.

44. José Casanova, *Public Religions in the Modern World* (Chicago: University of Chicago Press, 1994).

45. Patricia J. Williams, *The Alchemy of Race and Rights* (Cambridge, Mass.: Harvard University Press, 1991).

46. This usage of *illiberal secularism* also differs from José Casanova's characterization of French attempts to regulate religious minorities through laws restricting Muslim dress as an "extreme form of illiberal secularism." As he explains, "While conservative religious people are

expected to tolerate behavior they may consider morally abhorrent such as homosexuality, liberal secular Europeans are openly stating that European societies ought not to tolerate religious behavior or cultural customs that are morally abhorrent insofar as far as they are contrary to modern liberal secular norms." José Casanova, "Religion, European Secular Identities, and European Integration," in *Religion in an Expanding Europe*, ed. Timothy A. Byrnes and Peter J. Katznelson (New York: Cambridge University Press, 2006), 79–80. Casanova's use of *illiberalism* is meant as a normative judgment of secular liberals who do not follow their own principles. I see this instead as a familiar feature of secular liberalism. Secular liberals often distinguish between good and bad religions and do not consistently apply their own principles. I am using the term *illiberalism* descriptively rather than normatively. For my purposes, *illiberal secularism* is a rejection of liberalism rather than a failure to live up to liberal principles. I would simply use the term *secular liberalism* to describe the latter.

47. For an empirical study that measures features of Christian nationalism, see Andrew L. Whitehead and Samuel L. Perry, *Taking America Back for God: Christian Nationalism in the United States* (New York: Oxford University Press, 2020). While Whitehead and Perry would not use the word *secular* to describe Christian nationalism, I believe that the characteristics they describe foster the turn toward private institutions that I am describing as illiberal secularism. Their data also show that a significant number of people who subscribe to Christian nationalism are not necessarily white evangelical Christians. I suggest that there is a secular logic that makes this multireligious coalition possible.

48. Lauren Berlant, *The Queen of America Goes to Washington City: Essays on Sex and Citizenship* (Durham, N.C.: Duke University Press, 1997), 5.

49. According to Corey Robin, conservative thought has long privileged private power over the state: "The priority of conservative political argument has been the maintenance of private regimes of power—even at the cost of the strength and integrity of the state." Corey Robin, *The Reactionary Mind: Conservatism from Edmund Burke to Donald Trump*, 2nd ed. (New York: Oxford University Press, 2018), 15. In this sense, the illiberal privatization of everything is not entirely new but is an exaggeration of long-standing tendencies in American politics.

50. Joshua Gunn, "On Political Perversion," *Rhetoric Society Quarterly* 48, no. 2 (2018): 178.

51. Evgeny Morozov, *The Net Delusion: The Dark Side of Internet Freedom* (New York: Public Affairs, 2011), 75.

52. Zeynep Tufekci, *Twitter and Tear Gas: The Power and Fragility of Networked Protest* (New Haven, Conn.: Yale University Press, 2017), 40.

53. In her study of search engines, Safiya Umoja Noble describes how purportedly neutral technologies like algorithms reproduce the racism and sexism of internet users. Safiya Umoja Noble, *Algorithms of Oppression: How Search Engines Reinforce Racism* (New York: New York University Press, 2018).

54. In their study of conspiracy theories, Russell Muirhead and Nancy Rosenblum note that internet truth is determined by popularity contests: "What mattered was not evidence but the number of retweets the president's post would enjoy; the more retweets, the more credible the charge. Forwarding, reposting, retweeting, and 'liking': these are how doubts are instilled and accusations are validated in the new media." They describe this process as "delegitimation," where recognized institutional gatekeepers lose their authority. Russell Muirhead and Nancy L. Rosenblum, *A Lot of People Are Saying: The New Conspiracism and the Assault on Democracy* (Princeton, N.J.: Princeton University Press, 2019), 3.

55. Jia Tolentino, *Trick Mirror: Reflections on Self-Delusion* (New York: Random House, 2020), 22.

56. This ethos of winning is reflected in Trump's word choices on Twitter. As one count reveals: "Before and during his presidency Donald Trump's preferred words were those that project strength, toughness, and most of all wins. In his tweets he used 'win' and 'won' 1,136 times; also prominent were the words 'strong' (551 times), 'tough' (326 times), 'fight' (279 times). He degraded his opponents as 'failing' 234 times, 'weak' 199 times, and 'loser' 128 times." Brigitte L. Nacos, Robert Y. Shapiro, and Yaeli Bloch-Elkon, "Donald Trump: Aggressive Rhetoric and Political Violence," *Perspectives on Terrorism* 14, no. 5 (October 2020), 15–16.

57. Brian L. Ott and Greg Dickinson suggest that there is a linguistic affinity between Twitter's grammatical transgressions and the incivility of the Trump presidency: "Twitter is decidedly informal. Its lack of

concern for proper grammar and style undermines norms that tend to enforce civility." Ott and Dickinson, *The Twitter Presidency*, 63.

58. Stefan Wojcik and Adam Hughes, "Sizing Up Twitter Users," *PEW Research Center*, April 24, 2019, https://www.pewresearch.org/internet /2019/04/24/sizing-up-twitter-users/.

59. Walter Benjamin, "The Work of Art in the Age of Mechanical Reproduction," trans. Harry Zohn, in *Illuminations*, ed. Hannah Arendt (New York: Schocken, 1985), 238.

60. Achille Mbembe, *Necropolitics* (Durham, N.C.: Duke University Press, 2019), 115.

61. Mbembe, *Necropolitics*, 115–116.

62. In his refusal to be constrained by the rules, Trump reinforced the image of himself as a strong sovereign in a way that fit with how Robert Yelle describes the correspondence between the sacred and the sovereign exception. The sovereign enforces rules but is also free from ordinary constraints on human beings: "We must acknowledge the existence of something wild—something untamed and spontaneous—in human nature. This something is what we call the sacred, although a better name for it might be sovereignty. It is not a question of endorsing this quality, but of facing up to it." Robert Yelle, *Sovereignty and the Sacred* (Chicago: University of Chicago Press, 2019), 184. Trump's wildness existed in tandem with his calls for law and order.

63. Greg Lukianoff and Jonathan Haidt, *The Coddling of the American Mind: How Good Intentions and Bad Ideas Are Setting Up a Generation for Failure* (New York: Penguin, 2018).

64. Michael Taussig, *Defacement: Public Secrecy and the Labor of the Negative* (Stanford, Calif.: Stanford University Press, 1999), 1.

1. THE REALITY OF DONALD J. TRUMP

1. Mara Liasson, "Trump's Reality Star Approach to the Real World," *National Public Radio*, July 12, 2017, https://www.npr.org/2018/07/12 /628578365/trumps-reality-star-approach-to-the-real-world.

2. George Will, "The Shabbiest U.S. President Ever Is an Inexpressibly Sad Specimen," *Washington Post*, January 18, 2019, https://www .washingtonpost.com/opinions/what-a-misery-it-must-be-to-be

-donald-trump/2019/01/18/d0e05eea-1a82-11e9-8813-cb9dec761e73
_story.html.

3. Stephen Miller, quoted in Philip Bump, "This Is the Best Argument
to Be Made for Trump's Political Greatness?" *Washington Post*, January 8, 2018, https://www.washingtonpost.com/news/politics/wp/2018
/01/08/this-is-the-best-argument-to-be-made-for-trumps-political
-greatness.

4. Peter Baker, "For Trump, A Year of Reinventing the Presidency," *New
York Times*, December 31, 2017, https://www.nytimes.com/2017/12/31
/us/politics/trump-reinventing-presidency.html.

5. Baker, "For Trump, a Year of Reinventing the Presidency."

6. Donald J. Trump with Tony Schwartz, *Trump: The Art of the Deal* (New
York: Ballantine, 1987), 56.

7. Corey R. Lewandowski and David N. Bossie, *Let Trump Be Trump: The
Inside Story of His Rise to the Presidency* (New York: Hachette, 2017), 170.

8. On the Republican Party's use of cultural issues to distract working-
class voters from their economic interests, see Thomas Frank, *What's
the Matter with Kansas? How Conservatives Won the Heart of America*
(New York: Holt, 2005). Ernesto Laclau, however, argues that one
problem with liberal critiques of populism is that accounts of rational
self-interests fail to explain how the people identify their interests in the
first place. That is, liberal critiques of populism do not account for the
affective bonds between human beings that lead people to see themselves as members of groups with shared interests. As he explains, "The
main difficulty with classical theories of political representation is
that most of them conceived the will of the people as something that
was constituted *before* representation." Ernesto Laclau, *On Populist
Reason* (New York: Verso, 2005), 163–164. This means that liberal critics
of populism offer no explanation for what produces a people in the first
place, and therefore make dispassionate political appeals that are unin-
teresting both because they fail to discern the people's interest and
because they are boring.

9. Reece Peck's study of what he calls "Fox Populism" suggests that
attention to visceral features of publicity like branding strategies is
especially necessary in the current mediated environment. As Peck
argues, "The presidential victory of Donald Trump punctuates the
necessity of style as an analytical category more than ever. Trump ran

one of the most unorthodox Republican campaigns in recent memory. Yet as a longtime tabloid figure, he was able to leverage his knowledge of media publicity to defeat more ideologically pure opponents in the Republican primary like Senator Ted Cruz." Reece Peck, *Fox Populism: Branding Conservatism as Working Class* (New York: Cambridge University Press, 2019), 17.

10. As Mabel Berezin notes, liberal condescension toward Trump's intellect only increased his appeal among voters who felt the same slights. As she explains, "The part of Trump's narrative that described America as a war between doers and thinkers; the builders versus the financiers; the Ivy educated versus the educated at the school of hard knocks— stuck, or stuck enough to let Trump slip into the White House." Mabel Berezin, "On the Construction Sites of History: Where Did Donald Trump Come From?" *American Journal of Cultural Sociology* 5, no. 3 (2017): 331.

11. Graydon Carter, "Steel Traps and Short Fingers," *Vanity Fair*, October 17, 2015. https://www.vanityfair.com/culture/2015/10/graydon -carter-donald-trump.

12. In response to his receiving the epithet "Little Marco," Senator Marco Rubio attempted to mimic his opponent's lowbrow politics by invoking the small appendage issue: "And you know what they say about men with small hands? You can't trust them." Rather than brush off the insult, Trump defiantly held up his hands in response. Gregory Krieg, "Donald Trump Defends Size of His Penis," *CNN*, March 4, 2016, https://www.cnn.com/2016/03/03/politics/donald-trump-small -hands-marco-rubio/index.html.

13. Seth Meyers, "2011 White House Correspondents Dinner," *C-SPAN*, April 30, 2011, https://www.c-span.org/video/?299256-1/2011-white -house-correspondents-dinner.

14. Adam Gopnik, "Trump and Obama: A Night to Remember," *New Yorker*, September 12, 2015, https://www.newyorker.com/news/daily -comment/trump-and-obama-a-night-to-remember.

15. Sianne Ngai, *Ugly Feelings* (Cambridge, Mass.: Harvard University Press, 2005), 128.

16. Lauren Berlant suggests that shamelessness was the most successful aspect of the Trump brand. More than tangible Trump products, the most appealing features of Trumpism was the liberation from shame:

"But virtually no one purchased the Big Man's stuff—his stakes [*sic*], his clothes, his university, many of his investments: they went fallow, it was bad design, bad business. But if the white BSE [Big Sovereign Electorate] is not sharing his taste, it is sharing his embrace of and intensity of appetite and his commitment to a shameless life." Lauren Berlant, "Big Man," *Social Text Online*, January 19, 2017. https:// socialtextjournal.org/big-man/.

17. Roxanne Roberts, who sat next to Trump during the 2011 dinner, disputes that he was as upset as others made him out to be and questions whether shame had anything to do with his run for the presidency. As she states,

> This narrative flies in the face of actual history: Trump mentioned running for president as far back as the 1980s, so the notion that this dinner was the single catalyst for this presidential campaign is absurd. He frequently used humor as part of his self-promotional tool kit and was the guest of honor at a 2011 Comedy Central roast just two months before the correspondents' dinner—an X-rated drubbing that made Obama and Meyers look like weenies.

Roxanne Roberts, "I Sat Next to Donald Trump at the Infamous 2011 White House Correspondents Dinner," *Washington Post*, April 28, 2016, https://www.washingtonpost.com/lifestyle/style/i-sat-next-to -donald-trump-at-the-infamous-2011-white-house-correspondents -dinner/2016/04/27/5cf46b74-0bea-11e6-8ab8-9ad05of76d7d_story.html.

18. Oprah Winfrey Show, "Donald Trump Teases a President Bid During a 1988 Oprah Show," *YouTube*, 3:09, June 15, 2015, https://www .youtube.com/watch?time_continue=3&v=SEPs17_AkTI.

19. On Trump's rhetoric as the opposite of common sense, see Russell Muirhead and Nancy L. Rosenblum, *A Lot of People Are Saying: The New Conspiracism and the Assault on Democracy* (Princeton, N.J.: Princeton University Press, 2019), 125–129.

20. Alex Swoyer, "Donald Trump Jr: 'We Learned From People with Doctorates in Common Sense,'" *Breitbart*, July 19, 2016, https://www .breitbart.com/politics/2016/07/19/donald-trump-jr-we-learned-from -people-with-doctorates-in-common-sense.

21. Nadia Marzouki, *Islam: An American Religion*, trans. C. Jon Delogu (New York: Columbia University Press, 2017), 160.

22. Thomas Reid, *An Inquiry into the Human Mind on the Principles of Common Sense*, ed. Derek R. Brookes (1764; repr. University Park: Pennsylvania State Press, 2000), 18.

23. Reid, *Inquiry into the Human Mind*, 18.

24. Reid, *Inquiry into the Human Mind*, 52.

25. As Henry May argues in his classic study of Enlightenment thought in America, "Common Sense had begun its conquests just before and during the American Revolution. This should not be at all surprising. . . . Those who are daring enough to pull down established institutions have to believe in what they are doing; they cannot afford to be skeptics." Henry F. May, *The Enlightenment in America* (New York: Oxford University Press, 1976), 346.

26. Thomas Paine, *Common Sense* (1776; repr., Mineola: Dover, 1997), 5.

27. Walter Russell Mead described Trumpism as a "Jacksonian revolt." This Jacksonian turn was evident in Trump's embrace of an "America First" philosophy in which the defense of national honor was the president's first priority:

> Many Americans with cosmopolitan sympathies see their main ethical imperative as working for the betterment of humanity in general. Jacksonians locate their moral communities closer to home, in fellow citizens who share a common national bond. If the cosmopolitans see the Jacksonians as backward and chauvinistic, Jacksonians return the favor by seeing the elite as near treasonous— people who think it is morally questionable to put their own country, and its citizens, first.

Walter Russell Mead, "The Jacksonian Revolt: American Populism and the Liberal Order," *Foreign Affairs* 96, no. 2 (March/April 2017), 4.

28. Donald Trump, quoted in Tim Hains, "Trump: Andrew Jackson Defied 'Arrogant Elites'—'I Know the Feeling, Andrew,'" *RealClear Politics*, March 15, 2017, https://www.realclearpolitics.com/video/2017/03/15/trump_andrew_jackson_defied_an_arrogant_elite_---_i_know_the_feeling_andrew.html#!.

29. According to Antti Lepistö, appeals to the Scottish common sense tradition helped neoconservative critics to move from their elitist suspicion of uneducated publics to an embrace of populist rhetoric. As he suggests,

"The neoconservatives suggested, explicitly or implicitly, that American moral and social order depended on the rather delicate moral sense, or common sense, of ordinary people, and in doing so, they fused Scottish moral philosophy with a conservative understanding of civilization as fragile, easily disrupted, and in need of protection by every new generation." Antti Lepistö, *The Rise of Common-Sense Conservatism: The American Right and the Reinvention of the Scottish Enlightenment* (Chicago: University of Chicago Press, 2021), 13. The desire to harmonize populism with a shared moral sense might be one reason why neoconservatives were disproportionately represented among Never Trumpers.

30. Trump's use of a repertoire of cartoonish gestures and mimicry is one example of his use of natural signs to connect with his supporters. As Kira Hall, Donna M. Goldstein, and Matthew Bruce explain,

> When used in coordination with verbal strategies similarly designed to lampoon opponents, Trump's enactments craft essentialized characterizations of identity categories that simultaneously cast their members as problematic citizens, whether Democrats, disabled, lower class, Muslim, Mexican, or women. These depictive gestures operate cross-modally to signal to Trump's base that he challenges what is widely viewed as the political establishment's debilitating rhetoric of political correctness.

> Kira Hall, Donna M. Goldstein, and Matthew Bruce Ingram, "The Hands of Donald Trump: Entertainment, Gesture, Spectacle," *HAU: Journal of Ethnographic Theory* 6, no. 2 (Autumn 2016): 74.

31. As William Connolly observes, the connection between affect and precritical responses are shaped by identity: "The affect-imbued ideas that compose them are installed in the soft tissues of affect, emotion, habit, and posture, as well as the upper reaches of the intellect. Once installed, these sensibilities trigger preliminary responses to new events, even before the respondents think consciously about the events." William E. Connolly, *Christianity and Capitalism, American Style* (Durham, N.C.: Duke University Press, 2008), 44.

32. Donovan Schaefer, "Whiteness and Civilization: Shame, Race, and the Rhetoric of Donald Trump," *Communication and Critical/Cultural Studies* 17, no 1 (2020): 6.

33. Lauren Berlant, "Trump, or Political Emotions," *Supervalent Thought*, August 4, 2016, https://supervalentthought.com/2016/08/04/trump-or -political-emotions/.

34. Joshua Hawley, "The Age of Pelagius," *Christianity Today*, June 4, 2019, https://www.christianitytoday.com/ct/2019/june-web-only/age-of -pelagius-joshua-hawley.html.

35. Equating secularism with elitism is a feature that Daniel Steinmetz Jenkins and Anton Jäger see as a rhetorical plank within a "global theo-logical counter-revolution." As they explain,

> The Eurasian traditionalism of Vladimir Putin, the Christian-Democracy of Orbán, the Judeo-Christianity of Trump, the pros-perity Pentecostalism of Bolsonaro, the populist Catholicism of Salvini and the Hindu-nationalism of Modi, all speak of a reli-giously infused reaction to secular governance. What has been eroding for the past few decades is not simply democratic or liberal values per se; there has also been a growing suspicion of secularism and the secular elites who propagate it.

Daniel Steinmetz Jenkins and Anton Jäger, "The Populist Right Is Forging an Unholy Alliance with Religion," *Guardian*, June 11, 2019, https://www.theguardian.com/commentisfree/2019/jun/11/populists -right-unholy-alliance-religion. I agree that Trumpism could be part of a global response to secular liberalism (although I am not compe-tent to evaluate other national contexts), but in the case of the United States, it does this in a way that is consistent with secular privatiza-tion of religion. Much of this could be a semantic difference about what you choose to call secular.

36. The logic of common sense holds that Trump's freewheeling style allows him to articulate what everyone secretly feels to be true. In revealing what people really feel, common sense promises to bring everything out into the open. According to Lauren Berlant, this amounts to an ironic usage of the liberal ideal of a commons: "The Big Sovereign Electorate (BSE) makes a revolutionary use of the *commons* concept. Its commons is affective: its version of the commons pre-serves freedom as a feeling of unencumbrance; as a tool their com-mons sucks difference into the fantasy of an 'America' that is also

well-known to liberals as a utopia for unconstrained thinking, feeling, and speaking." Lauren Berlant, "Big Man."

37. Trump, *Art of the Deal*, 85.

38. Trump, *Art of the Deal*, 87.

39. Trump, *Art of the Deal*, 139.

40. Trump, *Art of the Deal*, 104.

41. Donald Trump, quoted in Amita Kelly, "Trump to Jewish Republicans: 'I'm a Negotiator Like You Folks,'" *NPR*, December 3, 2015, https://www.npr.org/2015/12/03/458329895/trump-to-jewish-republicans -im-a-negotiator-like-you-folks. Trump's rhetoric often blurred the lines between philo-Semitism and anti-Semitism. He appeared to believe antisemitic tropes that held that Jews cared only about money and that they controlled the media. It is just that in Trump's mind these were good qualities.

42. Trump, *Art of the Deal*, 90.

43. Elyse Goldwater, quoted in David A. Graham, Adrienne Green, Cullen Murphy, and Parker Reynolds, "An Oral History of Trump's Bigotry," *Atlantic Monthly*, June 2019, 55.

44. Chris Cillizza, "Donald Trump's Birther Event Is the Greatest Trick He Ever Pulled," *Washington Post*, September 16, 2016, https://www .washingtonpost.com/news/the-fix/wp/2016/09/16/donald-trumps -birther-event-is-the-greatest-trick-hes-ever-pulled/.

45. As Emily Ogden suggests, Trump's mastery of lying makes him all the more appealing when it is one tool in an arsenal to defeat enemies: "Even if Mr. Trump's audience retains a suspicion that he himself might be a swindler, that doesn't necessarily work to his disadvantage. The attacks on his truthfulness have an alarming tendency to reinforce his message that he's a master of the deceptive arts. In a treacherous world, you need a treacherous ally—treacherous, at least, to your mutual enemies." Emily Ogden, "Donald Trump, Mesmerist," *New York Times*, August 4, 2018, https://www.nytimes.com/2018/08/04 /opinion/sunday/donald-trump-mesmerist.html.

46. Trump's trickery has a magical power to best liberal critics that Michael Taussig observes in the futility of enlightenment attempts to debunk magicians, shamans, and sorcerers:

> The very notion of the trick, we might say, seems to sabotage binary logic, let alone reality, and does so most pointedly by making a

clever mess of good and evil in relation to ontology and technology. Might it be that reality itself is one big trick, and the professional responsible for relating to this, such as the shaman, entertains such cosmic trickery while extracting a small profit in the form of healing power and sorcery? It makes a lot of sense, then, to think of magic as mimesis, imitating reality so as to deceive it.

Michael Taussig, "Viscerality, Faith, and Skepticism: Another Theory of Magic," in *In Near Ruins: Cultural Theory at the End of the Century*, ed. Nicholas B. Dirks (Minneapolis: University of Minnesota Press, 1998), 251.

47. Trump, *Art of the Deal*, 214–215.
48. Donald J. Trump with Meredith McIver, *How to Get Rich* (New York: Ballentine, 2004), 153.
49. Trump, *Art of the Deal*, 58.
50. In the section preceding the above quotation, Lofton discusses how Trump manages these multiple senses of celebrity:

> To understand Donald Trump, you need to understand how popular media in the United States organizes around certain risk economies and certain gender paradigms, but also around the proud exposure of human self-deception. Scholars of popular culture know the weird crooked affinities between fan and celebrity. We know that fan worship of a celebrity is not just about admiring the celebrity but also about hating the celebrity, or liking the way that hate makes us feel superior, or how love and hate are tangled up in a mesh of intimate commiseration between one person who nobody knows and somebody who everybody does.

Kathryn Lofton, *Consuming Religion* (Chicago: University of Chicago Press, 2017), 168.

51. Corey Robin, *The Reactionary Mind: Conservatism from Edmund Burke to Donald Trump*, 2nd ed. (New York: Oxford University Press, 2018), 258.
52. Lucas Mann, "The Problem with Calling Trump a 'Reality-TV President,'" *Atlantic*, April 30, 2018, https://www.theatlantic.com /entertainment/archive/2018/04/what-exactly-makes-trump-a-reality -tv-president/558626/.
53. Mark Burnett, quoted in Patrick Radden Keefe, "Winning," *New Yorker*, January 7, 2019, 36.

54. As Masha Gessen points out, this invention of reality also extended to Trump's ability to make some aspects of unpleasant reality disappear. One example of this is Trump's response to criticism of migrant detention centers. By defining migrants as subhuman, the human suffering in the camps could be safely ignored. As Gessen notes, "Through his tweets, his attacks on the media, and his lying, Trump has been waging a battle to define reality to the exclusion of documented facts. In Trump's reality, it's not just that the Administration refuses to be held accountable for running concentration camps—it's that the camps, and the suffering in them, do not exist." Masha Gessen, "Donald Trump's Inoffensive War on Reality," *New Yorker*, July 5, 2019, https://www.newyorker.com/news/our-columnists/donald-trumps-inoffensive-war-on-reality.

55. Hall, Goldstein, and Ingram, "The Hands of Donald Trump," 80.

56. Lewandowski and Bossie, *Let Trump Be Trump*, 164.

57. Donald J. Trump (@realDonaldTrump), "I wonder if the New York Times will apologize to me a second time, as they did after the 2016 Election," Tweet, April 23, 2019, 5:08 a.m., https://twitter.com/realDonaldTrump/status/1120630405831569408.

58. Steve King, quoted in Caroline Summerfield, "Steve King: Bring Pride Back to Austria," *Unzensuriert*, September 2, 2018.

59. Daniella Diaz, "Miss Universe Strikes Back," *CNN*, September 28, 2016, https://www.cnn.com/2016/09/27/politics/alicia-machado-donald-trump-2016-election-anderson-cooper/index.html.

60. Alex Ross, "The Frankfurt School Knew Donald Trump Was Coming," *New Yorker*, December 5, 2016, https://www.newyorker.com/culture/cultural-comment/the-frankfurt-school-knew-trump-was-coming.

61. Jason Stanley, *How Fascism Works: The Politics of Us and Them* (New York: Random House, 2018), 57–58.

62. There are some who see this anticonservatism as a relative benefit of Trumpism. That is, precisely because Trump is so shameless, he lacks the secrecy and competence of Bush-era state surveillance apparatus. As Nicholas Lemann asserts, Trump is less powerful precisely because everything is out in the open: "Trumpism is public. It carries the risk of reawakening hateful public sentiments that had been temporarily quieted. Cheneyism is private. It carries the risk of a vast, consequential

government project being initiated before anybody has realized what the United States has committed itself to. Trumpism is politics. Cheneyism is government. Cheneyism is scarier." Nicholas Lemann, "'Vice' vs. the Real Dick Cheney," *New Yorker*, January 3, 2019, https:// www.newyorker.com/news/daily-comment/vice-vs-the-real-dick -cheney.

63. John Fea, *Believe Me: The Evangelical Road to Donald Trump* (Grand Rapids, Mich.: Eerdmans, 2018), 177.

64. As Tony Michaels argued, Trump might be the ultimate beneficiary of the liberal refusal to defend liberalism. If anything makes Donald Trump a conservative, it is his embodiment of the refusal to compromise with any aspect of liberalism. Indeed, liberal values of compromise and finding common ground have managed only to cede political territory to conservatives who see no value in such reciprocity: "Instead of liberalism, Democrats were more likely to use the language of efficiency and productivity to describe their proposals. Republicans, by contrast, surrendered no ideological terrain, even when they had to compromise politically. They consistently and proudly proclaimed their conservatism, all the while stretching its meaning to distant extremes." Tony Michaels, "Donald Trump and the Triumph of Antiliberalism," *Jewish Social Studies* 22, no. 3 (Spring/Summer 2017), 189.

65. As Christopher Craig Brittain notes in his study of evangelical support for Trump, "The content of both public policy and theological doctrine is marginalized in Trump's populist movement, as its sole content is occupied by the personality of the man himself." Christopher Craig Brittain, "Racketeering in Religion: Adorno and Evangelical Support for Trump," *Critical Research on Religion* 6, no. 3 (2018): 283.

66. The desire for a strong leader even led some Christians to prefer Trump over a more clearly self-identified evangelical like Mike Pence. As one supporter explained, "The president is having to deal with a den of vipers. I'm not sure Pence could do that." Bob Collins, quoted in Elizabeth Breunig, "In God's Country," *Washington Post*, August 14, 2019, https://www.washingtonpost.com/opinions/2019/08/14/evangelicals -view-trump-their-protector-will-they-stand-by-him/.

67. William E. Connolly, "Trump, the Working Class, and Fascist Rhetoric," *Theory and Event* 20, no. 1 (January 2017): 28.

68. One interpretation of the emphasis on strength is that it appeals to the dominionist strain among conservative Christians who place a messianic hope in a strong leader to restore Christian rule. According to Anthea Butler, "In their theology, God can use any male leader to achieve God's purpose. To put it one way, Jesus cares more for the wolf than the sheep. A strong man can make things happen." Anthea Butler, "Why Trump—And Some of His Followers—Believe He Is the Chosen One," *Religion News Service*, August 25, 2019, https://religionnews.com/2019/08/23/why-trump-and-some-of-his-followers-believe-he-is-the-chosen-one/.

69. Jerry Falwell Jr. (@JerryFalwellJr), "Conservatives & Christians need to stop electing 'nice guys,'" tweet, September 28, 2018, 8:50 p.m., https://twitter.com/JerryFalwellJr/status/1045853333007798272.

70. This might also account for the noted tie between the refusals to apologize for Trump's possible incitements of violence against his supporters. Indeed, the promise of extralegal violence might be part of what makes Trump particularly popular among those dissatisfied with procedural liberalism. This would be consistent with Walter Benjamin's suggestion that there is political insight to be gained from the popularity of the daring criminal: "Violence, when not in the hands of the law, threatens it not by the ends that it may pursue but by its mere existence outside the law. The same may be more drastically suggested, for one reflects how often the figure of the 'great' criminal, however repellent his ends may have been, has aroused the secret admiration of the public." Walter Benjamin, "Critique of Violence," trans. Harry Zohn, in *Walter Benjamin, Selected Writings*, ed. Marcus Bullock and Michael W. Jennings, vol. 1 (Cambridge: Harvard University Press, 1996), 239.

71. Laclau, *On Populist Reason*, 123.

72. House Speaker Paul Ryan's habit of criticizing Trump but nevertheless failing to challenge Trump's takeover over the Republican Party earned him particular scorn for spinelessness. As Alp Ozcelik notes, one anonymous critic went so far as to edit the Wikipedia page for invertebrates to include Ryan. Alp Ozcelik (@alplicable), "It's gone now but someone had edited the Wikipedia page for invertebrates to include Paul Ryan," tweet, January 26, 2017, https://twitter.com/alplicable/status/824742568852353026.

73. Alain Badiou, *Trump*, trans. Joseph Litvak (Medford, Mass.: Polity, 2019), 14.

74. Jamelle Bouie, "The Joy of Hatred," *New York Times*, July 19, 2019, https://www.nytimes.com/2019/07/19/opinion/trump-rally.html.

75. Laurie Penny, "No, I Won't Debate You," *Longreads*, September 18, 2018, https://longreads.com/2018/09/18/no-i-will-not-debate-you/.

76. As Roger Eatwell and Matthew Goodwin argue in their study of national populism that places the United States in comparison to Europe: "But while he held that America was ailing, Trump clearly did not, and does not, seek to forge a 'holistic nation,' let alone a radically 'new man' in a country whose culture is characterized by rugged and self-confident individualism. Although Trump's statements have given succor to racists, his views are a far cry from fascist racism, let alone Nazi anti-Semitism." Roger Eatwell and Matthew Goodwin, *National Populism: The Revolt Against Liberal Democracy* (New York: Penguin, 2018), 66.

77. Badiou, *Trump*, 15

78. Jasbir K. Puar, *Terrorist Assemblages: Homonationalism in Queer Times*, exp. ed. (Durham, N.C.: Duke University Press, 2017), 224.

79. J. Kameron Carter, "Behind Christianity Today's Editorial Is a Deeper Crisis of America's Religion of Whiteness," *Religion News Service*, December 24, 2019, https://religionnews.com/2019/12/24/behind -christianity-todays-editorial-is-a-deeper-crisis-of-americas-religion -of-whiteness.

80. Donald J. Trump, quoted in "Transcript: Donald Trump's RNC Speech," *CNN*, August 28, 2020, https://www.cnn.com/2020/08/28 /politics/donald-trump-speech-transcript/index.html.

81. Jeffrey Goldberg, "Trump: Americans Who Died in War Are 'Losers' and 'Suckers,'" *Atlantic*, September 3, 2020, https://www.theatlantic .com/politics/archive/2020/09/trump-americans-who-died-at-war -are-losers-and-suckers/615997/.

82. Donald J. Trump, (@realDonaldTrump), "We are winning, and will win, the war on the invisible enemy," tweet, April 12, 2020, 3:25 p.m., https://twitter.com/realdonaldtrump/status/1249418405951799309.

83. Warren Goldstein suggests that the coup itself could be read as a reality show spectacle: "While he told his supporters to march on the Capitol and said he would be there with him, he went back to the White

House to watch it on TV. In this respect, it was barely an attempted coup, but rather reality television, Trump style." Warren Goldstein, "Trump, the Religious Right, and the Spectre of Fascism," *Critical Research on Religion* 9, no. 1 (April 2021): 6.

84. In an essay comparing Trump's challenge to the legitimacy of what she called a "stupid coup" in Sri Lanka, Indi Samarajiva notes that one function of coups is to upset the norms and rituals surrounding the transfer of power: "This is precisely *why* we have elections, and why both sides accept the results. To keep the chaos at bay. The whole point is that you have a regular, ritual fight rather than fighting all the time. Once one side breaks ritual then you're on the way to civil war. Once you break the rules then chaos ensues. What exactly happens? I don't know. It's chaos." Indi Samarajiva, "I Lived Through a Stupid Coup. America is Having One Now,"' *Medium*, November 10, 2020, https://indica.medium.com/i-lived-through-a-coup-america-is-having-one-now-437934b1dac3.

85. Michael Gerson, "Trump's Evangelicals Were Complicit in the Desecration of Our Democracy," *Washington Post*, January 7, 2021, https://www.washingtonpost.com/opinions/trumps-evangelicals-were-complicit-in-the-desecration-of-our-democracy/2021/01/07/69a51402-5110-11eb-83e3-322644d82356_story.html.

86. Jelani Cobb, "Georgia, Trump's Insurrectionists, and Lost Causes," *New Yorker*, January 8, 2021, https://www.newyorker.com/news/daily-comment/georgia-trumps-insurrectionists-and-lost-causes.

2. STEVE BANNON AND THE CLASH OF CIVILIZATIONS

1. "The Crazy Nastyass Honey Badger," YouTube video, 3:20, January 18, 2011. https://www.youtube.com/watch?v=4r7wHMg5Yjg.

2. Milo Yiannopoulos, "Why Equality and Diversity Departments Should Only Hire Rich, Straight White Men," *Breitbart*, December 29, 2015, https://www.breitbart.com/tech/2015/12/29/why-equality-and-diversity-departments-should-only-hire-rich-straight-white-men/; and Tom Tancredo, "Political Correctness Protects Muslim Rape Culture," *Breitbart*, January 3, 2016.

3. J. Lester Feder, "This Is How Steve Bannon Sees the Entire World," *BuzzFeed News*, November 15, 2016, https://www.buzzfeed.com /lesterfeder/this-is-how-steve-bannon-sees-the-entire-world.

4. Bannonism was the culmination of decades of consumption of conservative media that became what Molly Worthen describes as "a profane devotional practice." Molly Worthen, "Idols of the Trump Era," in *Evangelicals: Who They Have Been, Are Now, and Could Be*, ed. Mark A. Noll, David W. Bebbington, and George M. Marsden (Grand Rapids, Mich.: Eerdmans, 2019), 257.

5. The idea that giving offense could be a Christian vocation was not necessarily new. In her study of early modern concepts of civility, for example, Teresa Bejan notes that an American advocate for religious toleration like the seventeenth-century Calvinist Roger Williams thought it was a Christian duty to inform others that they were damned. Evangelical zeal coexisted with religious difference in a civil society so that saints could witness to sinners. Civility, in this case, did not mean avoiding conflict as much as it referred to the minimal level of civic tolerance necessary for people to live together. As she explains, "And yet unlike hypocrisy, mere civility does not aim to deceive. As Williams knew well, it is often a more effective way of communicating our contempt for others *to* them than the most inventive insult." Obnoxious disagreement was more likely to lead to the truth. Insulting people was a better form of Christian witness than the hypocrisy of maintaining polite appearances to avoid discomfort. Teresa Bejan, *Mere Civility: Disagreement and the Limits of Toleration* (Cambridge, Mass.: Harvard University Press, 2017), 160.

6. It is possible that practices of sharing information with like-minded people on social media is behind much of the construction of conservative (or liberal) bias. That is, it is not just that conservatives are biased toward conservative media, they are biased toward information that comes from friends and family members who they trust. In their quantitative analysis of who was more likely to believe fake news, economists Hunt Allcott and Matthew Gentzkow note that while most fake news did lean toward Trump (or at least was anti-Clinton), this might have correlated with other factors such as education level and prior media consumption. Social media, because it was passed along by

friends, made everything believable: "As with Republicans relative to Democrats, people who report that social media were their most important sources of election news were more likely both to correctly believe true headlines and to incorrectly believe false headlines." Hunt Allcott and Matthew Gentzkow, "Social Media and Fake News in the 2016 Election," *Journal of Economic Perspectives* 31, no. 2 (Spring 2017): 228.

7. I make no analytic distinction between "Western" civilization and "Christian" civilization because I do not believe that Bannon's rhetoric makes any meaningful distinction. As I argue in this chapter, the concept of civilization has no analytic or descriptive coherency, so it makes little difference how it is qualified.

8. On the refusal to follow the rules for evaluating truth claims within democratic discourse, see Ryan Neville-Shepard, "Post-Presumption Argumentation and the Post-Truth World: On the Conspiracy Rhetoric of Donald Trump," *Argumentation and Advocacy* 55, no. 3 (2019): 175–193.

9. Nicole Hemmer, *Messengers of the Right: Conservative Media and the Transformation of American Politics* (Philadelphia: University of Pennsylvania Press, 2016), xiii.

10. William E. Connolly, "Trump, the Working Class, and Fascist Rhetoric," *Theory and Event* 20, no. 1 (January 2017), 31.

11. Michael Wolff, *Fire and Fury: Inside the Trump White House* (New York: Henry Holt, 2018), 61.

12. As Sarah Sobieraj and Jeffrey M. Berry explain, "Outrage sidesteps the messy nuances of complex political issues in favor of melodrama, misrepresentative exaggeration, mockery, and improbable forecasts of impending doom. Outrage talk is not so much discussion as it is verbal competition, political theater with a scorecard." Sarah Sobieraj and Jeffrey M. Berry, "From Incivility to Outrage: Political Discourse in Blogs, Talk Radio, and Cable News," *Political Communication* 28, no. 1 (2011): 20. Sobieraj and Berry attempt to quantify the frequency of outrage talk in different media outlets and find that while outrage appears in programs or essays they identify as either liberal or conservative, outrageous speech does indeed appear more frequently on conservative media. The point here is not so much to hold conservative

outlets more culpable as it is to suggest that audience for liberal media might be more likely to be drawn to media that at least presents itself as objective. This might have the ironic effect of framing the aspiration to objectivity as itself a sign of liberal bias.

13. Neil Midgley, "Word of the Year 2016 Is . . .," *Oxford Dictionaries*, https://en.oxforddictionaries.com/word-of-the-year/word-of-the -year-2016.

14. On his show in 2016, Colbert suggested that *post-truth* is a rip-off of his term. Stephen Colbert, "'Post-Truth' Is Just a Rip-Off of Truthiness," *YouTube* video, 7:09, November 18, 2016, https://www.youtube .com/watch?v=CkoyqUoBY7M.

15. As one essay asserts, the 1979 publication of *The Postmodern Condition* played a crucial role in shaping American public opinion:

> Under the terms of this outlook, all claims on truth are relative to the particular person making them; there is no position outside our own particulars from which to establish universal truth. This was one of the key tenets of postmodernism, a concept which first caught on in the 1980s after publication of Jean-Francois Lyotard's *The Postmodern Condition: A Report on Knowledge* in 1979. In this respect, for as long as we have been postmodern, we have been setting the scene for a "post-truth" era.

Andrew Calcutt, "The Surprising Origins of 'Post-Truth'—and How It Was Spawned by the Liberal Left," *The Conversation*, November 18, 2016, https://theconversation.com/the-surprising -origins-of-post-truth-and-how-it-was-spawned-by-the-liberal-left -68929.

16. Daniel Dennett, quoted in Carole Cadwalladr, "Daniel Dennett: 'I Begrudge Every Hour I Have to Spend Worrying about Politics,'" *Guardian*, February 12, 2017, https://www.theguardian.com/science /2017/feb/12/daniel-dennett-politics-bacteria-bach-back-dawkins -trump-interview.

17. According to Chantal Mouffe, people like Dennett, who believe that the reassertion of principles of dispassionate reason can serve as a rebuttal to populist appeals to emotion, are one of the ironic sources of the growth of right-wing populism:

Far from being a return of the archaic and irrational forces, an anachronism in times of "post-conventional" identities, to be fought through more modernisation and "Third Way" policies, right-wing populism is the consequence of the post-political consensus. Indeed, it is the lack of an effective democratic debate about possible alternatives that has led in many countries to the success of political parties claiming to be the "voice of the people."

Chantal Mouffe, "The 'End of Politics' and the Challenge of Right-Wing Populism," in *Populism and the Mirror of Democracy*, ed. Francisco Panizza (New York: Verso, 2005), 51.

18. Max Read, "How Much of the Internet Is Fake? Turns Out, a Lot of It, Actually," *New York Magazine*, December 26, 2018, http://nymag .com/intelligencer/2018/12/how-much-of-the-internet-is-fake.html.

19. For a former *Breitbart* editor's insistence on the opposition between hard facts and soft feelings, see Ben Shapiro, *Facts Don't Care About Your Feelings* (Hermosa Beach, Calif.: Creators, 2019).

20. Aisling McCrea, "The Magical Thinking of Guys Who Love Logic," *Outline*, February 15, 2019, https://theoutline.com/post/7083/the -magical-thinking-of-guys-who-love-logic.

21. McCrea, "The Magical Thinking of Guys Who Love Logic."

22. One of the more prominent examples of the embrace of hard reason over soft emotion is in the "Red Pill" philosophy prominent on the internet "manosphere." This is a reference to the 1999 film *The Matrix*, in which taking the red pill means choosing to confront the harsh reality of the world. In this case, harsh reality is the truth that feminism has robbed men of their masculinity. As Debbie Ging explains, "Taking the blue pill means switching off and living a life of delusion; taking the red pill means becoming enlightened to life's ugly truths. The Red Pill philosophy purports to awaken men to feminism's misandry and brainwashing." Debbie Ging, "Alphas, Betas, and Incels: Theorizing the Masculinities of the Manosphere," *Men and Masculinities* 22, no. 4 (2019): 640.

23. Daniel C. Dennett, *Breaking the Spell: Religion as a Natural Phenomenon* (New York: Penguin, 2006), 260.

24. Adam Wren, "What I Learned Binge-Watching Steve Bannon's Documentaries," *Politico*, December 2016, https://www.politico.com

/magazine/story/2016/12/steve-bannon-films-movies-documentaries
-trump-hollywood-214495.

25. Stephen K. Bannon, dir., *The Undefeated* (Washington, D.C.: Victory
Film Group, 2011).

26. One reviewer argues that this ending undoes the prior narrative celebrating Palin's strength: "Breitbart undercuts the entire Palin-as-
feminist-icon premise of the picture by excoriating the male politicians
who never defended her from criticism as 'eunuchs.'" Robert Levin,
"Sarah Palin's 'The Undefeated': Bad Propaganda, Worse Filmmaking," *Atlantic*, July 15, 2011, https://www.theatlantic.com/entertainment
/archive/2011/07/sarah-palins-the-undefeated-bad-propaganda-worse
-filmmaking/241975/.

27. For more on the development of civilized manliness as an ideology
grounded in the ability of white men to protect white women, see Gail
Bederman, *Manliness and Civilization: A Cultural History of Gender and
Race in the United States, 1880–1917* (Chicago: University of Chicago
Press, 1995).

28. Stephen K. Bannon, dir., *Occupy Unmasked* (Washington, D.C.:
Citizens United, 2012).

29. Michael Tracy, "'Occupy Unmasked'—Unmasked," *The Nation*,
October 9, 2012, https://www.thenation.com/article/occupy-unmasked
-unmasked/.

30. The refusal to see Occupy Wall Street as comparable to antiestablish-
ment protest on the right informs the distinction between the incivility of occupy protesters with the civility and decency of Tea Party
activists. As Ruth Braunstein notes, Tea Party activists insist that
their respect for authority means that they still observed civil protest.
As one protester stated, "We don't have to get into it with the police
with all those arrests. You know, we believe in laws, and we believe in
God, most of us believe in God, and believe in the laws of the Constitution and stuff like that." Ruth Braunstein, "Boundary Work and the
Demarcation of Civil from Uncivil Protest in the United States: Control, Legitimacy, and Political Inequality," *Theory and Society* 47, no. 5
(October 2018): 620.

31. Stephen K. Bannon, dir., *Generation Zero* (Washington, D.C.: Citizens United, 2010).

32. Like many complaints about coddled kids, the film tells a white, middle-class story. The exception here is that African Americans now play on liberal guilt to compel banks to loan to persons from minority groups who lack the financial resources to repay their loans.

33. This four-part meta-historical thesis is based on Neil Howe and William Strauss's theory of "turnings." Howe serves as one of the film's commentators. Neil Howe and William Strauss, *The Fourth Turning: What the Cycles of History Tell Us About America's Next Rendezvous with Destiny* (New York: Broadway, 1997).

34. Michael Graziano, "The Steve Bannon School of American History," *Religion in American History*, January 31, 2017, httpt://usreligion .blogspot.com/2017/01/the-steve-bannon-school-of-american.html.

35. Melinda Cooper notes that the expectation that families voluntarily constrain capitalist freedom is a common thread in neoliberalism and neoconservatism, and this is often missed by liberal critics who do not understand how conservatives can embrace free markets while advocating for state regulations of bodies. Whereas some neoconservatives criticize neoliberal commitment to unrestricted markets as an embrace of hedonist individualism, neoliberals expect that families would teach virtues as long as social welfare programs do not undermine family structures by creating dependence on the state. The difference between neoliberals and neoconservatives was that the latter believes that the state needs to actively protect the family from corrosive market forces in order to restore communal forms of solidarity. Melinda Cooper, *Family Values: Between Neoliberalism and the New Social Conservatism* (New York: Zone, 2017), 56–63. In his suspicion of globalism, Bannon would fit more closely with neoconservatism, except for his commitment to an uncivil Trumpism that does not give a shit about neoconservative decorum. In a sense, Bannon replaces the more polite, restrained, and virtuous forms of conservative communitarianism with the solidarity of a people united in battle against enemies.

36. Wendy Brown, *In the Ruins of Neoliberalism: The Rise of Antidemocratic Politics in the West* (New York: Columbia University Press, 2019), 90.

37. As Quinn Slobodian notes, the transformation of "globalist" from "a rather obscure term of academic analysis to a target of right-wing opprobrium" is one sign of a populist pushback against the hold

neoliberalism has had on conservative economic politics. Quinn Slobodian, *Globalists: The End of Empire and the Birth of Neoliberalism* (Cambridge, Mass.: Harvard University Press, 2018), 25.

38. Norbert Elias, *The Civilizing Process*, trans. Edmund Jephcott, eds. Eric Dunning, Johan Goudsblom, and Stephen Mennell (1939; repr. Malden, Mass.: Blackwell, 2000), 5; emphasis in the original.

39. Charles Long, *Significations: Signs, Symbols, and Images in the Interpretation of Religion* (Philadelphia: Fortress, 1986), 94.

40. Steve Bannon, quoted in James McAuley, "'Let Them Call You Racists': Steve Bannon Delivers Fighting Speech to France's National Front," *Washington Post*, March 10, 2018, https://www.washingtonpost.com/world/the-tide-of-history-is-with-us-steve-bannon-delivers-rhetoric-filled-speech-to-frances-national-front/2018/03/10/4f21e016-2480-11e8-946c-9420060cb7bd_story.html.

41. Steven Bannon, quoted in Elizabeth Zerofsky, "The Illiberal State," *New Yorker*, January 14, 2019, 47.

42. While Bannon rejects the label "white nationalism" in favor of "economic nationalism," it is not clear if the various nations grouped under Western civilization have shared economic interests. For example, Bannon's complaint that global markets allow underpaid labor to steal jobs from first-world workers might make sense to an audience of unemployed factory workers in Ohio, but it overlooks how Eastern European countries like Hungary, Poland, and the Czech Republic seek to benefit from precisely these trade arrangements. Tim Gosling points out that a similar problem exists for Bannon's anti-China sentiment, which is not shared by Eastern European populists. As he explains, "Bannon, who left the White House last summer, is so clueless about the needs and priorities of Eastern European nations that right-wing commentators in Budapest were quick to express frustration. Why, they asked, would Bannon parrot the White House line that China and Iran threaten Western civilization when those countries are currently a cornerstone of Orban's foreign and economic policy ambitions?" Tim Gosling, "The Nationalist Internationale Is Crumbling," *Foreign Policy*, July 20, 2018, https://foreignpolicy.com/2018/07/20/the-nationalist-internationale-is-crumbling-steve-bannon-eastern-europe-hungary-czech-republic-slovakia-trade/.

43. Patrick J. Buchanan, "Memo to Trump: Declare an Emergency," *CNSNews*, January 11, 2019, https://www.cnsnews.com/commentary /patrick-j-buchanan/patrick-buchanan-memo-trump-declare -emergency.

44. Great Replacement theory has played an increasingly prominent role in shaping the rhetoric of white nationalist movements. In a manifesto titled "An Inconvenient Truth," for example, a mass shooter in El Paso, Texas, cited concerns about the Great Replacement when he stated that his attempts to kill as many people as possible in a Walmart was a response to the "Hispanic invasion of Texas." Tim Arango, Nicholas Bogel-Burroughs, and Katie Benner, "Minutes Before El Paso Killing, Hate-Filled Manifesto Appears Online," *New York Times*, August 3, 2019, https://www .nytimes.com/2019/08/03/us/patrick-crusius-el-paso-shooter -manifesto.html.

45. Buchanan, "Memo to Trump." Buchanan does not mention specific Democratic policies designed to achieve the aim of increasing the proportion of women in America.

46. Rogers Brubaker, "Between Nationalism and Civilizationalism: The European Populist Movement in Comparative Perspective," *Ethnic and Racial Studies* 40, no. 8 (2017): 1193. Brubaker draws a distinction between European populist movements and Trumpism on the grounds that Trump's rhetoric is too antiliberal as well as "not culturally embedded in a broader civilizationalism; it is almost entirely U.S. focused." Bannon's interest in Europe might complicate this. Rather than see nationalism as contrary to civilization, Bannon views the nation-state as part of the genius of Western civilization.

47. Among contemporary right-wing populist movements, there can often be a thin line between anti-Semitism and philo-Semitism. For one thing, the philo-Semitism in this populist context is almost entirely a matter of defense of Israel rather than any love for the religion of Judaism or the Jewish people. While populism often reproduces many of the tropes of explicit and implicit antisemitic rhetoric, many populists see Israel as a figure of strength in the global war against Islam. This tension is particular prominent among the leadership of Breitbart itself. As Wil S. Hylton points out,

No criticism of Breitbart irritates its leadership more than the charge of anti-Semitism. That's partly because many of the top figures at Breitbart, including Andrew Breitbart, Larry Solov and the entire editorial team when the site relaunched in 2012—Joel Pollak, Ben Shapiro and Alex [Marlow]—were all of Jewish descent, but also because a fundamental commitment on the site is to a borderline fanatical advocacy for Israel.

Wil S. Hylton, "Down the Breitbart Hole," *New York Times Magazine*, August 16, 2017, https://www.nytimes.com/2017/08/16/magazine/breitbart-alt-right-steve-bannon.html.

48. Joan Wallach Scott notes that the interest in gender equity has more to do with a project to mark Islam as uncivilized rather than any sustained commitment to women's rights. As she notes, "As the phrase 'clash of civilizations' gained prominence, especially after 9/11, secularism and gender equality became increasingly emphasized as the basis for Western superiority to all of Islam." Joan Wallach Scott, *Sex and Secularism* (Princeton, N.J.: Princeton University Press, 2018), 2.

49. One variant of philo-Semitic posturing is when right-wing activists selectively target leftist critics of Israel for anti-Semitism. This was especially evident in attacks on U.S. representatives Alexandria Ocasio-Cortez, Ilhan Omar, Rashida Tlaib, and Ayanna Pressley. As Talia Lavin argues, "the Republican establishment makes public statements about its superglued-to-Netanyahu foreign policy as if it inoculates them against anti-Semitism." Talia Lavin, "When Non-Jews Wield Anti-Semitism as Political Shield," *GQ*, July 17, 2019, https://www.gq.com/story/anti-semitism-political-shield.

50. According to one appraisal of Trump's influence: "This is Trump's presidency, but even more so, it is Huntington's America. Trump may believe himself a practical man, exempt from any intellectual influence, but he is the slave of a defunct political scientist." Carlos Lozada, "Samuel Huntington: A Prophet for the Trump Era," *Washington Post*, July 18, 2017, https://www.washingtonpost.com/news/book-party/wp/2017/07/18/samuel-huntington-a-prophet-for-the-trump-era.

51. Samuel Huntington, "The Clash of Civilizations?" *Foreign Affairs* 72, no. 3 (1993): 21–49.

52. Edward Said, "A Clash of Ignorance," *The Nation*, October 4, 2001. https://www.thenation.com/article/clash-ignorance/.
53. Samuel Huntington, *The Clash of Civilizations and the Remaking of World Order* (New York: Simon & Schuster, 2003), 43.
54. Huntington, *Clash of Civilizations*, 43.
55. Huntington, *Clash of Civilizations*, 21.
56. William Smith has argued that the equation of Bannon and Huntington is based on caricature of Huntington's ideas. As he argues,

> But these commentators misunderstand the connection between Huntington's views and Bannon's. While Bannon does follow Huntington in seeing the world order as marked by civilizational clashes, the most prominent being the clash between Islam and the West, he has not adopted Huntington's remedies for these clashes. Huntington forcefully argued that the leaders of the great world civilizations must seek common ground; Bannon's focus is upon the clash itself.

> William S. Smith, "Samuel Huntington Was Not Like Steve Bannon," *Center for the Study of Statesmanship*, https://css.cua.edu/ideas _and_commentary/samuel-huntington-was-not-like-steve-bannon/.

57. It is possible that I am giving Bannon too much credit. Adam Shatz has argued that one feature of contemporary defenses of Western civilizations is that they have abandoned even the pretense of academic sophistication:

> The Orientalism of today, the Orientalism of Fox News, Bat Ye'or's "Eurabia," and Steve Bannon, is an Orientalism based not on tendentious scholarship but on an absence of scholarship. Its Eurocentrism, which feeds off the idea that Europe is under threat from Muslim societies and other shit-hole countries, is an undisguised conspiracy theory. It has spread not by way of bookshops and libraries but Twitter, Facebook, and the Dark Web.

> Adam Shatz, "'Orientalism' Then and Now," *New York Review of Books*, May 20, 2019, https://www.nybooks.com/daily/2019/05/20 /orientalism-then-and-now/. Shatz has a point, but Bannon's posturing as a widely read intellectual is a crucial part of his view of himself.

58. The equation of Christianity with illiberalism is evident in the rhetoric of Fidesz, another European group with which Bannon has worked. As Liz Fekete explains,

> Fidesz defines itself as a Christian nationalist party but Orbán is clear that the Christianity he espouses is one that despises liberal values, particularly internationalism and compassion for global humanity. . . . In effect, Orbán has argued that compassion towards non-native is a form of political correctness. He emphasised, instead, order and responsibility as the foundational values of a patriarchal Christianity, one that starts from the protection of kith and kin and proceeds to love of country and culture.

Liz Fekete, "Hungary: Power, Punishment, and the 'Christian-national idea,'" *Race & Class* 57, no. 4 (2016), 43.

59. Ervand Abrahamian argues that part of the reason for Huntington's popularity is his ability to simplify the complex politics of numerous nation-states into sweeping claims about cultural essences: "His forte lies in the ability to analyse international politics without discussing real politics, especially the Arab-Israeli conflict. It is international relations with politics taken out." Ervand Abrahamian, "The US Media, Huntington, and September 11," *Third World Quarterly* 24, no. 3 (June 2003): 535.

60. Steve King, quoted in Caroline Summerfield, "Steve King: Bring Pride Back to Austria," *Unzensuriert*, September 2, 2018, https://www.unzensuriert.at/content/0027654-Steve-King-Bring-Pride-back-Austria.

61. One notable feature of this feature is how it holds children culpable for the supposed crimes of their parents. In a rebuttal to critics of the administration's enthusiasm for imprisoning children, Trump stated: "They look so innocent. They're not innocent." According to Trump, migrants from Central America would be likely to grow up to be violent gang members. "They're not people. These are animals, and we have to be very, very tough." Donald Trump, quoted in Seung Min Kim, "Trump Warns Against Admitting Unaccompanied Migrant Children: 'They're Not Innocent,'" *Washington Post*, May 23, 2018, https://www.washingtonpost.com/politics/trump-warns-against

-admitting-unaccompanied-migrant-children-theyre-not-innocent
/2018/05/23/e4b24a68-5ec2-11e8-8c93-8cf33c21da8d_story.html.

62. Joshua Green, *Devil's Bargain: Steve Bannon, Donald Trump, and the Storming of the Presidency* (New York: Penguin, 2017), 204.

63. Jungian thought found a home among right-wing intellectuals on the internet such as the Canadian psychologist Jordan Peterson, who fashions masculinist posturing into a theory of timeless gender differences. Typical of guys who love logic, Peterson shares Bannon's penchant for sweeping defenses of Western civilization. As Pankaj Mishra suggests in an essay on Peterson, Jungian mysticism offers a spiritual antidote to soothe the souls of men who feel like they are losing control of the world: "Hailing myth and dreams as the repository of fundamental human truths, they became popular because they addressed a widely felt spiritual hunger: of men looking desperately for maps of meaning in a world they found opaque and uncontrollable." Pankaj Mishra, *Bland Fanatics: Liberals, Race, and Empire* (New York: Farrar, Straus and Giroux, 2020), 127.

64. Corey R. Lewandowski and David N. Bossie, *Let Trump Be Trump: The Inside Story of His Rise to the Presidency* (New York: Hachette, 2017), 102.

65. In his own (or his ghostwriter's) words, Trump notes: "The relatively small number of hours I've spent reading Jung have been more than worth it." Donald J. Trump with Meredith McIver, *How to Get Rich* (New York: Ballantine, 2004), 95.

66. Stanley Fish, *The First: How to Think About Hate Speech, Campus Speech, Religious Speech, Fake News, Post-Truth, and Donald Trump* (New York: One Signal, 2019), 182–183.

67. Ethan Kleinberg, "Pandering to the Timid: The Truth About Post-Truth," *Theory Revolt*, February 1, 2019, https://www.academia.edu /38283250/Pandering_to_the_Timid_the_truth_about_post_truth.

68. Sara Ahmed, "Affective Economies," *Social Text* 22, no. 2 (Summer 2004): 133.

69. One consistent feature of Bannon is that he respects fighters regardless of whether they are on the right or left. About populist nemesis George Soros, for example, Bannon states: "Soros has done an amazing job. . . . He's created cadres, and those cadres have immense political power. To me he's a role model in that regard." Steve Bannon, quoted in Elizabeth Zerofsky, "Steve Bannon's Roman Holiday," *New Yorker*,

April 11, 2019, https://www.newyorker.com/news/dispatch/steve
-bannons-roman-holiday.

70. Kate Maltby, "Expose Steve Bannon for What He Is," *CNN*, September 19, 2018, https://www.cnn.com/2018/09/18/opinions/expose-steve
-bannon-opinion-maltby/index.html.

71. Laurie Penny, "No, I Will Not Debate You," *Longreads*, September 18, 2018, https://longreads.com/2018/09/18/no-i-will-not-debate
-you/.

72. Nesrine Malik, "Indulging Steve Bannon Is Just a Form of Liberal Narcissism," *Guardian*, September 13, 2018, https://www.theguardian
.com/commentisfree/2018/sep/13/indulge-steve-bannon-liberal
-narcissism.

73. Aleksandar Hemon, "Fascism Is Not an Idea to Be Debated, It's a Set of Actions to Fight," *Literary Hub*, November 1, 2018, https://lithub
.com/fascism-is-not-an-idea-to-be-debated-its-a-set-of-actions-to
-fight.

3. CARTOONS AND GUNS

1. Elias Groll, "Meet the Man Who Put the 'Je Suis' in the 'Je Suis Charlie,'" *Foreign Policy*, January 19, 2015, http://foreignpolicy.com/2015/01
/19/meet-the-man-who-put-the-je-suis-in-the-je-suis-charlie/.

2. Olivier Tonneau, "On Charlie Hebdo: A Letter to My British Friends," *Mediapart*, January 11, 2015, https://blogs.mediapart.fr/olivier-tonneau
/blog/110115/charlie-hebdo-letter-my-british-friends.

3. To be clear, my own interest in this chapter is not to explain the intent of the cartoonists as much as to consider the reception of the attacks in the United States. I am not myself competent to offer an analysis of the French context.

4. Adam Gopnik, "Satire Lives," *New Yorker*, January 19, 2015, https://
www.newyorker.com/magazine/2015/01/19/satire-lives.

5. Talal Asad, "Free Speech, Blasphemy, and Secular Criticism," in *Is Critique Secular? Blasphemy, Injury, and Free Speech*, by Talal Asad, Wendy Brown, Judith Butler, and Saba Mahmood (Berkeley: University of California Press, 2009), 55–56.

6. As Christine Agius notes, Danish reaction to the 2006 cartoon controversy also contains this conflation of the supposed Muslim

inability to understand satire with the inability to be fully competent secular citizens. As she explains,

> Muslims are largely seen to be different subjects within the Danish state: easily susceptible to extremism and radicalization and unable to separate their private (religious) and public (rational) lives. As a visual discourse, the crisis replicated this divide via the different types of visual representations at play. The cartoons were seen to represent opinion, a form of critique against authority, free speech and satire, contrasted against factual photographic depictions and video footage of violent protest.

Christine Agius, "Performing Identity: The Danish Cartoon Controversy and Discourses of Identity and Security," *Security Dialogue* 44, no. 3 (June 2013): 248.

7. Rafia Zakaria, "Writing while Muslim: The Freedom to be Offended," *Los Angeles Review of Books*, May 8, 2015, https://lareviewofbooks.org/article/writing-while-muslim-the-freedom-to-be-offended-charlie-hebdo/.

8. Adam Sherwin, "Salman Rushdie: The Authors Boycotting Event Awarding Charlie Hebdo Are 'Pussies,'" *Independent* April 27, 2015, http://www.independent.co.uk/news/salman-rushdie-the-authors-boycotting-event-awarding-charlie-hebdo-a-prize-for-free-speech-are-pussies-10207871.html.

9. Henry Samuel, "French Cartoonist Sine on Trial on Charges of Anti-Semitism over Sarkozy Jibe," *Telegraph*, January 27, 2009, http://www.telegraph.co.uk/news/worldnews/europe/france/4351672/French-cartoonist-Sine-on-trial-on-charges-of-anti-Semitism-over-Sarkozy-jibe.html.

10. There are diverse positions within the liberal tradition about whether reasonable arguments will win. For John Stuart Mill, for example, one of the arguments for the liberty of speech was that truth sometimes does not win, and therefore unpopular opinions need to be protected from persecution so that it might win out in the end. As he explains, "The real advantage which truth has, consists in this, that when an opinion is true, it may be extinguished once, twice, or many times, but in the course of ages there will generally be some persons to rediscover

it, until some one of its reappearances falls on a time when from favorable circumstances it escapes persecution until it has made such head as to withstand all subsequent attempts to suppress it." John Stuart Mill, *On Liberty*, ed. Alburey Castell (1859; repr. Arlington Heights, IL: Harland Davidson, 1947), 28. However, not all popular liberal commentators share Mill's restrained view about whether truth will always dispel error.

11. Quoted in Saba Mahmood, "Religious Reason and Secular Affect: An Incommensurable Divide?" in *Is Critique Secular? Blasphemy, Injury, and Free Speech*, by Talal Asad, Wendy Brown, Judith Butler, and Saba Mahmood (Berkeley: University of California Press, 2009), 75.

12. On insult, masculinity, and religious identity, see Jay Geller, "The Godfather of Psychoanalysis: Circumcisions, Antisemitism, and Freud's 'Fighting Jew,'" *Journal of the American Academy of Religion* 67, no. 2 (June 1999): 355–385.

13. Garry Trudeau, "The Abuse of Satire," *Atlantic Monthly*, April 11, 2015, https://www.theatlantic.com/international/archive/2015/04/the -abuse-of-satire/390312/.

14. Not everyone agrees on the criteria for identifying when satire punches down or up. As Jane Weston Vauclair points out, *Charlie Hebdo* satirists, like many secularists, saw Islam in particular and religion in general as a powerful target. As she notes, "The team saw itself as punching up, lampooning a strong ideology and a faith of 1.5 billion people, imposing its power like other churches or religions." Jane Weston Vauclair, "Local Laughter, Global Politics: Understanding *Charlie Hebdo*," *European Comic Art* 8, no. 1 (Spring 2015): 12.

15. Talal Asad, *Secular Translations: Nation-State, Modern Self, and Calculative Reason* (New York: Columbia University Press, 2018), 32.

16. The comedian Joan Rivers, for example, described Lenny Bruce's use of racist language as "healthy and cleansing." Emily Nussbaum, "Last Girl in Larchmont," *New Yorker*, February 16, 2015, https://www .newyorker.com/magazine/2015/02/23/last-girl-larchmont.

17. For more on how the cartoon controversy played out in Europe and the United States, see Peter Gottschalk and Gabriel Greenberg, *Islamophobia and Anti-Muslim Sentiment: Picturing the Enemy*, 2nd ed. (New York: Rowman & Littlefield, 2019), 11–21.

18. Pamela Geller, quoted in Anne Barnard and Alan Feuer, "Outraged, and Outrageous," *New York Times*, October 8, 2010, https://www .nytimes.com/2010/10/10/nyregion/10geller.html.

19. Rogers Brubaker, "Between Nationalism and Civilizationalism: The European Populist Movement in Comparative Perspective," *Ethnic and Racial Studies* 40, no. 8 (2017): 1204.

20. On this point, Representative Steve King asks: "So how is it, that the liberals, the leftists, on the one side, could build an alliance with the misogynistic hard core rightist Islamic people that have no tolerance for anything? These are the alliances that are squeezing Western civilization from either side, the right and the left. How can the women's movement embrace a misogynist religion? That's indeed stunning. It means to me, they hate Western civilization more than anything." Steve King, in an interview with Caroline Summerfield, "Steve King: Bring Pride Back to Austria," *Unzensuriert*, September 2, 2018.

21. Theodore Schleifer, "Donald Trump: 'I Think Islam Hates Us,'" *CNN*, March 10, 2016. https://www.cnn.com/2016/03/09/politics/donald -trump-islam-hates-us/index.html.

22. Nadia Marzouki, *Islam: An American Religion*, trans. C. Jon Delogu (New York: Columbia University Press, 2017), 128.

23. Donald J. Trump, quoted in Jenna Johnson, "Donald Trump Says Tough Gun Control Laws in Paris Contributed to Tragedy," *Washington Post*, November 14, 2015, https://www.washingtonpost.com/news /post-politics/wp/2015/11/14/donald-trump-says-tough-gun-control -laws-in-paris-contributed-to-tragedy/.

24. One example of the relationship between speech and property are libel and slander laws that address slights to reputation as matters to be rectified through the exchange of money. The amount of payment is calculated not by the economic costs of the damage to a citizen's reputation.

25. I am also following Achille Mbembe's suggestion that slavery plays a crucial role in the development of modernity: "Any historical account of the rise of modern terror needs to address slavery, which could be considered one of the first instances of biopolitical experimentation." Achille Mbembe, *Necropolitics* (Durham, N.C.: Duke University Press, 2019), 74.

26. John Locke, *Two Treatises of Government*, ed. Peter Laslett (1698; repr. New York: Cambridge University Press, 1988), 284.

27. Antony Anghie argues that attempts to obscure the colonial past play an integral role in imagining modern ideas of sovereignty within international law. This is accomplished in part by framing the era of conquest that produced inequalities as in the past, whereas present sovereign states are legitimated through the liberal logic of contract. As Anghie explains, "The old international law of conquest creates the inequalities that the new international law of contracts perpetuates, legalises and substantiates when it 'neutrally' enforces the agreements, however one sided, entered into by sovereign Third World states. It is in this way that the 'old' international law of imperialism, based on conquest, is connected with the new international law of imperialism, based on contract." Antony Anghie, *Imperialism, Sovereignty and the Making of International Law* (New York: Cambridge University Press, 2004), 241.

28. As Anshuman A. Mondal notes in his critique of free speech absolutism, the weakness of liberal attempts to harmonize commitments to free speech with multiculturalism have "become more pronounced now in a World in which 'the West' is so unquestionably dominant over, and can no longer afford to be so parochial about and aloof from, 'the Rest.'" Anshuman A. Modal, *Islam and Controversy: The Politics of Free Speech after Rushdie* (New York: Palgrave Macmillan, 2014), 1–2.

29. Walter Benjamin, "On the Concept of History," trans. Harry Zohn, in *Walter Benjamin: Selected Writings*, vol. 4, ed. Howard Eiland and Michael W. Jennings, 389–400 (Cambridge, Mass.: Harvard University Press, 2003), 392.

30. Sara Ahmed, "Affective Economies," *Social Text* 22, no. 2 (Summer 2004): 132.

31. Mbembe, *Necropolitics*, 27.

32. Mbembe, *Necropolitics*, 40; emphasis in the original.

33. For more on different frames of analysis for the *Charlie Hebdo* killings, see Russell Brand, "Charlie Hebdo: Whose Fault Is It?" YouTube video, 8 minutes, January 12, 2015, https://www.youtube.com/watch?v=Dg8YoWpbfZw.

34. Russell T. McCutcheon, "Context Matters (Sometimes)," *Culture on the Edge*, January 11, 2015, https://edge.ua.edu/russell-mccutcheon /context-matters-sometimes/.

35. As Didier Fassin notes, celebrations of free speech in the wake of the Charlie Hebdo shooting coexisted with calls to further restrict any speech taken to be a "vindication of terrorism." For example, some French schools responded with suspensions and expulsions in cases where "there has been too much questioning from students." Didier Fassin, "In the Name of the Republic: Untimely Meditations on the Aftermath of the Charlie Hebdo Attack," *Anthropology Today* 31, no. 2 (April 2015): 4.

36. As Teju Cole stated in the wake of the *Charlie Hebdo* attacks, "The West is a variegated space, in which both freedom of thought and tightly regulated speech exist, and in which disavowals of deadly violence happen at the same time as clandestine torture. But, at moments when Western societies consider themselves under attack, the discourse is quickly dominated by an ahistorical fantasy of long-suffering serenity and fortitude in the face of provocation." Teju Cole, "Unmournable Bodies," *New Yorker*, January 9, 2015, https://www .newyorker.com/culture/cultural-comment/unmournable-bodies.

37. john a. powell, "As Justice Requires/Permits: The Delimitation of Harmful Speech in a Democratic Society," *Law and Inequality* 16, no. 1 (1998): 109.

38. While the focus of this chapter is responses to cartoon controversies in the United States, it is worth noting that any consensus that legal censorship is a bad idea works differently in other national contexts. There are differences between American and European responses to religious offenses due to some country's considerations of group dignity as an issue for religious freedom. On divergent legal responses to religious defamation, see Peter Danchin, "Defaming Muhammad: Dignity, Harm, and Incitement to Religious Hatred," *Duke Forum for Law and Social Change* 2 (2010): 5–38. This is not to say that state attempts to regulate speech necessarily reduce violence. According to C. S. Adcock, the legacies of European colonialism also continue to shape free speech in the Indian context. She notes that a set of concerns about the violent nature of insulting speech has created a

perverse incentive for some religious groups to threaten violence on the grounds that their own threats would be the legitimate basis for restricting some forms of offensive speech. C. S. Adcock, "Violence, Passion, and the Law: A Brief History of Section 295A and Its Antecedents," *Journal of the American Academy of Religion* 84, no. 2 (June 2016): 337–351. On the unintended consequences of state regulations of speech in other national contexts, see Kari Telle, "Faith on Trial: Blasphemy and 'Lawfare' in Indonesia," *Ethnos* 83, no. 2 (2018): 371–391; and Benjamin Schonthal, "Environments of Law: Islam, Buddhism, and the State in Contemporary Sri Lanka," *Journal of Asian Studies* 75, no. 1 (February 2016): 137–156.

39. The latent violence in the distribution of property in the state of war resembles what Benjamin observed in liberalism's inability to come to terms with the constituting violence of the state. Walter Benjamin, "Critique of Violence," trans. Harry Zohn, in *Walter Benjamin: Selected Writings*, vol. 1, ed., Marcus Bullock and Michael W. Jennings, 236–252 (Cambridge: Harvard University Press, 1996).

40. The nexus of private security and the need to defend civilization is viscerally tied to the perception that good guys with guns will be white. As Jamil Smith points out,

> Guns are inherently a tool of death, if not mere intimidation, so it isn't just an expression of First Amendment rights when folks exploit their Second Amendment rights in this way. It is extreme, if not classifiable as extremism, when white men react to a small-d democratic result with the threat of violence. In last November's election, Virginia put Democrats in charge of the state legislature for the first time in 26 years. Since then, pro-gun activists have threatened to kill a state lawmaker, and others have intimated that civil war is afoot.

Jamil Smith, "Trump, Guns, and White Fragility," *Rolling Stone*, January 23, 2020, https://www.rollingstone.com/politics/political -commentary/richmond-gun-rally-trump-impeachment-mitch -mcconnell-941512/.

41. Part of what this chapter has argued is that the state of emergency that requires private security is not foreign to civilization but an ongoing

presence within it. As Giorgio Agamben explains, "In truth, the state of exception is neither external nor internal to the juridical order, and the problem of defining it concerns precisely a threshold, or a zone of indifference, where inside and outside do not exclude each other but rather blur with each other." Giorgio Agamben, *State of Exception*, trans. Kevin Attell (Chicago: University of Chicago Press, 2005), 23.

42. Gavan Titley, *Is Free Speech Racist?* (Medford, Mass.: Polity, 2020), 23.

4. CHRISTIAN VALUES AND THE WHITE EVANGELICAL

1. Christopher Harress, "Jake Byrd Heckles Roy Moore: Jimmy Kimmel Comedian Crashes Roy Moore Rally," *Advance Local*, November 30, 2017, https://www.al.com/news/2017/11/jake_byrd_heckles_roy_moore_ji.html.

2. Stephanie McCrummen, Beth Reinhard, and Alice Crites, "Woman Says Roy Moore Initiated Sexual Encounter When She Was 14, He Was 32," *Washington Post*, November 9, 2017, https://www.washingtonpost.com/investigations/woman-says-roy-moore-initiated-sexual-encounter-when-she-was-14-he-was-32/2017/11/09/1f495878-c293-11e7-afe9-4f60b5a6c4a0_story.html.

3. Jimmy Kimmel (@jimmykimmel), "Sounds great Roy—let me know when you get some Christian values and I'll be there!," tweet, November 30, 2017, 11:57 a.m., https://twitter.com/jimmykimmel/status/936323360694222848.

4. Jimmy Kimmel (@jimmykimmel), "OK Roy, but I'm leaving my daughters at home! P.S.—wear that cute little leather vest," tweet, November 30, 2017, 1:43 p.m., https://twitter.com/jimmykimmel/status/936349997112557568.

5. To compound Moore's bad Twitter week, several observers noted that he was also bad at riding horses. Hannah Keyser, "Roy Moore Doesn't Even Ride a Horse Well," *Deadspin*, December 12, 2017, https://deadspin.com/roy-moore-doesnt-even-ride-a-horse-well-1821227240.

6. Jimmy Kimmel, quoted in Marissa Martinelli, "Jimmy Kimmel Teaches Roy Moore a Thing or Two About 'Christian Values,'" *Slate*, December 12, 2017, http://www.slate.com/blogs/browbeat/2017/12/01/jimmy_kimmel_on_roy_moore_s_christian_values.html.

7. One feature that was absent from the debate between Kimmel and Moore was any suggestion of a theological difference between Catholicism and evangelicalism. Up until the mid-twentieth century, Kimmel's Catholicism might have marked him as a religious outsider in the United States. His invocation of his Catholic identity did not signal any denominational dispute, however, as much as it set up an opposition between Moore and a generic liberal Christian ethos that Nancy Ammerman has described as "Golden Rule Christianity." Christians who cite the Golden Rule as a central feature of their religiosity often play down doctrinal orthodoxy in favor of practical habits of leading a good life. As Ammerman explains, "The most frequently mentioned characterization of the Christian life was that people should seek to do good, to make the world a better place, to live by the golden rule." Judged by the Golden Rule standard, Moore's mistreatment of others undermined the central point of Christianity. Nancy T. Ammerman, "Golden Rule Christianity: Lived Religion in the American Mainstream," in *Lived Religion in America*, ed. David D. Hall, 196–216 (Princeton, N.J.: Princeton University Press, 1997), 197.

8. Judge Roy Moore (@MooreSenate), "Despite D.C. and Hollywood Elites' bigotry towards southerners, Jimmy, we'll save you a seat on the front pew," tweet, November 30, 2017. Sadly, this tweet is no longer accessible as the Moore for Senate Twitter account was deactivated after the election and has been taken over by an account titled "Best Attitude Status" that tweets in Hindi.

9. One notable defense came from the Alabama state auditor, who compared Moore to Joseph: "Mary was a teenager and Joseph was an adult carpenter. They became parents of Jesus." Jim Ziegler, quoted in Philip Wegman, "Alabama State Auditor Defends Roy Moore Against Sexual Allegations, Invokes Mary and Joseph," *Washington Examiner*, November 9, 2017, https://www.washingtonexaminer.com/alabama -state-auditor-defends-roy-moore-against-sexual-allegations -invokes-mary-and-joseph.

10. Leslie Dorrough Smith, *Compromising Positions: Sex Scandals, Politics, and American Christianity* (New York: Oxford University Press, 2020), 57.

11. Daniel Cox and Robert P. Jones, "The High Correlation Between Percentage of White Christians, Support for Trump in Key States," *Public Religion Research Institute*, November 17, 2016, https://www.prri.org

/spotlight/trump-triumphed-white-christian-states/; and Gregory A. Smith and Jessica Martinez, "How the Faithful Voted: A Preliminary 2016 Analysis," *Pew Research Center*, November 9, 2016, https://www.pewresearch.org/fact-tank/2016/11/09/how-the-faithful-voted-a-preliminary-2016-analysis/.

12. On the role of polls in inventing American religious categories, see Robert Wuthnow, *Inventing American Religion: Polls, Surveys, and a Tenuous Quest for a Nation's Faith* (New York: Oxford University Press, 2015).

13. A common feature of scholarship on evangelicalism is to note this definitional difficulty and recognize that this means there will be a great variety of evangelicals in practice, but then insist on a basic coherency that makes the term usable. One example of this would come from historian Mark Noll, who insists that evangelicalism "should never be looked on as a hard-edged, narrowly defined denomination. Rather, evangelicalism was and is a set of defining beliefs and practices easier to see as an adjective (e.g., evangelical Anglicans, evangelical missionary efforts, and evangelical doctrine) than as a simple noun. Yet cohesion has always been present, both from the common original commitment to revival and from the strength of shared convictions." Mark A. Noll, *The Rise of Evangelicalism: The Age of Edwards, Whitefield and the Wesleys* (Downers Grove, Ill.: InterVarsity, 2003), 21.

14. On the often-pejorative connotations of the label fundamentalist, see David Harrington Watt, *Anti-Fundamentalism in Modern America* (Ithaca, N.Y.: Cornell University Press, 2017).

15. George M. Marsden, *Understanding Fundamentalism and Evangelicalism* (Grand Rapids, Mich.: Eerdmans, 1991), 1.

16. D. W. Bebbington, *Evangelicalism in Modern Britain: A History from the 1730s to the 1860s* (New York: Routledge, 1988), 3.

17. Part of what this historical qualification accomplishes is to make contemporary evangelicalism equivalent to the consensus in nineteenth-century protestantism. As Marsden asserts, "Roughly speaking, evangelicalism today includes any Christians traditional enough to affirm the basic beliefs of the old nineteenth-century evangelical consensus." Marsden, *Understanding Fundamentalism and Evangelicalism*, 4.

18. According to Marsden, the threats to evangelical orthodoxy were particularly prominent in institutions of higher education: "Three strong concussions were felt almost simultaneously—evolutionary naturalism, higher criticism of the Bible, and the newer Idealistic philosophy and theology." George M. Marsden, *Fundamentalism and American Culture*, 2nd ed. (New York: Oxford University Press, 2006), 26.

19. For a classic account of fundamentalist/modernist battles within different denominations, see Norman F. Furniss, *The Fundamentalist Controversy, 1918–1931* (Hamden, Conn.: Archon, 1963).

20. To be clear, I am attempting to trace a conventional narrative for the purposes of understanding how the term *evangelical* has been deployed. Several scholarly accounts have challenged this narrative by documenting the political activism of conservative protestants in the mid-twentieth century. For example, see Kevin M. Kruse, *One Nation Under God: How Corporate American Invented Christian America* (New York: Basic Books, 2016).

21. Graham's international success led him to "the conviction that he could make marvelous inroads into America's major denominations if he could only jettison the disastrous fundamentalist images of separatism, anti-intellectualism, and contentiousness." George M. Marsden, *Reforming Fundamentalism: Fuller Seminary and the New Evangelicalism* (Grand Rapids, Mich.: Eerdmans, 1987), 159.

22. For his account of the federal government's threat to the sanctity of the family, see Jerry Falwell, *Listen, America!* (New York: Bantam, 1980), 112–118.

23. John Fea dedicated his book on Trump to the "19 percent," which was meant as a rebuke to racist Trumpism but did have the ironic effect of endorsing his membership in a tautologically all-white group. Even when challenging Trump, the 19 percenters did not fundamentally challenge the category of white evangelicalism. John Fea, *Believe Me: The Evangelical Road to Donald Trump* (Grand Rapids, Mich.: Eerdmans, 2018).

24. Mark Galli, "Trump Should Be Removed from Office," *Christianity Today*, December 19, 2019, https://www.christianitytoday.com/ct/2019/december-web-only/trump-should-be-removed-from-office.html.

25. Jim Wallis, "Reclaiming Jesus from the Trump Evangelicals," *Sojourners*, March 29, 2018, https://sojo.net/articles/reclaiming-jesus-trump -evangelicals.

26. David Gushee, "In the Ruins of White Evangelicalism: Interpreting a Compromised Christian Tradition Through the Witness of African American Literature," *Journal of the American Academy of Religion* 87, no. 1 (March 2019): 15.

27. Michael Gerson, "The Last Temptation," *Atlantic Monthly*, April 2018, https://www.theatlantic.com/magazine/archive/2018/04/the-last -temptation/554066/. It is not clear what Nietzsche text Gerson has in mind here. It is probable that, like many commentators, he confused Zarathustra's Ape with Zarathustra.

28. As Christopher Craig Brittain speculates, Trump's campaign resonated because it promised a departure from jeremiads about America's religious decline: "The lamentations of some leaders of the Religious Right over the failure of America to become a 'Christian nation' appear to sound to Trump supporters like the cries of losers. Many evangelicals long to belong to a winning racket—to Trump nation—whose leader may not have a salvation story, but he certainly looks and feels to them like a savior." Christopher Craig Brittain, "Racketeering in Religion: Adorno and Evangelical Support for Donald Trump," *Critical Research on Religion* 6, no. 3 (2018): 282.

29. Fea clarified who the court evangelicals were by providing a list:

> The roster of court evangelicals includes Liberty University president Jerry Falwell, Jr., Southern Baptist pastor and Fox News commentator Robert Jeffress, radio host and 'family values' advocate James Dobson, evangelist Franklin Graham, Christian public relations guru Johnnie Moore (who claims to be a 'modern-day Dietrich Bonhoeffer'), longtime Christian Right political operative Ralph Reed, culture warrior Paula White, former presidential candidate Gary Bauer, and megachurch pastor Mark Burns.
>
> Fea, *Believe Me*, 118.

30. Thomas S. Kidd, *Who Is an Evangelical? The History of a Movement in Crisis* (New Haven: Yale University Press, 2019), 155.

31. Francis Fukuyama, "Against Identity Politics: The New Tribalism and the Crisis of Democracy," *Foreign Affairs* 97, no. 5 (September/ October 2018), 104.

32. Not all analysts who use the term *culture wars* focus on conflicts over values. In his history of culture wars from the 1960s to the present, for example, Andrew Hartman surveys a variety of contests over religious, racial, and sexual identities. Andrew Hartman, *A War for the Soul of America: A History of the Culture Wars*, 2nd ed. (Chicago: University of Chicago Press, 2015).

33. James Davison Hunter, *Culture Wars: The Struggle to Define America* (New York: Basic Books, 1991), 33.

34. Hunter, *Culture Wars*, 44.

35. Arlie Russell Hochschild describes her own difficulty in trying to account for why conservative Louisiana residents who had suffered the destruction of their environments seemed to vote against their own interests by opposing government efforts to regulate pollution. She refers to this as the "great paradox" but comes to recognize that there are significant emotional benefits that might be just as important as economic interests. She calls this "emotional self-interest." As she explains, "While economic self-interest is never entirely absent, what I discovered was the profound importance of emotional self-interest—a giddy release from the feeling of being a stranger in one's own land." Arlie Russell Hochschild, *Strangers in Their Own Land: Anger and Mourning on the American Right* (New York: New Press, 2018), 228.

36. For a critique of the economic anxiety analysis, see Diana C. Mutz, "Status Threat, Not Economic Hardship, Explains the 2016 Presidential Vote," *PNAS* 115, no. 19 (2018): 4330–4339. www.pnas.org/cgi/doi /10.1073/pnas.1718155115.

37. In a reflection on his hometown of Yakima, Washington, Patrick Wyman describes local elites as the owners of business and property who enjoy relative affluence in places that coastal elites tend to see as economically and culturally impoverished. The relative affluence of local elites is tied to an economic and social status quo to a far greater degree that upwardly mobile urban professionals who benefit from economic and social change. Patrick Wyman, "Local Gentry: Local

Power and the Social Order," *Perspectives: Past, Present, and Future*, September 17, 2020, https://patrickwyman.substack.com/p/american -gentry. The class that Wyman identifies tends to harbor a suspicion of urban liberals as well as progressive economic reforms that might raise wages or otherwise increase the cost of doing business. For this reason, it is not correct to see Trump supporters in the heartland as universally voting against their economic interests.

38. While the small-town environment plays a significant role in Moore's evangelical imagination, this is not to say that evangelicalism is absent from cities. Even in urban settings, however, the city is often imagined as enemy territory. One particularly intense version of spiritual warfare in the city is the subject of Jessica Johnson's study of the Mars Hill Church in Seattle, Washington. She chronicles how Pastor Mark Driscoll went on the offensive to defend a Christian masculinity that is challenged by a changing urban sexual landscape. Driscoll made his mark with media-savvy performances that use deliberately profane sexual language designed to grab the attention of urban hipsters. As Johnson notes, "If pedagogy is about transforming the way the world feels such that bodies learn by switching affections, Driscoll's bomb throwing while trolling online to save a 'pussified nation' was a crusade of shock and awe." Jessica Johnson, *Biblical Porn: Affect, Labor, and Pastor Mark Driscoll's Evangelical Empire* (Durham, N.C.: Duke University Press, 2018), 60.

39. On the evangelical culture of fear and safety, see Jason Bivins, *Religion of Fear: The Politics of Horror in Conservative Evangelicalism* (New York: Oxford University Press, 2008).

40. While rejecting the vision of private freedom as well as nationalism espoused by people like Moore, Wendell Berry does suggest that abstraction and anonymity are why public goods often fail to have purchase among people who identify primarily in terms of local communities. As Berry argues, "When a public government becomes identified with a public economy, a public culture, and public fashions of thought, it can become the tool of a public process of nationalism or 'globalization' that is oblivious of local differences and therefore destructive of communities." Wendell Berry, *Sex, Economy, Freedom, and Community* (New York: Pantheon, 1993), 148.

41. As Sorcha Brophy notes, this division between public appearance and private belief is a familiar feature of maintaining denominational orthodoxy. Rather than seen as signs of hypocrisy, the willingness to adopt denominational positions in public despite private disagreements is a sign of character. One of her interlocutors suggests "that these individuals had freedom to explore contrary positions in private arenas because they were already committed to denominational positions." Sorcha A. Brophy, "Orthodoxy as Project: Temporality and Action in an American Protestant Denomination," *Sociology of Religion* 77, no. 2 (2016): 137.

42. Moore had previously lost his job as Alabama chief justice because he refused to obey a court order to remove from his courthouse a large monument inscribed with the Ten Commandments. In that case, Moore argued that the Commandments are religiously neutral because they articulate a moral foundation that unifies all Americans. As the opinion notes, "Chief Justice argues that the Ten Commandments, as he has presented them in the monument, do not involve duties individuals owe the Creator, and therefore are not religious; instead, he says, they represent the moral foundation of secular duties that individuals owe society." *Glassroth v. Moore*, 335 F. 3rd 1282, 1295 (2003).

43. Roy Moore with John Perry, *So Help Me God: The Ten Commandments, Judicial Tyranny, and the Battle for Religious Freedom* (Nashville: Broadman and Holman, 2005), 128.

44. As Smith explains, "Chaos rhetoric is a type of declension speech that attempts to persuade an audience by stressing an imminent threat to a beloved entity (which could include everything from children, to liberty, to the nation itself). In claiming the deterioration of this entity, chaos rhetoric portrays a world where threat, disorder, fear, and chaos reign." Leslie Dorrough Smith, *Righteous Rhetoric: Sex, Speech, and the Politics of Concerned Women for America* (New York: Oxford University Press, 2014), 5.

45. Amy Chua, *Political Tribes: Group Instinct and the Fate of Nations* (New York: Penguin, 2018), 41.

46. Gerardo Martí, "The Unexpected Orthodoxy of Donald J. Trump: White Evangelical Support for the 45th President of the United States," *Sociology of Religion* 80, no. 1 (Spring 2019): 7. Italics in original.

47. Christine Mungai, "Pundits Who Decry Tribalism Know Nothing About Real Tribes," *Washington Post*, January 30, 2019, https://www .washingtonpost.com/outlook/pundits-who-decry-tribalism-know -nothing-about-real-tribes/2019/01/29/8d14eb44-232f-11e9-90cd -dedb0c92dc17_story.html.

48. Charles McCrary, "The Trump Era's Tribalism Discourse: Reflections on a 'Weird Euphemism,'" *Revealer*, May 6, 2020, https://therevealer .org/the-trump-eras-tribalism-discourse-reflections-on-a-weird -euphemism/.

49. My thinking about the limits of culture wars is indebted to Jean-François Bayart's critique of the illusion of cultural identity. I would suggest that it is helpful to think of evangelicalism as a political rather than a cultural category. Moore's evangelicalism would meet the criteria for what Bayart calls a "political performance." As Bayart suggests, political performance could be a substitute for the concept of culture:

> For their part, geologists have abandoned the hypothesis of an 'igneous core' at the centre of the earth. But culturalists still believe firmly in the incandescent cores at the heart of cultures. Ultimately, it is this very concept that is the problem, and the word culture should incontestably be jettisoned if vocabulary were biodegradable. . . . Perhaps we should . . . refer to "political performance" in order to emphasise that the reception of cultural phenomena, ideologies, and institutions is never passive and contributes to their "formation."

Jean-François Bayart, *The Illusion of Cultural Identity*, trans. Steven Rendall, Janet Roitman, Cynthia Schoch, and Jonathan Derrick (Chicago: University of Chicago Press, 2005), 108–109.

50. Noting the role that threats play in shaping white evangelical identity, Kristin Kobes Du Mez suggests that the Obama administration strengthened the resolve of evangelicals. As she explains, "The Religious Right had always thrived on a sense of embattlement, and in that respect, the Obama White House was heaven-sent." Kristin Kobes Du Mez, *Jesus and John Wayne: How Evangelicals Corrupted a Faith and Captured a Nation* (New York: Liveright, 2020), 248.

51. On the function of *evangelicalism* as a term designed to distinguish between "us and them," see Michael J. Altman, "'Religion, Religions,

Religious' in America: Toward a Smithian Account of Evangelicalism," *Method and Theory in the Study of Religion* 31, no. 1 (2019): 71–82.

52. In a campaign stop in Fairhope, Alabama, Moore, wearing his leather vest and cowboy hat, waved a gun and proclaimed his support for the Second Amendment. John Sharp, "Roy Moore Flashing Gun at a Rally Not a Crime, Police Say after Complaint," *Advance Local*, September 27, 2017, https://www.al.com/news/mobile/2017/09/fairhope_police_receive_compla.html.

53. According to Jason Bivins, conservative Christians embrace the role of "martyrs" through a rhetoric of embattlement. Jason C. Bivins, *Embattled Majority: Religion and its Despisers in America* (New York: Oxford University Press, forthcoming).

54. As one of the formative voices in the 1920s fundamentalist movement, J. Gresham Machen, argued, liberalism is an entirely new religion that attempts to place good behavior and social well-being ahead of the reality of sin. Reducing Christianity to people's good behavior is antithetical to the idea of God's grace and Christian freedom:

> The grace of God is rejected by modern liberalism. And the result is slavery—the slavery of the law, the wretched bondage by which man undertakes the impossible task of establishing his own righteousness as a ground of acceptance of God. It may seem strange at first sight that "liberalism," of which the very name means freedom, should in reality be wretched slavery. But the phenomenon is not really so strange. Emancipation from the blessed will of God always involves bondage to some worse taskmaster.

J. Gresham Machen, *Christianity and Liberalism* (1923; new ed., Grand Rapids, Mich.: Eerdmans, 2009), 121.

55. While focusing on a different set of epistemic problems than those discussed in this chapter, John Lardas Modern uses the term *evangelical secularism* to describe this public management of private sentiments. While evangelicalism is often defined as something interior, Modern notes that it measures its success by its ability to produce and maintain public norms designed to govern a diverse population. As he points out, "The statistically driven methods of evangelical media did not seek to eradicate the idiosyncrasies of everyday life (sin was, after all, originary). On the contrary, they sought to account for the private realm

in such a way as to bring it into the orbit of a community that was in the process of being imagined." John Lardas Modern, *Secularism in Antebellum America* (Chicago: University of Chicago Press, 2011), 51.

56. The threat of evangelicalism might also be a constitutive feature of secular liberalism. As Susan Friend Harding notes, modern secularism often identifies itself in relation to a fundamentalist threat: "It was as if there were a weird kind of contract between fundamentalists and the mainstream. Much of the power of fundamentalists in the public arena came from the extent to which they were a modern nightmare come true, but public appearances also triggered fierce remarginalizing practices that discredited them and limited their efficacy." Susan Friend Harding, *The Book of Jerry Falwell: Fundamentalist Language and Politics* (Princeton, N.J.: Princeton University Press, 2000), 79. In his study of People for the American Way in the 1970s, L. Benjamin Rolsky extends this analysis when he demonstrates that a religious left defined itself over and against an intolerant Christian right. L. Benjamin Rolsky, *The Rise and Fall of the Religious Left: Politics, Television, and Popular Culture in the 1970s and Beyond* (New York: Columbia University Press, 2019).

57. In her comparative study of evangelical congregations in Canada and the United States, Lydia Bean shows how people were shaped by the rhetoric of the respective social and national contexts. The reason that culture wars rhetoric resonates far more in the United States than in Canada has less to do with different evangelical faith commitments than with different views of the relationship between religious and political institutions. As she argues, "For culture war captains, parachurch and interest groups served as important agents of religious *socialization*, rather than as a vehicle to act of preexisting religious commitments." Lydia Bean, *The Politics of Evangelical Identity: Local Churches and Partisan Divides in the United States and Canada* (Princeton, N.J.: Princeton University Press, 2014), 222.

58. Smith, *Righteous Rhetoric*, 168.

59. James Dobson, quoted by *Christianity Today* editors, "James Dobson: Why I am Voting for Donald Trump," *Christianity Today*, September 23, 2016, https://www.christianitytoday.com/ct/2016/october/james -dobson-why-i-am-voting-for-donald-trump.html.

60. Randall Balmer, "The Real Origins of the Religious Right," *Politico*, May 27, 2014, https://www.politico.com/magazine/story/2014/05/religious-right-real-origins-107133.

61. In his study of what motivated voters in the 2016 election, Ryan Claassen notes that fear of minorities appears to be the best predictor of white evangelical voting habits: "If blaming minority groups for social problems is a key element in populist and nationalist rhetoric, Trump may have harnessed an important and often overlooked public-opinion trend among white evangelicals." Ryan L. Claassen, "Understanding the Political Motivations of Evangelical Voters," in *The Evangelical Crackup? The Future of the Evangelical-Republican Coalition*, eds. Paul A. Djupe and Ryan L. Claassen, 49–62 (Philadelphia, Temple University Press, 2018), 61.

62. According to Jemar Tisby, evangelical persecution narratives deflect from reckoning with their own complicity with racism. Trump has been especially adept at mirroring white evangelical racism while tapping into this sentiment. As Tisby notes, "Trump tapped into the latent sense among some evangelicals that they were losing influence in American culture and politics. Increasingly, evangelicals believe they are the ones experiencing persecution." Jemar Tisby, *The Color of Compromise: The Truth About the American Church's Complicity in Racism* (Grand Rapids, Mich.: Zondervan, 2019), 188–189.

63. Anthea Butler, *White Evangelical Racism: The Politics of Morality in America* (Chapel Hill: University of North Carolina Press, 2021), 10–11.

64. Hannah Dick suggests that one reason political analysts are confused by Trump support is that they focus on evangelicalism as a distinctly religious movement. She suggests that a better approach would be to consider white evangelicalism as a set of interlocking identities: "There has been a specific historical alignment between white evangelicalism as a cultural framework, a religious affiliation, a class-based category, and a political orientation." Hannah Dick, "Framing Faith During the 2016 Election: Journalistic Coverage of the Trump Campaign and the Myth of the Evangelical Schism," in *Evangelicals and Presidential Politics: From Jimmy Carter to Donald Trump*, ed. Andrew S. Moore (Baton Rouge: Louisiana State University Press, 2021), 174.

65. On the intersection of racial and religious identities within the rhetoric of family values, see Sophie Bjork-James, *The Divine Institution: White Evangelicalism's Politics of the Family* (New Brunswick, N.J.: Rutgers University Press, 2020).

66. Janet Jakobsen notes that the discourse of family values arose at a moment when national identity was under threat by transnational economic forces. Rather than advocate for public regulation of the economy, appeals to the family could be a stabilizing force that provided forms of regulation and stability acceptable to fiscal and social conservatives suspicious of the state. Family values, then, allowed white Christians to equate their own sexual norms with national stability in a way that advanced their own economic and cultural interests at the expense of others. As she explains, "'Family values' mediates between the economy and the 'American' nation under contemporary market conditions by offering a discourse that can mediate between exploitation and domination. In other words, 'family' (rather than the state) mediates between economy and nation, and 'values' mediates between exploitation and domination." Janet R. Jakobsen, "Can Homosexuals End Western Civilization as We Know It? Family Values in a Global Economy," in *Queer Globalizations: Citizenship and the Afterlife of Colonialism*, ed. Arnaldo Cruz-Malavé and Martin F. Manalansan (New York: New York University Press, 2002), 50.

67. In addition to mobilizing support for the Republican Party, appeals to the protections of the Christian values of white Americans are also politically effective because Democrats take these values seriously. As Jamelle Bouie notes, the perceived electoral power of white rural voters makes Democratic leadership more likely to attack progressive critics of racism than to alienate white voters. As Bouie states, "What's more striking than the president's blood-and-soil racism is how Democratic Party elites—or at least one group of them—are playing with similar assumptions. No, they haven't held out the white working property owner as the only citizen of value, but they're obsessed with winning that voter to their side—convinced that this group is the path to victory." Jamelle Bouie, "Trump's America is a White Man's Country," *New York Times*, July 15, 2019, https://www.nytimes.com/2019/07/15/opinion/trump-aoc-omar-pelosi.html.

5. *MASTERPIECE CAKESHOP* AND THE ART OF RELIGIOUS FREEDOM

1. Donald J. Trump, quoted in Paul Alexander, "Trump Towers," *Advocate*, February 15, 2000, 23.
2. Rebecca Savransky, "Trump: 'I'm Much Better for the Gays,'" *The Hill*, April 16, 2016, http://thehill.com/blogs/ballot-box/presidential-races/283498-trump-says-he-shamed-clinton-into-saying-radical-islam.
3. *Obergefell v. Hodges*, 576 U.S. 644 (2015).
4. *Masterpiece Cakeshop v. Colorado Civil Rights Commission*, 584 U.S. ____ (2018).
5. Oral Argument at 4, *Masterpiece Cakeshop v. Colorado Civil Rights Commission* 137 S.Ct. 2290 (2017).
6. *Masterpiece Cakeshop* is technically a Fourteenth Amendment case because it involves Colorado law, but the logic of Phillips's argument invokes the First Amendment's pairing of free speech and freedom of religion.
7. Oral Argument at 13, *Masterpiece Cakeshop v. Colorado Civil Rights Commission* 137 S.Ct. 2290 (2017).
8. Oral Argument at 18, *Masterpiece Cakeshop v. Colorado Civil Rights Commission* 137 S.Ct. 2290 (2017).
9. Sarah Posner, "An Army of Christian Lawyers," *The Nation*, January 1–8, 2018, 12–26.
10. As it turned out, the 7–2 decision meant that Gorsuch's vote was not required for a majority. Gorsuch did, however, write a concurring opinion that advanced a stronger defense of Phillips's religious freedom claim than Kennedy made in his majority opinion.
11. For an account of how different groups produce religion in response to contests over religious freedom, see Tisa Wenger, *Religious Freedom: The Contested History of an American Ideal* (Chapel Hill: University of North Carolina Press, 2017).
12. Many critics, including Jonathan Greenblatt of the Anti-Defamation League, were able to identify the flaw of the Nazi analogy in the space of a tweet. Responding to a *Chicago Tribune* editorial that advanced the comparison, Greenblatt explained: "The Tribune should know better: Nazis are not protected by anti-discrimination laws! To compare

baking a cake for a gay couple to baking a cake with a swastika is beyond offensive to the #LGBTQ community." Jonathan Greenblatt (@GreenblattADL), tweet, December 8, 2017, 1:22 p.m., https://twitter .com/JGreenblattADL/status/939243850622820357.

13. Colorado Civil Code, 24-34-601, 2a.

14. On the use of religious freedom arguments by segregationists, see Tisa Wenger, "Discriminating on the Basis of Religion? Segregationists and Slaveholders Did It Too," *Washington Post*, December 5, 2017, https:// www.washingtonpost.com/news/made-by-history/wp/2017/12/05 /discriminating-in-the-name-of-religion-segregationists-and -slaveholders-did-it-too.

15. One exception has been in the case of Pastafarians, who claim to believe in a Flying Spaghetti Monster who created the universe. A Nebraska judge ruled that Pastafarianism is a parody of religious beliefs in scientific creation and that no one sincerely believes in the Spaghetti Monster. Therefore, Pastafarians are not entitled to free exercise exemptions. This challenge to sincerity, however, is more the exception than the rule. *Cavanaugh v. Bartelt*, 178 F. Supp. 3d 819—Dist. Court, D. Nebraska 2016.

16. *Newman v. Piggie Park Enterprises, Inc.*, 256 F. Supp. 941, 945 (1966).

17. In *Arlene's Flowers Inc. v. Washington*, for example, a Washington florist lost her case when she refused to provide flowers for a same-sex marriage. The Court remanded the case to the Supreme Court of Washington to consider in light of *Masterpiece Cakeshop*. Rather than reverse its decision, the Washington court argued that it found no evidence of hostility to religion. Therefore, it held that *Masterpiece Cakeshop* did not require reversing its decision. The Supreme Court refused to grant cert on this case in July of 2021, thus leaving the issue unresolved. As Kristen Waggoner complained, the refusal violated the florist's free speech: "This is the worst example of cancel culture, weaponized through the court system by state governments and gigantic corporations, and it is an insult to our nation's founding principles." Kristen Waggoner, "Supreme Court Leaves Americans Guessing about the Meaning of Tolerance," *Newsweek*, July 7, 2021, https://www.newsweek.com/supreme-court-leaves-americans -guessing-about-meaning-tolerance-opinion-1607243.

18. On the internal tensions within complicity arguments that use religious freedom arguments to be "left alone" by the state while reserving the right to judge the immorality of other people's actions, see Mary Ann Case, "Why 'Live and Let Live' Is Not a Viable Solution to the Difficult Problems of Religious Accommodation in the Age of Sexual Civil Rights," *Southern California Law Review* 88 (2015): 463–492.

19. *Burwell v. Hobby Lobby Stores, Inc.*, 134 S.Ct. 2751 (2014).

20. Winnifred Fallers Sullivan, "Is Masterpiece Cakeshop a Church?" *Immanent Frame*, June 8, 2018. https://tif.ssrc.org/2018/06/08/is-masterpiece -cakeshop-a-church/.

21. David Mullins, quoted in David G. Savage, "Colorado Cake Maker Asks Supreme Court to Provide a Religious Liberty Right to Refuse a Gay Couple," *Los Angeles Times*, September 12, 2007, http://www .latimes.com/politics/la-na-pol-court-religion-gays-20170912-story .html.

22. In his discussion of the tension between "rights" and "rites," Marco Derks considers how the ritual dimensions of marriage have received relatively little attention in the analysis of same-sex marriage controversies. Marco Derks, "Conscientious Objectors and the Marrying Kind: Rights and Rites in Dutch Public Discourse on Marriage Registrars with Conscientious Objections Against Conducting Same-Sex Weddings," *Theology and Sexuality* 23 (2017): 209–228.

23. Whether a nonreligious conscience claim can merit a religious exemption is the subject of a 1965 case where a man sought conscientious objector status even though he did not identify with an organized religion. While the court recognized his right to conscientious objection, it did so because the convictions in question occupied the same place as religion. As Justice Willian O. Douglas's concurring opinion explains, "None comes to us an avowedly irreligious person or as an atheist, one as a sincere believer in 'goodness and virtue for their own sakes.' His questions and doubts on theological issues, and his wonder, are no more alien to the statutory standard than are the awe-inspired questions of a devout Buddhist." *United States v. Seeger*, 380 US 163, 193 (1965).

24. *Reynolds v. United States*, 98 U.S. 145, 166 (1879).

25. For more on the centrality of belief in religious freedom cases, see Sarah Imhoff, "Belief," in *Religion, Law, USA*, ed. Joshua Dubler and Isaac Weiner (New York: New York University Press, 2019), 26–39.

26. *Minersville School District v. Gobitis*, 310 U.S. 586 (1940).

27. *West Virginia State Board of Education v. Barnette*, 319 U.S. 624 (1943).

28. For an account of how Jehovah's Witnesses shaped mid-twentieth century free exercise interpretation, see Sarah Barringer Gordon, *The Spirit of the Law: Religious Voices in the Constitution in Modern America* (Cambridge, Mass.: Harvard University Press, 2010), 15–55.

29. *Sherbert v. Verner*, 374 U.S. 398 (1963).

30. *Employment Division v. Smith*, 494 U.S. 872 (1990).

31. *City of Boerne v. Flores*, 521 U.S. 507 (1997).

32. Douglas NeJaime and Reva B. Siegel, "Conscience Wars: Complicity-Based Conscience Claims in Religion and Politics," *Yale Law Journal* 124, no. 7 (2014): 2553.

33. *Masterpiece Cakeshop v. Colorado Civil Rights Commission*, 584 U.S. ____ (2018).

34. Jean L. Cohen argues that granting corporate exemptions from laws designed to protect people from harm is part of a strategy to erode liberal democratic constitutionalism in favor of a "political theological" conception of sovereignty. Corporations and churches are seeking rights not within the constitutional order but by referring to a sovereign power that exists apart from and above such constitutional framework. As she states, *"But a political theological conception of the corporate is operative here, for churches allegedly enjoy these privileges whether or not they are incorporated via a civil law procedure.* The deep structure of this sort of accommodation is not a matter of self-limitation of government but of deference to another sovereign's jurisdiction." Jean L. Cohen, "Freedom of Religion, Inc.: Whose Sovereignty," *Netherlands Journal of Legal Philosophy* 44, no. 3 (2015): 200; emphasis in original. I agree with Cohen that corporate exemptions seek to erode liberal democracy and that corporations hope to govern themselves as political theological sovereigns, but the price of this is to carve out an exception from state sovereignty in a way that is consistent with secular divisions between the politics and religion.

35. *Masterpiece Cakeshop v. Colorado Civil Rights Commission*, 584 U.S. ____, 16 (2018).

36. On the history of the category of religion, see Tomoko Masuzawa, *The Invention of World Religions; Or, How European Universalism Was Preserved in the Language of Pluralism* (Chicago: University of Chicago Press, 2005).

37. On privacy's dependence on property, see Patricia J. Williams, *The Alchemy of Race and Rights* (Cambridge, Mass.: Harvard University Press, 1991), 15–43.

38. Wendy Brown, *In the Ruins of Neoliberalism: The Rise of Antidemocratic Politics in the West* (New York: Columbia University Press, 2019), 141.

39. In addition to privileging some conscience claims over others, the *Masterpiece Cakeshop* ruling also picks a side in determining whose economic rights have priority. The case takes as self-evident that economic freedom is exercised by owners of private businesses in a way that deflects from their interaction with the public. As Lawrence B. Glickman argues, "Viewing the desires of consumers not as the engine of the economy, but as a potential constraint upon the autonomy and selfhood of the business owner, the Court drew upon a conservative history of defining free enterprise as freedom for sellers and manufacturers rather than liberty for customers." Lawrence B. Glickman, "Don't Let Them Eat Cake," *Boston Review*, June 7, 2018, https://bostonreview.net/law-justice/lawrence-glickman-masterpiece -cakeshop.

40. For a critique of the limits of liberal concepts of tolerance, see Janet R. Jakobsen and Ann Pellegrini, *Love the Sin: Sexual Regulation and the Limits of Tolerance* (Boston: Beacon, 2004).

41. As Sullivan explains, "An increasingly common critique of the *Hobby Lobby* decision is that it reveals the triumph of neoliberalism and the capitalist colonization of our lives—seen, as it often is, to be of a piece with the corrupt reasoning of *Citizens United*. Too great an emphasis on an economic reading of these opinions, however, reflects an impoverished understanding of christian theology and of the relationship between religion and the economy, as well as a misreading of U.S. religious and legal history." Winnifred Fallers Sullivan, *Church State Corporation: Construing Religion in US Law* (Chicago: University of Chicago Press, 2020), 15–16.

42. Sullivan, *Church State Corporation*, 16.

43. Sullivan, *Church State Corporation*, 175.

44. Cathleen Kaveny, "The Ironies of the New Religious Liberty Litigation," *Daedalus* 149, no. 3 (Summer 2020): 78.

45. A useful point of contrast to the embrace of legal victories at the expense of moral and theological impoverishment is found in Méadhbh McIvor's study of Christian legal activism in contemporary England. While McIvor's interlocutors share many of the religious convictions of Jack Phillips, they have ambivalent feelings about pursuing an American-style litigation strategy focusing on religious freedom rights. While Christian activists wanted to win cases, they were worried about arguments that undermined the common good. As McIvor explains, "They worry, however, that society has embraced a rights-based system without understanding the origin of these rights or the responsibilities that might accompany them. Rather than grounding them in a notion of the common good based on the teachings of the Bible, rights had become individual, fragmented, and mutually exclusive." In their desire to articulate an alternative vision of public goods, McIvor suggests that conservative Christian legal activists articulate what Michael Warner would call a "counter-public." I suggest that a Christian counter-public differs from the private freedom sought by illiberal secularism because the former has not abandoned a moral and theological basis for the common good. Méadhbh McIvor, *Representing God: Christian Legal Activism in Contemporary England* (Princeton, N.J.: Princeton University Press, 2020), 94.

46. Jack Phillips, *The Cost of My Faith: How a Decision in My Cake Shop Took Me to the Supreme Court* (Washington, D.C.: Salem, 2021), 3.

47. Phillips, *Cost of My Faith*, 76.

48. Sue Selasky, "Lesbian Baker in Detroit Got Homophobic Cake Order: Why She Made It Anyway," *Detroit Free Press*, August 13, 2020, https://www.freep.com/story/news/local/michigan/detroit/2020/08/13/detroit-baker-april-anderson-homophobic-cake-david-gordon/3343464001/.

49. According to the would-be customer who ordered the cake: "Every day, overtly Christian companies are in danger of falling victim to the 'cancel culture' and bleeding sponsors and industry partners if they dare voice a collective opinion in favor of the timeless and authentic definition of marriage—that it's between one man and one woman." David Gordon, "The Gay Rainbow Is a Mark of the Beast," *Church Militant*,

July 21, 2020, https://www.churchmilitant.com/news/article/the-gay
-rainbow-is-a-mark-of-the-beast#.

50. Jay Kaplan, quoted in Selasky, "Lesbian Baker in Detroit Got Homo-
    phobic Cake Order."

51. Phillips, *Cost of My Faith*, 185.

52. April Anderson, quoted in Alyssa Newcomb, "A Lesbian Baker in
    Detroit Got an Anti-Gay Cake Order. She Baked It Anyway," *Today*,
    August 14, 2020, https://www.today.com/food/why-lesbian-baker
    -detroit-filled-anti-gay-cake-order-t189491.

53. The Alliance Defending Freedom still insisted that the principle held
    as the bakers did not bake the requested cake. "April could not—and
    did not—create *the requested* cake because it would have expressed a
    message that conflicts with her core beliefs. Instead, she created a *dif-
    ferent* cake with a message she liked." Sarah Kramer, "Read Past the
    Headline: This LGBT Cake Artist Declined to Express a Message Just
    Like Jack Phillips," *Alliance Defending Freedom*, August 18, 2020,
    https://adflegal.org/blog/read-past-headline-lgbt-cake-artist
    -declined-express-message-just-jack-phillips. The cake itself did not
    have a message, but the baker did include an accompanying note.

54. Jeff Sessions, "Prepared Remarks of the Attorney General to the Alli-
    ance Defending Freedom on July 11, 2017," *Federalist*, July 13, 2017,
    http://thefederalist.com/2017/07/13/heres-the-speech-jeff-sessions
    -delivered-to-christian-first-amendment-lawyers/.

6. NFL PROTESTS AND THE PROFANE RITES OF SOMETHING

1. Donald Trump, quoted in Aric Jenkins, "Read President Trump's
   NFL Speech on National Anthem Protests," *Time*, September 23,
   2017, http://time.com/4954684/donald-trump-nfl-speech-anthem
   -protests/.

2. Colin Kaepernick, quoted in Nick Wagoner, "Transcript of Colin Kaepernick's Comments after Preseason Finale," *ESPN*, September 2,
   2016, http://www.espn.com/blog/san-francisco-49ers/post/_/id/19126
   /transcript-of-colin-kaepernicks-comments-after-preseason-finale.

3. John Branch, "The Awakening of Colin Kaepernick," *New York Times*,
   September 7, 2017, https://www.nytimes.com/2017/09/07/sports/colin

-kaepernick-nfl-protests.html; and Elliott Almond, "Colin Kaepernick's Tattoos More Than Skin Deep," *Mercury News*, January 25, 2013, https://www.mercurynews.com/2013/01/25/super-bowl-2013-colin-kaepernicks-tattoos-more-than-skin-deep/.

4. Ruth Braunstein, "Boundary Work and the Demarcation of Civil from Uncivil Protest in the United States: Control, Legitimacy, and Political Inequality," *Theory and Society* 47, no. 2 (October 2018): 623.

5. William C. Rhoden, "Westbrook-Fan Incident May Spur NBA to Do More to Shield Players," interview by David Greene, *NPR*, March 13, 2019, https://www.npr.org/2019/03/13/702908728/westbrook-fan-incident-may-spur-nba-to-do-more-to-shield-players.

6. C. C. J. Carpenter, Joseph A. Durick, Milton L. Grafman, Paul Hardin, Nolan B. Harmon, George M. Murray, Edward V. Ramage, and Earl Stallings, "Letter to Martin Luther King," April 12, 1963, reprinted at *Teaching American History*, https://teachingamericanhistory.org/library/document/letter-to-martin-luther-king/.

7. Martin Luther King Jr., "Letter from Birmingham City Jail," in *A Testament of Hope: The Essential Writings and Speeches of Martin Luther King, Jr.*, ed. James M. Washington (San Francisco: HarperSanFrancisco, 1986), 294–295.

8. Jean-Jacques Rousseau, *The Social Contract and Discourses*, trans. G. D. H. Cole (New York: Everyman's Library, 1973), 276.

9. Micah Watson suggests that Rousseau attempts to resolve the tension between force and freedom by stressing the educational work necessary to make the general will internal to every citizen. Including the citizen within the general will in the first place still requires a kind of miracle, and this is part of the religious aspect of civil religion. As Watson explains,

> If it is man's nature to be free, then there is nothing to say that we cannot consciously attempt to remake man's nature so as to ameliorate his miserable condition. The most difficult and miraculous task the Legislator must perform is to persuade men and women to join the social contract. Rousseau writes that this transformation is impossible without religion. Thus Rousseau's civil religion does more than just maintain the just society; it is an essential component of creating it in the first place.

Micah Watson, "The Damned Neighbors Problem: Rousseau's Civil Religion Revisited," *Religions* 10, no. 6 (2019), 349.

10. Rousseau, *The Social Contract*, 177.

11. As Jean-Luc Nancy points out, the apparent necessity of civil religion demonstrated that liberal models of self-interest provided an insufficient ground for citizenship. Citizenship required affective bonds and sentiments that reflect deeper commitments than the willingness of liberal subjects to respect each other's rights: "Rousseau's civil religion is not something added in the manner of a more or less gratuitous ornament to the edifice constructed by the contract. On the contrary, it comes to try and repair the intrinsic flaw of the contract, which does not know how to bring about a regime of assembly (*régime d'assemblement*) other than on the basis of interest—even as this contract forms man himself at the same time it forms the citizen." Civil religion goes beyond mere rational interest to provide affective qualities of belonging such as fervor, desire, and sentiment. Jean-Luc Nancy, "Church, State, Resistance," *Journal of Law and Society* 34, no. 1 (March 2007): 9.

12. Robert Bellah, "Civil Religion in America," *Daedalus* 96, no. 1 (Winter 1967): 14.

13. Writing fifty years after Bellah's essay, sociologist Philip Gorski echoes this distinction between civil religion and divisive forms of racial and religious identification. To this end, he distinguishes between civil religion and religious nationalism: "The religious nationalist wishes to fuse religion and politics, to make citizenship in one a mark of citizenship in the other, with violent means if necessary." Following this logic, Trump's divisive Christian nationalism would be disqualified as civil religion. Trump's predecessor, Barack Obama, with his call to unify blue states and red states, would be a better exemplar of civil religiosity. Philip Gorski, *American Covenant: A History of Civil Religion from the Puritans to the Present* (Princeton, N.J.: Princeton University Press, 2017), 17.

14. Bellah, "Civil Religion in America," 4.

15. A number of observers registered Trump's hugging the flag as a profane gesture. As comedian Stephen Colbert suggested, "He is dry humping old glory." Stephen Colbert, quoted in Laura Bradley, "Colbert Rips into Trump's 'Historically Long and Epically Weird' CPAC Speech," *Vanity Fair*, March 5, 2019, https://www.vanityfair.com

/hollywood/2019/03/donald-trump-cpac-speech-colbert-late-show.
Over on social media, people noted that the president's brand of flag
fetishism was foretold by the Twitter prophet @dril in a 2012 tweet:
"another day volunteering at the betsy ross museum. everyone keeps
asking if they can fuck the flag. buddy, they wont even let me fuck it."
Wint (@dril), Tweet, February 19, 2012, 8:27 p.m., https://twitter.com
/dril/status/171450835388203008.

16. The divisiveness of symbolism led Trump's border wall led Lloyd Barba
to suggest that it might be useful to analyze Trumpism as a form of
(un)civil religion. Lloyd D. Barba, "Trump's Wall: A Monument of
(Un)Civil Religion?" Mediation, *MAVCOR Journal* 3, no. 1 (2019),
http://dx.doi.org/10.22332/mav.med.2019.1.

17. Robert Bellah, *The Broken Covenant: American Civil Religion in a Time
of Trial*, 2nd ed. (Chicago: University of Chicago Press, 1992), 179.

18. Leilah Danielson suggests that civil religion is a mythmaking project
rather than historical analysis. Therefore, the scholarly literature on
civil religion is a primary source that is "best understood as a mani-
festation of growing concern by many white Americans in the 1960s
and 1970s that the social fabric of the country was unravelling, becoming corrupted, and that the solution was to revive patriotism and
'traditional' religious and moral values." Leilah Danielson, "Civil
Religion as Myth, Not History," *Religions* 10, no. 6 (2019): 375–376.

19. According to Russell McCutcheon, the persistence of civil religion
demonstrates that scholars continue to invest religious language with
a special status that distinguishes it from ordinary politics. Rather than
try to locate civil religion, it would be more useful to simply study
nationalism or ideology:

> So, even the historically-rigorous types, who see themselves as, say,
> sociologists, still won't simply dissolve, for instance, the late Robert
> Bellah's notion of civil religion into nationalism or ideology. No,
> because for them there's something unique or different about the
> former that is lost if we just see this or that reference to God in a
> politician's speech or a constitution as being nothing more or less
> than another mundane nationalist convention.
>
> Russell McCutcheon, quoted in Andie Alexander, "On the Spot
> with Russell McCutcheon," *Culture on the Edge*, September 30, 2013,

https://edge.ua.edu/russell-mccutcheon/on-the-spot-with-russell
-mccutcheon/.

20. On the tendency of civil religion to privilege minority activists who
can frame their work in terms of a contribution to a broader civic good
rather than advance a conflictual politics in service to particular communities, see Rudiger V. Busto, "'In the Outer Boundaries:' Pentecostalism, Politics, and Reies López Tijerina's Civic Activism," in *Latino
Religions and Civic Activism in the United States*, ed. Gastón Espinosa,
Virgilio P. Elisondo, and Jesse Miranda (New York: Oxford University Press, 2005), 72–73.

21. According to Michael Angrosino, one effect of this ideal of perfected
nationalism is to endow democratic institutions with their own sacred
aura: "American civil religion has been based on the elevation of the
democratic system to a sacred status. In treating democratic principles,
institutions, and the voice of the people as sacred elements in an over-
arching religious faith, civil religion in America has infused the
democratic system with an aura not shared by most other civil poli-
ties." Michael Angrosino, "Civil Religion Redux," *Anthropological
Quarterly* 75, no. 2 (Spring 2002): 249.

22. On this point, L. Benjamin Rolsky suggests that classifying the protests as religious runs the risk of depoliticizing the players' actions in
favor of an essentialized connection between religion and black community activism: "To render Kaepernick simply as an actor of religious
dissent ignores how his kneeling participated in a longer tradition of
black community activism that has taken place outside the confines of
the Black Church, real or imagined." L. Benjamin Rolsky, "Colin Kaepernick, Religion, and the Academic Think Piece," *Marginalia: Los
Angeles Review of Books*, September 10, 2016.

23. Nicolas Howe, *Landscapes of the Secular: Law, Religion, and American
Sacred Space* (Chicago: University of Chicago Press, 2016), 18.

24. Christopher J. Lebron, *The Making of Black Lives Matter: A Brief History of an Idea* (New York: Oxford University Press, 2017), 133.

25. Barbara Ransby, *Making All Black Lives Matter: Reimagining Freedom
in the 21st Century* (Berkeley: University of California Press, 2018), 1–2.

26. In his study of soccer in France, Paul Silverstein notes that sports func-
tioned as a national project to assimilate religious and racial minorities by presenting an idealized vision of an inclusive nation that was

in tension with sociological reality. In speaking of the Paris-Saint Germain team, he notes: "Such a universalist conception of French citizenship (or, in any event, Parisian metropolitan belonging) as embodied in soccer play extends to the multiracial character of the PSG itself, a club that recruited players from throughout Europe, Latin America, and Africa." Paul A. Silverstein, "Sporting Faith: Islam, Soccer, and the French Nation-State," *Social Text* 18, no. 4 (Winter 2000): 36.

27. For some creative attempts to apply religious studies categories to the analysis of sports, see Paul Christopher Johnson, "The Fetish and McGwire's Balls," *Journal of the American Academy of Religion* 68, no. 2 (June 2000): 243–264; and Sean McCloud, "Popular Culture Fandoms, the Boundaries of Religious Studies, and the Project of the Self," *Culture and Religion* 4, no. 2 (2003): 187–206.

28. Michael Novak, *The Joy of Sports: End Zones, Bases, Baskets, Balls, and the Consecration of the American Spirit*, rev. ed. (Lanham, Md.: Madison, 1994), 3.

29. As Benjamin Zeller argues, "If we wanted proof of the robustness of American civil religion—with its totem of a flag and hymn-like national anthem—the public flare-up that greeted Kaepernick's dissent offers a powerful reminder." Benjamin Zeller, "Why Kaepernick's Refusal to Stand Is an Act of Religious Dissent," *Religion Dispatches*, August 31, 2016, http://religiondispatches.org/why-kaepernicks-refusal -to-stand-was-an-act-of-religious-dissent/.

30. In his discussion of reactions to the NFL protests, Michael Serazio notes that this officially apolitical quality of mediated sports serves to make conservative politics into common sense. As Serazio notes, "These voices have resisted the intrusion of *explicit* politics into the arena of play—even as implicit ideological messages about economic inequality and militaristic nationalism circulate almost totally unremarked." Michael Serazio, *The Power of Sports: Media and Spectacle in American Culture* (New York: New York University Press, 2019), 225.

31. Trips to the White House by sports teams that had won national championships became a recurring site of contest under Trump when athletes of color refused to attend. As Jemele Hill notes, the assertion that the trip was not political was often cited by white coaches and athletes in defense of their attendance. This apolitical stance absolved

them of responsibility to support their teammates because those refusing to attend introduced divisive politics into an otherwise apolitical event. Hill argues, however, that disjuncture between political and apolitical athletes serves to highlight the reality of social inequality: "In team sports, the concept of putting team before self is preached ad nauseam. Solidarity is supposed to be paramount, but clearly in this situation the solidarity doesn't run both ways. If you're one of the athletes of color on a team, how can you not wonder how your white teammates feel about people like you?" Jemele Hill, "Why Don't White Athletes Understand What's Wrong with Trump?" *Atlantic*, May 7, 2019, https://www.theatlantic.com/ideas/archive/2019/05/red-sox -divided -racial-lines-white-house-visit/588856/.

32. Douglas Hartmann, *Race, Culture, and the Revolt of the Black Athlete* (Chicago: University of Chicago Press, 2003), xv.

33. Jackie Robinson as told to Alfred Duckett, *I Never Had It Made* (New York: Putnam, 1972), 12.

34. Part of American civil religion can be seen in battlefield commemorations. Venerative consumption is a familiar feature that at once demonstrates respect for but also runs the risk of profaning the object of reverence:

> Like other American battlefields, this memorial site has been ritualized by its demarcation from profane space, by its ceremonial displays, and by the pilgrimages to its sacred precincts of tourists, veterans, survivors, and other devotees of an American patriotic faith. Tourist pilgrims come to pay their respects, but also to buy such relics as T-shirts, books, slides, videotapes, maps, and photographs, illustrating "venerative consumption" that enables visitors to take some part of the sacred shrine back home.

David Chidester and Edward T. Linenthal, eds. *American Sacred Space* (Bloomington: Indiana University Press, 1995), 3–4.

35. One typical response from an offended veteran described Kaepernick's high salary as a kind of insult to injury: "As a veteran of this great nation, I am personally insulted. Mr. Kaepernick: You overpaid, prissy-assed, self-entitled son of a bitch!" Clay Martin, "Former Green Beret Has Message for NFL QB Colin Kaepernick," *Guns America Digest*,

August 30, 2016, https://www.gunsamerica.com/digest/green-beret
-kaepernick/.

36. Robinson, *I Never Had It Made*, 10.

37. For Novak, the unseemly mixture of money and sports devalues
athletic competition by reducing it to mere entertainment. As he
explains, "Sports, in a word, are a form of godliness. That is why the
corruptions of sports in our day, by corporations and television and
glib journalism and cheap public relations, are so hateful. If sports
were entertainment, why should we care? They are far more than that.
So when we see them abused, our natural response is the rise of vomit
in the throat." Novak, *Joy of Sports*, 27.

38. Michael Bennett and Dave Zirin, *Things That Make White People
Uncomfortable* (Chicago: Haymarket, 2018), xxvii.

39. Jonathan Z. Smith, *Imagining Religion: From Babylon to Jonestown*
(Chicago: University of Chicago Press), 63.

40. This gap is what some ritual theorists describe as the "subjunctive
dimension" of ritual. The subjunctive refers to the "as if" of ritual that
is always in distinction with "as it is" of social life. According to
Adam B. Seligman and colleagues, "The subjunctive world created by
ritual is always doomed ultimately to fail—the ordered world of flaw-
less repetition can never fully replace the broken world of experience.
This is why the tension between the two is inherent and ultimately
unbridgeable." Adam B. Seligman, Robert P. Weller, Michael J. Puett,
and Bennett Simon, *Ritual and Its Consequences: An Essay on the Limits
of Sincerity* (New York: Oxford University Press, 2008), 30.

41. Eddie S. Glaude Jr. *Democracy in Black: How Race Still Enslaves the
American Soul* (New York: Crown, 2016), 49.

42. Colin Kaepernick (@Kaepernick7), "Believe in something. Even if it
means sacrificing everything. #JustDoIt," tweet, September 5, 2018,
10:11 a.m., https://twitter.com/kaepernick7/status/1037387722107830272.

43. Nathaniel Friedman, "Something for Nothing: The High Formalist
Branding of Nike's Kaepernick Campaign," *Baffler*, September 5, 2018,
https://thebaffler.com/latest/something-for-nothing-friedman.

44. Dave Zirin, "On Colin Kaepernick's Nike Ad: Will the Revolution
Be Branded?" *The Nation*, September 4, 2018, https://www.thenation
.com/article/on-colin-kaepernicks-nike-ad-will-the-revolution-be
-branded/.

45. Walter Benjamin argues that capitalism's lack of dogma makes it a particularly extreme form of cultic religion: "Capitalism is a purely cultic
religion, perhaps the most extreme that ever existed. In capitalism,
things have a meaning only in their relationship to the cult; capitalism
has no specific body of dogma, no theology." Walter Benjamin, "Capitalism as Religion," trans. Rodney Livingstone, in *Walter Benjamin:
Selected Writings*, vol. 1, eds., Marcus Bullock and Michael W. Jennings,
288–291 (Cambridge, Mass.: Harvard University Press, 1996), 288.

46. Jemele Hill, "Kaepernick Won. The NFL Lost," *Atlantic*, February 17, 2019,
https://www.theatlantic.com/ideas/archive/2019/02/colin-kaepernick
-won-his-settlement-nfl/582994/.

47. Daniel Trotta, "Kaepernick Ads Spark Boycott Calls, But Nike Is Seen
as Winning in the End," Reuters, September 4, 2018, https://www
.reuters.com/article/us-nike-kaepernick/kaepernick-ads-spark
-boycott-calls-but-nike-is-seen-as-winning-in-the-end
-idUSKCN1LK1DK.

48. Donald J. Trump (@realDonaldTrump), "Just like the NFL, whose
ratings have gone WAY DOWN, Nike is getting absolutely killed with
anger and boycotts," tweet, September 5, 2018, https://twitter.com
/realDonaldTrump/status/1037334510159966214.

7. FEAR AND SAFETY ON CAMPUS

1. Judith Shapiro, "From Strength to Strength," *Inside Higher Ed*, December 15, 2014, https://www.insidehighered.com/views/2014/12/15/essay
-importance-not-trying-protect-students-everything-may-upset
-them; and Judith Shulevitz, "In College and Hiding from Scary
Ideas," *New York Times*, March 21, 2015, https://www.nytimes.com/2015
/03/22/opinion/sunday/judith-shulevitz-hiding-from-scary-ideas.html.

2. John Ellison, quoted in Scott Jaschik, "U Chicago to Freshmen: Don't
Expect Safe Spaces," *Inside Higher Ed*, August 25, 2016, https://www
.insidehighered.com/news/2016/08/25/u-chicago-warns-incoming
-students-not-expect-safe-spaces-or-trigger-warnings.

3. Caitlin Flanagan, "That's Not Funny!" *Atlantic*, September 2015,
https://www.theatlantic.com/magazine/archive/2015/09/thats-not
-funny/399335/.

4. In response to critics like Flanagan who claim that the inability to take offense imperils irreverent art and comedy, Laura Miller suggests that what is instead at work is a more subtle distinction between offense and harm:

> Much of what transgressive art rebels against is *politeness*, but politeness has many dimensions. It may dictate that you never swear or discuss sex, religion, or politics in "mixed company." And it also decrees that you don't use racial slurs when referring to groups you don't belong to. The first restriction, however practical it may be, would strike a lot of people as a prime example of phony bourgeois manners, ripe for skewering in the defense of truth. The second example feels like another, more fundamental standard of decency and morality, and breaking that rule a very different way of being bad. The first is a strategy for not offending people; the second, a policy of not hurting them.

Laura Miller, "How to Be Bad," *Slate*, January 28, 2019, https://slate .com/culture/2019/01/transgressive-art-political-correctness-vanessa -place-louis-ck-hannah-gadsby.html. Much of this chapter considers how different people draw lines between offense and harm.

5. Some comedians disagree with the appraisal of oversensitive students. Sarah Silverman, for example, sees student activists in continuity with students of the past: "You have to listen to the college-aged because they lead the revolution. They're pretty much always on the right side of history." Sarah Silverman, quoted in Caroline Siede, "Sarah Silverman Sides with College Students in the Great PC Wars," *AV Club*, September 16, 2015, https://news.avclub.com/sarah-silverman-sides -with-college-students-in-the-grea-1798284415.

6. Chris Rock, quoted in Frank Rich, "In Conversation," *New York Magazine*, December 1, 2014, https://www.vulture.com/2014/11/chris-rock -frank-rich-in-conversation.html.

7. Dave Urbanski, "Professor's Contract with Students: Drop the Class Immediately if You Are Triggered by Free Speech." *Blaze*, August 23, 2018, https://www.theblaze.com/news/2018/08/23/professors-contract -with-students-drop-the-class-immediately-if-you-are-triggered-by -free-speech.

8. Greg Lukianoff and Jonathan Haidt, "The Coddling of the American Mind," *Atlantic Monthly*, September 2015, https://www.theatlantic.com /magazine/archive/2015/09/the-coddling-of-the-american-mind /399356/.

9. Greg Lukianoff and Jonathan Haidt, *The Coddling of the American Mind: How Good Intentions and Bad Ideas Are Setting Up a Generation for Failure* (New York: Penguin, 2018), 30.

10. Taves refers "special things" instead of sacred to avoid postulating that the sacred is a timeless essence. According to her, special things are deemed sacred in sociologically and historically specific contexts. Ann Taves, *Religious Experience Reconsidered: A Building-Block Approach to the Study of Religion and Other Special Things* (Princeton, N.J.: Princeton University Press, 2009), 35.

11. On the source of religion in the hazard protection system, see Pascal Boyer, *Religion Explained: The Evolutionary Origins of Religious Thought* (New York: Basic Books, 2001).

12. Lukianoff and Haidt, *Coddling of the American Mind*, 4.

13. David French, "FIRE's Guide to Religious Liberty on Campus," Philadelphia: Foundation for Individual Rights in Education, 2002. http://thefire.org/public/pdfs/religious-liberty.pdf.

14. French, "FIRE's Guide to Religious Liberty on Campus."

15. In previous years, some non–religiously affiliated schools like Vassar and Worcester Polytechnic Institute were assigned blue lights because they clearly advertised their lack of commitment to free speech. According to FIRE, WPI got a blue light because it clearly advertised that students do not enjoy First Amendment rights. Vassar promised no free speech because it identifies as a "voluntary association of persons" who agree to follow university policies that affirm diversity and prohibit hate speech. The Vassar faculty handbook explains: "As a private institution, Vassar is a voluntary association of persons invited to membership on the understanding that they will respect the principles by which it is governed." In other words, an orthodoxy about racial or sexual equality was acceptable for a private institution if such commitments were part of a quasi-religious belief system. "Statement on Civility and Responsibility in an Academic Community," *Faculty Handbook at Vassar College*, http://facultysites.vassar.edu/paruud/docs

/fpcc/governance/fac09-10tocwhite.html. By 2021 Vassar had been assigned a yellow light while WPI received a red light.

16. Erwin Chemerinsky and Howard Gillman, *Free Speech on Campus* (New Haven, Conn.: Yale University Press, 2017), 117.

17. Edward Schlosser, "I'm a Liberal Professor, and My Liberal Students Terrify Me," *Vox*, June 3, 2015, https://www.vox.com/2015/6/3/8706323 /college-professor-afraid.

18. The coddled student narrative assumes that students are liberal in a way that does not necessarily reflect the views of most college students. One self-described liberal professor complained instead of "conservative fragility" that became especially vindictive after the 2016 election. Jason McCormick, "I'm a Liberal Professor and My Conservative Students Terrify Me," *Medium*, December 1, 2016. https://medium .com/the-coffeelicious/im-a-liberal-professor-and-my-conservative -students-terrify-me-f4ce5ece0549.

19. Lukianoff and Haidt, "The Coddling of the American Mind."

20. In another popular critique of call-out culture, Jon Ronson has also argued that public shaming on a medium like Twitter makes people less likely to take risks. As he laments, "We are defining the boundaries of normality by tearing apart the people outside of it." Jon Ronson, *So You've Been Publicly Shamed* (New York: Riverhead, 2015), 281.

21. Lukianoff and Haidt, *Coddling*, 58.

22. Jonathan Haidt, *The Righteous Mind: Why Good People Are Divided by Politics and Religion* (New York: Vintage, 2012), 262.

23. Lukianoff and Haidt, *Coddling of the American Mind*, 56–57.

24. Erika Christakis, "Dressing Yourselves," Email to Silliman College (Yale) Students on Halloween Costumes, reprinted at *FIRE*, October 30, 2015, https://www.thefire.org/email-from-erika-christakis -dressing-yourselves-email-to-silliman-college-yale-students-on -halloween-costumes/.

25. On the tie between Christakis's arguments and institutional racism, see Aaron Z. Lewis, "What's Really Going on at Yale," *Medium*, November 8, 2015, https://medium.com/@aaronzlewis/what-s-really -going-on-at-yale-6bdbbeeb57a6; and Larissa Pham, "The Architecture of Racism at Yale University," *Guernica*, November 18, 2015, https://www.guernicamag.com/larissa-pham-the-architecture-of -racism-at-yale-university/.

26. Erika Christakis, "My Halloween Email Led to a Campus Firestorm—
and a Troubling Lesson About Self-Censorship," *Washington Post*,
October 28, 2016, https://www.washingtonpost.com/opinions/my
-halloween-email-led-to-a-campus-firestorm—and-a-troubling
-lesson-about-self-censorship/2016/10/28/70e55732-9b97-11e6-aoed
-abo774c1eaa5_story.html.

27. Sigal R. Ben-Porath, *Free Speech on Campus* (Philadelphia: University
of Pennsylvania Press, 2017), 30. Ben-Porath is guided by her desire to
create an environment of inclusive freedom.

28. Amy Wax and Larry Alexander, "Paying the Price for Breakdown of
the Country's Bourgeois Culture," *Philadelphia Inquirer*, August 9,
2017, https://www.inquirer.com/philly/opinion/commentary/paying
-the-price-for-breakdown-of-the-countrys-bourgeois-culture
-20170809.html.

29. Lukianoff and Haidt, *Coddling of the American Mind*, 108.

30. According to Farhana Sultana, rehashing intellectually and ethically
discredited arguments that are bound to face intense resistance is a way
for far-right intellectuals to fashion themselves as heroes. When the
witch hunts begin, a persecuted academic "dog-whistles the far-right
to attack critical scholars with their outrage machine of ad hominem
threats, harassment, falsifications, while the Academic claims victimhood and persecution, and continues to use the far-right to garner support." Farhana Sultana, "The False Equivalence of Academic Freedom
and Free Speech: Defending Academic Integrity in the Age of White
Supremacy, Colonial Nostalgia, and Anti-Intellectualism," *ACME:
An International Journal for Critical Geographies* 17, no. 2 (2018): 247.

31. In a similar vein, anthropologist Jessica Johnson notes that an inflam-
matory speech by Milo Yiannopoulos at the University of Washington contained no information or ideas that everyone did not already
know: "The script was ugly but predictable. After watching a few vid-
eos of his talks at other campuses, there was nothing shocking about
his language or surprising about his tactics." Jessica Johnson, "When
Hate Circulates on Campus to Uphold Free Speech," *Studies in Law,
Politics, and Society* 80 (2019): 115.

32. Discounting harm also landed Wax in controversy when she defended
Brett Kavanaugh against charges that he had sexually assaulted Christine Blasey Ford. Wax was willing to concede that the attack might

have happened, but she did not think it was a big deal because the attack "didn't create any permanent harm, except through this manufactured idea that this is such a horrible, traumatic thing." Amy Wax, quoted in Juliana Feliciano Reyes, "The Internet Wants Penn Prof Amy Wax Fired (Again)—This Time for Her Comments on the Kavanaugh Hearing," *Philadelphia Inquirer*, October 3, 2018, https://www.inquirer.com/philly/news/amy-wax-firing-kavanaugh-ford-hearing-online-petition-law-professors-20181003.html. These sorts of statements prompted the National Association of Scholars to give Wax an award for "her continued academic courage in the face of threats to her livelihood and attacks on her integrity."

33. Porochista Khakpour, "On a Collective Morality," *Sicker/Sickest*, June 8, 2020, https://porochista.substack.com/p/on-a-collective-morality.

34. As Danielle Butler asserts, sounding alarms about cancel culture amounts to a dog whistle that says as much about discomfort over speech that threatens to redistribute power and resources: "However, what people do when they invoke dog whistles like 'cancel culture' and 'culture wars' is illustrate their discomfort with the kinds of people who now have a voice and their audacity to direct it toward figures with more visibility and power." Danielle Butler, "The Misplaced Hysteria about a 'Cancel Culture' That Doesn't Actually Exist," *The Root*, October 23, 2018, https://verysmartbrothas.theroot.com/the-misplaced-hysteria-about-a-cancel-culture-that-do-1829563238.

35. Lukianoff and Haidt, *Coddling of the American Mind*, 72.

36. Kelly J. Baker, *Sexism Ed: Essays on Gender and Labor in Academia* (Chapel Hill, N.C.: Blue Crow, 2018), 110.

37. "A Letter on Justice and Open Debate," *Harper's Magazine*, July 7, 2020, https://harpers.org/a-letter-on-justice-and-open-debate/.

38. One tangible effect of efforts to deplatform Yiannopoulos is that he has indeed lost much of his public platform. As Rachel Kraus argues, "Milo only makes news when something or someone cancels him; when people say 'no' to his insistences that white privilege is fake or that black lives matter is a hate group. The fact that Yiannopoulos has found his reach and influence so depleted that he can't get new gigs and takes to comments on Facebook to complain shows the real world effect that de-platforming a toxic public figure can actually have."

Rachel Kraus, "Milo Yiannopoulos Facebook Rant Shows that De-Platforming Actually Works," *Mashable*, August 27, 2018, https://mashable.com/article/milo-yiannopoulos-deplatforming-alex-jones/.

39. Donald J. Trump, quoted in Linda Qiu, "Trump Asks, 'What About the Alt-Left?' Here's an Answer," *New York Times*, August 15, 2017, https://www.nytimes.com/2017/08/15/us/politics/trump-alt-left-fact-check.html.

40. As one critic of the University of Chicago's policing practices noted, it is not self-evident that everyone's safety is equally protected by placing increased resources into police: "Safety is something that is grown from within a community, and it requires things like investment, and things like mental health. . . . Those are the things that when we start taking money away from these security institutions and start putting them into institutions like housing and jobs and education and mental health services, that then we can actually build safe communities." Schuyler Stallcup, quoted in Ashtini Kartik-Narayan, "The Fight Over Chicago's Largest Private Police Force," *South Side Weekly*, July 16, 2018, https://southsideweekly.com/the-fight-over-chicagos-largest-private-police-force-university-of-chicago-ucpd/.

41. As Sara Ahmed has observed, diversity initiatives can themselves be conservative forces designed to protect institutions from harm: "Diversity thus participates in the illusion of equality, fitting in with the university's social mission: the idea the university has of itself as doing good ('the great benefactor'). Diversity can allow organizations to retain their good idea of themselves." Sara Ahmed, *On Being Included: Racism and Diversity in Institutional Life* (Durham, N.C.: Duke University Press, 2012), 71.

42. Michael S. Roth, *Safe Enough Spaces: A Pragmatist's Approach to Inclusion, Free Speech, and Political Correctness on College Campuses* (New Haven, Conn.: Yale University Press, 2019), 29.

43. Hua Hsu, "The Year of the Imaginary College Student," *New Yorker*, December 31, 2015, https://www.newyorker.com/culture/cultural-comment/the-year-of-the-imaginary-college-student.

44. Nathan Heller, "Letter from Oberlin: The Big Uneasy," *New Yorker*, March 23, 2016, https://www.newyorker.com/magazine/2016/05/30/the-new-activism-of-liberal-arts-colleges.

45. Roth, *Safe Enough Spaces*, 48.

46. Jennie Capó Crucet, *My Time Among the Whites: Notes from an Unfinished Education* (New York: Picador, 2019), 174.

47. Sarah Smith and McClain Baxley, "Students Burn Author's Book Outside of Eagle Village," *George-Anne*, October 10, 2019, https://thegeorgeanne.com/1522/news/students-burn-authors-book-outside-of-eagle-village/.

48. Lukianoff and Haidt, *Coddling of the American Mind*, 175.

49. Lukianoff and Haidt, *Coddling of the American Mind*, 175.

50. As Jelani Cobb notes, public responses to protest that privilege free speech in ways that deflect from institutional racism share "themes of racial obtuseness, arthritic institutional responses to it, and the feeling, among students of color, that they are tenants rather than stakeholders in their universities." Jelani Cobb, "Race and the Free-Speech Diversion," *New Yorker*, November 10, 2015, https://www.newyorker.com/news/news-desk/race-and-the-free-speech-diversion.

51. Carl Takei, "Colleges and Universities Have a Racial Profiling Problem," *American Civil Liberties Union*, September 21, 2018, https://www.aclu.org/blog/racial-justice/race-and-inequality-education/colleges-and-universities-have-racial-profiling.

52. Marianna Najman-Franks and Karen Xia, "Black Columbia Student Physically Restrained on Countertop by Barnard Public Safety Requesting to See CUID," *Columbia Spectator*, April 12, 2019, https://www.columbiaspectator.com/news/2019/04/12/black-columbia-student-physically-restrained-on-countertop-by-barnard-public-safety-requesting-to-see-cuid/.

53. Brian N. Williams, Andrea M. Headley, Megan LePere-Schloop, "Smith College Incident Is Latest Case of Racial 'Profiling by Proxy,'" *The Conversation*, August 7, 2018, https://theconversation.com/smith-college-incident-is-latest-case-of-racial-profiling-by-proxy-101156; and Britton O'Daly, "Black Student Reported to YPD for Napping in Dormitory Common Room," *Yale Daily News*, May 8, 2018, https://yaledailynews.com/blog/2018/05/08/black-student-reported-to-ypd-for-napping-in-dormitory-common-room/.

54. Lukianoff and Haidt, *Coddling of the American Mind*, 103.

55. Lukianoff and Haidt, *Coddling of the American Mind*, 103.

56. As Brown explains,

> When the ideal or practice of tolerance is substituted for justice or
> equality, when sensitivity to or even respect for the other is substi-
> tuted for justice to the other, when historically induced suffering is
> reduced to "difference" or to a medium of "offense," when suffering
> as such is reduced to a problem of personal feeling, then the field
> of political battle and political transformation is replaced with an
> agenda of behavioral, attitudinal, and emotional practices.

    Wendy Brown, *Regulating Aversion: Tolerance in the Age of Identity
    and Empire* (Princeton, N.J.: Princeton University Press, 2006), 16.

57. Rei Terada suggests that much of what is at stake in the discourse of
    coddling kids is an unfamiliar sense of vulnerability on the part of pro-
    fessors who were accustomed to institutional protections. She sees
    this in particular in Laura Kipnis's reaction to finding herself the sub-
    ject of a formal legal complaint that threatened her job:

> Kipnis's original essay contends that "it's just as likely that a stu-
> dent can derail a professor's career *these days* as the other way
> around" ("Sexual Paranoia"; my italics), and at length this turn-
> about seems to be much of the problem. It's shocking to Kipnis
> that due to the animosities, "a tenured professor on [her] campus"
> might now lie "awake at night worrying" about losing her job ("My
> Title IX"); but the novelty of the experience suggests that the ten-
> ured professor does not lie awake worrying about others' losses, and
> doesn't find them intolerable."

    Rei Terada, "Recrimination and Ruined Hope," *New Inquiry*,
    May 31, 2015, https://thenewinquiry.com/blog/recrimination-and
    -ruined-hope/.

58. "A Letter on Justice and Open Debate," *Harper's Magazine.*

59. Osita Nwanevu, "The Willful Blindness of Reactionary Liberalism,"
    New Republic, July 6, 2020, https://newrepublic.com/article/158346
    /willful-blindness-reactionary-liberalism.

BIBLIOGRAPHY

Abdel-Fadil, Mona. "The Politics of Affect: The Glue of Religious and Identity Conflicts in Social Media." *Journal of Religion, Media, and Digital Culture* 8, no. 1 (2019): 11–34.

Abrahamian, Ervand. "The US Media, Huntington, and September 11." *Third World Quarterly* 24, no. 3 (June 2003): 529–544.

Adcock, C. S. "Violence, Passion, and the Law: A Brief History of Section 295A and Its Antecedents." *Journal of the American Academy of Religion* 84, no. 2 (June 2016): 337–351.

Agamben, Giorgio. *Profanations.* Trans. Jeff Fort. New York: Zone, 2007.

——. *State of Exception.* Trans. Kevin Attell. Chicago: University of Chicago Press, 2005.

Agius, Christine. "Performing Identity: The Danish Cartoon Controversy and Discourses of Identity and Security," *Security Dialogue* 44, no. 3 (June 2013): 241–258.

Ahmed, Sara. "Affective Economies." *Social Text* 22, no. 2 (Summer 2004): 117–139.

——. *On Being Included: Racism and Diversity in Institutional Life.* Durham, N.C.: Duke University Press, 2012.

Alexander, Paul. "Trump Towers." *The Advocate*, February 15, 2000.

Allcott, Hunt, and Matthew Gentzkow. "Social Media and Fake News in the 2016 Election," *Journal of Economic Perspectives* 31, no. 2 (Spring 2017): 211–236.

Altman, Michael J. "'Religion, Religions, Religious' in America: Toward a Smithian Account of Evangelicalism." *Method and Theory in the Study of Religion* 31, no. 1 (2019): 71–82.

Ammerman, Nancy T. "Golden Rule Christianity: Lived Religion in the American Mainstream." In *Lived Religion in America*, edited by David D. Hall, 196–216. Princeton, N.J.: Princeton University Press, 1997.

Anderson, Luvell, and Ernie Lepore. "Slurring Words." *Noûs* 47, no. 1 (March 2013): 25–48.

Anghie, Antony. *Imperialism, Sovereignty and the Making of International Law*. New York: Cambridge University Press, 2004.

Angrosino, Michael. "Civil Religion Redux." *Anthropological Quarterly* 75, no. 2 (Spring 2002): 239–267.

Asad, Talal. "Free Speech, Blasphemy, and Secular Criticism." In *Is Critique Secular? Blasphemy, Injury, and Free Speech*, by Talal Asad, Wendy Brown, Judith Butler, and Saba Mahmood, 20–63. Berkeley: University of California Press, 2009.

——. *Secular Translations: Nation-State, Modern Self, and Calculative Reason*. New York: Columbia University Press, 2018.

Badiou, Alain. *Trump*. Trans. Joseph Litvak. Medford, Mass.: Polity, 2019.

Baker, Kelly J. *Sexism Ed: Essays on Gender and Labor in Academia*. Chapel Hill, N.C.: Blue Crow, 2018.

Bannon, Stephen K., dir. *Generation Zero*. Washington, D.C.: Citizens United, 2010.

——, dir. *Occupy Unmasked*. Washington, D.C.: Citizens United, 2012.

——, dir. *The Undefeated*. Washington, D.C.: Victory Film Group, 2011.

Barba, Lloyd D. "Trump's Wall: A Monument of (Un)Civil Religion?" Mediation, *MAVCOR Journal* 3, no. 1 (2019). http://dx.doi.org/10.22332/mav.med.2019.1.

Barton, Carlin A., and Daniel Boyarin. *Imagine No Religion: How Modern Abstractions Hide Ancient Realities*. New York: Fordham University Press, 2016.

Bayart, Jean-François. *The Illusion of Cultural Identity*. Trans. Steven Rendall, Janet Roitman, Cynthia Schoch, and Jonathan Derrick. Chicago: University of Chicago Press, 2005.

Bean, Lydia. *The Politics of Evangelical Identity: Local Churches and Partisan Divides in the United States and Canada*. Princeton, N.J.: Princeton University Press, 2014.

Bebbington, D. W. *Evangelicalism in Modern Britain: A History from the 1730s to the 1860s*. New York: Routledge, 1988.

Bederman, Gail. *Manliness and Civilization: A Cultural History of Gender and Race in the United States, 1880–1917.* Chicago: University of Chicago Press, 1995.

Bejan, Teresa. *Mere Civility: Disagreement and the Limits of Toleration.* Cambridge, Mass.: Harvard University Press, 2017.

Bellah, Robert. *The Broken Covenant: American Civil Religion in a Time of Trial.* 2nd ed. Chicago: University of Chicago Press, 1992.

——. "Civil Religion in America." *Daedalus* 96, no. 1 (Winter 1967): 1–14.

Ben-Porath, Sigal R. *Free Speech on Campus.* Philadelphia: University of Pennsylvania Press, 2017.

Benjamin, Walter. "Capitalism as Religion." Trans. Rodney Livingstone. In *Walter Benjamin: Selected Writings,* vol. 1, ed. Marcus Bullock and Michael W. Jennings, 288–291. Cambridge, Mass.: Harvard University Press, 1996.

——. "Critique of Violence." Tran. Harry Zohn. In *Walter Benjamin, Selected Writings,* vol. 1, ed. Marcus Bullock and Michael W. Jennings, 236–252. Cambridge, Mass.: Harvard University Press, 1996.

——. "On the Concept of History." Trans. Harry Zohn. In *Walter Benjamin: Selected Writings,* vol. 4, ed. Howard Eiland and Michael W. Jennings, 389–400. Cambridge, Mass.: Harvard University Press, 2003.

——. "The Work of Art in the Age of Mechanical Reproduction." Trans. Harry Zohn. In *Illuminations,* ed. Hannah Arendt, 69–82. New York: Schocken, 1985.

Bennett, Michael, and Dave Zirin. *Things That Make White People Uncomfortable.* Chicago: Haymarket, 2018.

Berezin, Mabel. "On the Construction Sites of History: Where Did Donald Trump Come From?" *American Journal of Cultural Sociology* 5, no. 3 (2017): 322–337.

Berlant, Lauren. "Big Man." *Social Text Online,* January 19, 2017. https://socialtextjournal.org/big-man/.

——. *The Queen of America Goes to Washington City: Essays on Sex and Citizenship.* Durham, N.C.: Duke University Press, 1997.

Berry, Wendell. *Sex, Economy, Freedom, and Community.* New York: Pantheon, 1993.

Bivins, Jason C. *Embattled Majority: Religion and Its Despisers in America.* New York: Oxford University Press, forthcoming.

———. *Religion of Fear: The Politics of Horror in Conservative Evangelicalism.* New York: Oxford University Press, 2008.

Bjork-James, Sophie. *The Divine Institution: White Evangelicalism's Politics of the Family.* New Brunswick, N.J.: Rutgers University Press, 2020.

Boyer, Pascal. *Religion Explained: The Evolutionary Origins of Religious Thought.* New York: Basic Books, 2001.

Braunstein, Ruth. "Boundary Work and the Demarcation of Civil from Uncivil Protest in the United States: Control, Legitimacy, and Political Inequality." *Theory and Society* 47, no. 5 (October 2018): 603–633.

Brittain, Christopher Craig. "Racketeering in Religion: Adorno and Evangelical Support for Trump." *Critical Research on Religion* 6, no. 3 (2018): 269–288.

Brophy, Sorcha A. "Orthodoxy as Project: Temporality and Action in an American Protestant Denomination." *Sociology of Religion* 77, no. 2 (2016): 123–143.

Brown, Wendy. *In the Ruins of Neoliberalism: The Rise of Antidemocratic Politics in the West.* New York: Columbia University Press, 2019.

———. *Regulating Aversion: Tolerance in the Age of Identity and Empire.* Princeton, N.J.: Princeton University Press, 2006.

Brubaker, Rogers. "Between Nationalism and Civilizationalism: The European Populist Movement in Comparative Perspective." *Ethnic and Racial Studies* 40, no. 8 (2017): 1191–1226.

Busto, Rudiger V. "'In the Outer Boundaries:' Pentecostalism, Politics, and Reies López Tijerina's Civic Activism." In *Latino Religions and Civic Activism in the United States,* ed. Gastón Espinosa, Virgilio P. Elisondo, and Jesse Miranda, 65–75. New York: Oxford University Press, 2005.

Butler, Anthea. *White Evangelical Racism: The Politics of Morality in America.* Chapel Hill: University of North Carolina Press, 2021.

Callahan, Richard J., Jr. "The Study of American Religion: Looming Through the Glim." *Religion* 42, no. 3 (2012): 425–437.

Capó Crucet, Jennine. *My Time Among the Whites: Notes from an Unfinished Education.* New York: Picador, 2019.

Carpenter, C. C. J., Joseph A. Durick, Milton L. Grafman, Paul Hardin, Nolan B. Harmon, George M. Murray, Edward V. Ramage, and Earl Stallings. "Letter to Martin Luther King," April 12, 1963. Reprinted at *Teaching American History.* https://teachingamericanhistory.org/library/document/letter-to-martin-luther-king/.

Carter, Graydon. "Steel Traps and Short Fingers." *Vanity Fair*, October 17, 2015. https://www.vanityfair.com/culture/2015/10/graydon-carter-donald -trump.

Casanova, José. *Public Religions in the Modern World*. Chicago: University of Chicago Press, 1994.

———. "Religion, European Secular Identities, and European Integration." In *Religion in an Expanding Europe*, ed. Timothy A. Byrnes and Peter J. Katznelson, 65–92. New York: Cambridge University Press, 2006.

Case, Mary Ann. "Why 'Live and Let Live' Is Not a Viable Solution to the Difficult Problems of Religious Accommodation in the Age of Sexual Civil Rights." *Southern California Law Review* 88 (2015): 463–492.

Chemerinsky, Erwin, and Howard Gillman. *Free Speech on Campus*. New Haven, Conn.: Yale University Press, 2017.

Chidester, David, and Edward T. Linenthal, eds. *American Sacred Space*. Bloomington: Indiana University Press, 1995.

Chua, Amy. *Political Tribes: Group Instinct and the Fate of Nations*. New York: Penguin, 2018.

Claassen, Ryan L. "Understanding the Political Motivations of Evangelical Voters." In *The Evangelical Crackup? The Future of the Evangelical-Republican Coalition*, ed. Paul A. Djupe and Ryan L. Claassen, 49–62. Philadelphia: Temple University Press, 2018.

Cobb, Jelani. "Georgia, Trump's Insurrectionists, and Lost Causes." *New Yorker*, January 8, 2021. https://www.newyorker.com/news/daily-comment /georgia-trumps-insurrectionists-and-lost-causes.

———. "Race and the Free-Speech Diversion." *New Yorker*, November 10, 2015. https://www.newyorker.com/news/news-desk/race-and-the-free -speech-diversion.

Cohen, Jean L. "Freedom of Religion, Inc.: Whose Sovereignty." *Netherlands Journal of Legal Philosophy* 44, no. 3 (2015): 169–210.

Cole, Teju. "Unmournable Bodies." *New Yorker*, January 9, 2015. https://www .newyorker.com/culture/cultural-comment/unmournable-bodies.

Connolly, William E. *Christianity and Capitalism, American Style*. Durham, N.C.: Duke University Press, 2008.

———. "Trump, the Working Class, and Fascist Rhetoric." *Theory and Event* 20, no. 1 (January 2017): 23–37.

Cooper, Melinda. *Family Values: Between Neoliberalism and the New Social Conservatism*. New York: Zone, 2017.

Cox, Daniel, and Robert P. Jones. "The High Correlation Between Percentage of White Christians, Support for Trump in Key States." *Public Religion Research Institute*, November 17, 2016. https://www.prri.org/spotlight/trump-triumphed-white-christian-states.

Danchin, Peter. "Defaming Muhammad: Dignity, Harm, and Incitement to Religious Hatred." *Duke Forum for Law and Social Change* 2 (2010): 5–38.

Danielson, Leilah. "Civil Religion as Myth, Not History." *Religions* 10, no. 6 (2019): 374–389.

Davidson, Donald. *Inquiries into Truth and Interpretation*. New York: Oxford University Press, 1984.

DeHanas, Daniel Nilsson, and Marat Shterin. "Religion and the Rise of Populism." *Religion, State, and Society* 46, no. 3 (2018): 177–185.

Dennett, Daniel C. *Breaking the Spell: Religion as a Natural Phenomenon*. New York: Penguin, 2006.

Derks, Marco. "Conscientious Objectors and the Marrying Kind: Rights and Rites in Dutch Public Discourse on Marriage Registrars with Conscientious Objections against Conducting Same-Sex Weddings." *Theology and Sexuality* 23 (2017): 209–228.

Derrida, Jacques. *Of Grammatology*. Trans. Gayatri Chakravorty Spivak. Baltimore: Johns Hopkins University Press, 1997.

Dewey, John. *Liberalism and Social Action*. 1935. Reprint, Amherst, N.Y.: Prometheus, 2000.

Dick, Hannah. "Framing Faith During the 2016 Election: Journalistic Coverage of the Trump Campaign and the Myth of the Evangelical Schism." In *Evangelicals and Presidential Politics: From Jimmy Carter to Donald Trump*, ed. Andrew S. Moore, 166–184. Baton Rouge: Louisiana State University Press, 2021.

Du Mez, Kristin Kobes. *Jesus and John Wayne: How Evangelicals Corrupted a Faith and Captured a Nation*. New York: Liveright, 2020.

Durkheim, Émile. *The Elementary Forms of Religious Life*. 1912. Trans. Karen E. Fields. Reprint, New York: Free Press, 1995.

Eatwell, Roger, and Matthew Goodwin. *National Populism: The Revolt Against Liberal Democracy*. New York: Penguin, 2018.

Elias, Norbert. *The Civilizing Process*. Trans. Edmund Jephcott, Ed. Eric Dunning, Johan Goudsblom, and Stephen Mennell. 1939. Reprint, Malden, Mass.: Blackwell, 2000.

Falwell, Jerry. *Listen, America!* New York: Bantam, 1980.

Fassin, Didier. "In the Name of the Republic: Untimely Meditations on the Aftermath of the Charlie Hebdo Attack." *Anthropology Today* 31, no. 2 (April 2015): 3–7.

Fea, John. *Believe Me: The Evangelical Road to Donald Trump.* Grand Rapids, Mich.: Eerdmans, 2018.

Fekete, Liz. "Hungary: Power, Punishment, and the 'Christian-National Idea.'" *Race & Class* 57, no. 4 (2016): 39–53.

Fish, Stanley. *The First: How to Think About Hate Speech, Campus Speech, Religious Speech, Fake News, Post-Truth, and Donald Trump.* New York: One Signal, 2019.

——. *There's No Such Thing as Free Speech: And It's a Good Thing Too.* New York: Oxford University Press, 1994.

Flanagan, Caitlin. "That's Not Funny!" *Atlantic,* September 2015. https:// www.theatlantic.com/magazine/archive/2015/09/thats-not-funny/399335/.

Frank, Thomas. *What's the Matter with Kansas? How Conservatives Won the Heart of America.* New York: Holt, 2005.

French, David. *FIRE's Guide to Religious Liberty on Campus.* Philadelphia: Foundation for Individual Rights in Education, 2002. http://thefire.org /public/pdfs/religious-liberty.pdf.

Fukuyama, Francis. "Against Identity Politics: The New Tribalism and the Crisis of Democracy." *Foreign Affairs* 97, no. 5 (September/October 2018): 90–114.

Furniss, Norman F. *The Fundamentalist Controversy, 1918–1931.* Hamden, Conn.: Archon, 1963.

Galli, Mark. "Trump Should Be Removed from Office." *Christianity Today,* December 19, 2019. https://www.christianitytoday.com/ct/2019/december -web-only/trump-should-be-removed-from-office.html.

Geller, Jay. "The Godfather of Psychoanalysis: Circumcisions, Antisemitism, and Freud's 'Fighting Jew,'" *Journal of the American Academy of Religion* 67, no. 2 (June 1999): 355–385.

Gerson, Michael. "The Last Temptation." *Atlantic Monthly,* April 2018. https://www.theatlantic.com/magazine/archive/2018/04/the-last -temptation/554066/.

Gessen, Masha. "Donald Trump's Inoffensive War on Reality." *New Yorker,* July 5, 2019. https://www.newyorker.com/news/our-columnists/donald -trumps-inoffensive-war-on-reality.

Ging, Debbie. "Alphas, Betas, and Incels: Theorizing the Masculinities of the Manosphere," *Men and Masculinities* 22, no. 4 (2019): 638–657.

Glaude, Eddie S., Jr. *Democracy in Black: How Race Still Enslaves the American Soul*. New York: Crown, 2016.

Glickman, Lawrence B. "Don't Let Them Eat Cake." *Boston Review*, June 7, 2018. https://bostonreview.net/law-justice/lawrence-glickman-masterpiece-cakeshop.

Goldberg, Jeffrey. "Trump: Americans Who Died in War Are 'Losers' and 'Suckers.'" *Atlantic*, September 3, 2020. https://www.theatlantic.com/politics/archive/2020/09/trump-americans-who-died-at-war-are-losers-and-suckers/615997/.

Goldstein, Warren. "Trump, the Religious Right, and the Spectre of Fascism." *Critical Research on Religion* 9, no. 1 (April 2021): 3–7.

Goodwyn, Lawrence. *The Populist Moment: A Short History of the Agrarian Revolt in America*. New York: Oxford University Press, 1978.

Gopnik, Adam. "Satire Lives." *New Yorker*, January 19, 2015. https://www.newyorker.com/magazine/2015/01/19/satire-lives.

——. "Trump and Obama: A Night to Remember." *New Yorker*, September 12, 2015. https://www.newyorker.com/news/daily-comment/trump-and-obama-a-night-to-remember.

Gordon, Sarah Barringer. *The Spirit of the Law: Religious Voices in the Constitution in Modern America*. Cambridge, Mass.: Harvard University Press, 2010.

Gorski, Philip. *American Covenant: A History of Civil Religion from the Puritans to the Present*. Princeton, N.J.: Princeton University Press, 2017.

Gosling, Tim. "The Nationalist Internationale Is Crumbling." *Foreign Policy*, July 20, 2018. https://foreignpolicy.com/2018/07/20/the-nationalist-internationale-is-crumbling-steve-bannon-eastern-europe-hungary-czech-republic-slovakia-trade/.

Gottschalk, Peter, and Gabriel Greenberg. *Islamophobia and Anti-Muslim Sentiment: Picturing the Enemy*. 2nd ed. New York: Rowman & Littlefield, 2019.

Graham, David A., Adrienne Green, Cullen Murphy, and Parker Reynolds. "An Oral History of Trump's Bigotry." *Atlantic Monthly*, June 2019.

Green, Joshua. *Devil's Bargain: Steve Bannon, Donald Trump, and the Storming of the Presidency*. New York: Penguin, 2017.

Groll, Elias. "Meet the Man Who Put the 'Je Suis' in the 'Je Suis Charlie." *Foreign Policy*, January 19, 2015. http://foreignpolicy.com/2015/01/19/meet -the-man-who-put-the-je-suis-in-the-je-suis-charlie/.

Gunn, Joshua. "On Political Perversion." *Rhetoric Society Quarterly* 48, no. 2 (2018): 161–186.

Gushee, David. "In the Ruins of White Evangelicalism: Interpreting a Compromised Christian Tradition Through the Witness of African American Literature." *Journal of the American Academy of Religion* 87, no. 1 (March 2019): 1–17.

Haidt, Jonathan. *The Righteous Mind: Why Good People Are Divided by Politics and Religion*. New York: Vintage, 2012.

Hall, Kira, Donna M. Goldstein, and Matthew Bruce Ingram. "The Hands of Donald Trump: Entertainment, Gesture, Spectacle." *HAU: Journal of Ethnographic Theory* 6, no. 2 (Autumn 2016): 71–100.

Harding, Susan Friend. *The Book of Jerry Falwell: Fundamentalist Language and Politics*. Princeton, N.J.: Princeton University Press, 2000.

Hartman, Andrew. *A War for the Soul of America: A History of the Culture Wars*. 2nd ed. Chicago: University of Chicago Press, 2015.

Hartmann, Douglas. *Race, Culture, and the Revolt of the Black Athlete*. Chicago: University of Chicago Press, 2003.

Hawley, Joshua. "The Age of Pelagius," *Christianity Today*, June 4, 2019. https://www.christianitytoday.com/ct/2019/june-web-only/age-of -pelagius-joshua-hawley.html.

Heller, Nathan. "The Big Uneasy." *New Yorker*, March 23, 2016. https://www .newyorker.com/magazine/2016/05/30/the-new-activism-of-liberal-arts -colleges.

Hemmer, Nicole. *Messengers of the Right: Conservative Media and the Transformation of American Politics*. Philadelphia: University of Pennsylvania Press, 2016.

Hill, Jemele. "Kaepernick Won. The NFL Lost." *Atlantic*, February 17, 2019. https://www.theatlantic.com/ideas/archive/2019/02/colin-kaepernick -won-his-settlement-nfl/582994/.

——. "Why Don't White Athletes Understand What's Wrong with Trump?" *Atlantic*, May 7, 2019. https://www.theatlantic.com/ideas /archive/2019/05/red-sox-divided-racial-lines-white-house-visit /588856/.

Hochschild, Arlie Russell. *Strangers in Their Own Land: Anger and Mourning on the American Right.* New York: New Press, 2018.

Howe, Neil, and William Strauss. *The Fourth Turning: What the Cycles of History Tell Us About America's Next Rendezvous with Destiny.* New York: Broadway, 1997.

Howe, Nicolas. *Landscapes of the Secular: Law, Religion, and American Sacred Space.* Chicago: University of Chicago Press, 2016.

Hsu, Hua. "The Year of the Imaginary College Student." *New Yorker,* December 31, 2015. https://www.newyorker.com/culture/cultural-comment/the-year-of-the-imaginary-college-student.

Hunter, James Davison. *Culture Wars: The Struggle to Define America.* New York: Basic Books, 1991.

Huntington, Samuel. "The Clash of Civilizations?" *Foreign Affairs* 72, no. 3 (1993): 21–49.

——. *The Clash of Civilizations and the Remaking of World Order.* New York: Simon & Schuster, 2003.

Imhoff, Sarah. "Belief." In *Religion, Law, USA,* ed. Joshua Dubler and Isaac Weiner, 26–39. New York: New York University Press, 2019.

Ingersoll, Julie J. *Building God's Kingdom: Inside the World of Christian Reconstruction.* New York: Oxford University Press, 2015.

Jakobsen, Janet R. "Can Homosexuals End Western Civilization as We Know It? Family Values in a Global Economy." In *Queer Globalizations: Citizenship and the Afterlife of Colonialism,* ed. Arnaldo Cruz-Malavé and Martin F. Manalansan, 49–70. New York: New York University Press, 2002.

Jakobsen, Janet R., and Ann Pellegrini. *Love the Sin: Sexual Regulation and the Limits of Tolerance.* Boston: Beacon, 2004.

Jaschik, Scott. "U Chicago to Freshmen: Don't Expect Safe Spaces." *Inside Higher Ed,* August 25, 2016. https://www.insidehighered.com/news/2016/08/25/u-chicago-warns-incoming-students-not-expect-safe-spaces-or-trigger-warnings.

Jefferson, Thomas. *Notes on the State of Virginia.* 1785. Ed. Frank Shuffleton. New York: Penguin, 1999.

Jenkins, Aric. "Read President Trump's NFL Speech on National Anthem Protests." *Time,* September 23, 2017. http://time.com/4954684/donald-trump-nfl-speech-anthem-protests/.

Johnson, Jessica. *Biblical Porn: Affect, Labor, and Pastor Mark Driscoll's Evangelical Empire.* Durham, N.C.: Duke University Press, 2018.

——. "When Hate Circulates on Campus to Uphold Free Speech." *Studies in Law, Politics, and Society* 80 (2019): 113–130.

Johnson, Paul Christopher. "The Fetish and McGwire's Balls." *Journal of the American Academy of Religion* 68, no. 2 (June 2000): 243–264.

Kaveny, Cathleen. "The Ironies of the New Religious Liberty Litigation," *Daedalus* 149, no. 3 (Summer 2020): 72–86.

Kazin, Michael. *The Populist Persuasion: An American History.* Rev. ed. Ithaca, N.Y.: Cornell University Press, 1998.

Keefe, Patrick Radden. "Winning." *New Yorker,* January 7, 2019.

Kidd, Thomas S. *Who Is an Evangelical? The History of a Movement in Crisis.* New Haven, Conn.: Yale University Press, 2019.

King, Martin Luther, Jr. "Letter from Birmingham City Jail." In *A Testament of Hope: The Essential Writings and Speeches of Martin Luther King, Jr.,* ed. James M. Washington, 289–302. San Francisco: Harper-SanFrancisco, 1986.

Kruse, Kevin M. *One Nation Under God: How Corporate American Invented Christian America.* New York: Basic Books, 2016.

Laclau, Ernesto. *On Populist Reason.* New York: Verso, 2005.

Lavin, Talia "When Non-Jews Wield Anti-Semitism as Political Shield." *GQ,* July 17, 2019. https://www.gq.com/story/anti-semitism-political -shield.

Lebron. Christopher J. *The Making of Black Lives Matter: A Brief History of an Idea.* New York: Oxford University Press, 2017.

Landsbaum, Claire. "Donald Trump Uses Albany Rally to Criticize Delegate System Again." *New York Magazine,* April 12, 2016. http://nymag .com/daily/intelligencer/2016/04/trump-criticizes-delegate-system-at -albany-rally.html.

Lemann, Nicholas. "'Vice' vs. the Real Dick Cheney." *New Yorker,* January 3, 2019. https://www.newyorker.com/news/daily-comment/vice-vs-the-real -dick-cheney.

Lepistö, Antti. *The Rise of Common-Sense Conservatism: The American Right and the Reinvention of the Scottish Enlightenment.* Chicago: University of Chicago Press, 2021.

"A Letter on Justice and Open Debate." *Harper's Magazine,* July 7, 2020. https://harpers.org/a-letter-on-justice-and-open-debate/.

Levin, Robert. "Sarah Palin's 'The Undefeated': Bad Propaganda, Worse Filmmaking." *Atlantic,* July 15, 2011. https://www.theatlantic.com

/entertainment/archive/2011/07/sarah-palins-the-undefeated-bad
-propaganda-worse-filmmaking/241975/.

Lewandowski, Corey R., and David N. Bossie. *Let Trump Be Trump: The Inside Story of His Rise to the Presidency*. New York: Hachette, 2017.

Lilla, Mark. *The Once and Future Liberal: After Identity Politics*. New York: Harper, 2017.

Lincoln, Bruce. *Discourse and the Construction of Society: Comparative Studies of Myth, Ritual, and Classification*. New York: Oxford University Press, 1989.

Locke, John. "A Letter Concerning Toleration." In *Locke on Toleration*, ed. Richard Vernon, 3–46. New York: Cambridge University Press, 2010.

——. *Two Treatises of Government*. Ed. Peter Laslett. 1698. Reprint, New York: Cambridge University Press, 1988.

Lofton, Kathryn. *Consuming Religion*. Chicago: University of Chicago Press, 2017.

Long, Charles. *Significations: Signs, Symbols, and Images in the Interpretation of Religion*. Philadelphia: Fortress, 1986.

Lukianoff, Greg, and Jonathan Haidt. "The Coddling of the American Mind." *Atlantic Monthly*, September 2015. https://www.theatlantic.com /magazine/archive/2015/09/the-coddling-of-the-american-mind /399356/.

——. *The Coddling of the American Mind: How Good Intentions and Bad Ideas Are Setting Up a Generation for Failure*. New York: Penguin, 2018.

Machen, J. Gresham. *Christianity and Liberalism*. 1923. New ed. Grand Rapids, Mich.: Eerdmans, 2009.

MacKinnon, Catherine A. *Only Words*. Cambridge: Harvard University Press, 1996.

Mahmood, Saba. "Religious Reason and Secular Affect: An Incommensurable Divide?" In *Is Critique Secular? Blasphemy, Injury, and Free Speech*, by Talal Asad, Wendy Brown, Judith Butler, and Saba Mahmood, 64–92. Berkeley: University of California Press, 2009.

Mann, Lucas. "The Problem with Calling Trump a 'Reality-TV President.'" *Atlantic*, April 30, 2018. https://www.theatlantic.com/entertainment /archive/2018/04/what-exactly-makes-trump-a-reality-tv-president /558626/.

March, Andrew. "Speech and the Sacred: Does the Defense of Free Speech Rest on a Mistake about Religion?" *Political Theory* 40, no 3 (2012): 319–346.

Marsden, George M. *Fundamentalism and American Culture*. 2nd ed. New York: Oxford University Press, 2006.

———. *Reforming Fundamentalism: Fuller Seminary and the New Evangelicalism*. Grand Rapids, Mich.: Eerdmans, 1987.

———. *Understanding Fundamentalism and Evangelicalism*. Grand Rapids, Mich.: Eerdmans, 1991.

Martí, Gerardo. "The Unexpected Orthodoxy of Donald J. Trump: White Evangelical Support for the 45th President of the United States." *Sociology of Religion* 80, no. 1 (Spring 2019):1–8.

Martinéz, Jessica, and Gregory A. Smith. "How the Faithful Voted: A Preliminary 2016 Analysis." *Pew Research Center*, November 9, 2016. https://www.pewresearch.org/fact-tank/2016/11/09/how-the-faithful-voted-a -preliminary-2016-analysis/.

Marx, Karl, and Friedrich Engels. *The Communist Manifesto*. 1848. Reprint, New York: Signet Classic, 1998.

Marzouki, Nadia. *Islam: An American Religion*. Trans. C. Jon Delogu. New York: Columbia University Press, 2017.

Masuzawa, Tomoko. *The Invention of World Religions; Or, How European Universalism Was Preserved in the Language of Pluralism*. Chicago: University of Chicago Press, 2005.

May, Henry F. *The Enlightenment in America*. New York: Oxford University Press, 1976.

Mbembe, Achille. *Necropolitics*. Durham, N.C.: Duke University Press, 2019.

McCloud, Sean. "Popular Culture Fandoms, the Boundaries of Religious Studies, and the Project of the Self." *Culture and Religion* 4, no. 2 (2003): 187–206.

McIvor, Méadhbh. *Representing God: Christian Legal Activism in Contemporary England*. Princeton, N.J.: Princeton University Press, 2020.

McVicar, Michael J. *Christian Reconstruction: R. J. Rushdoony and American Religious Conservatism*. Chapel Hill: University of North Carolina Press, 2015.

Mead, Walter Russell. "The Jacksonian Revolt: American Populism and the Liberal Order." *Foreign Affairs* 96, no. 2 (March/April 2017): 2–7.

Michaels, Tony. "Donald Trump and the Triumph of Antiliberalism." *Jewish Social Studies* 22, no. 3 (Spring/Summer 2017): 186–192.

Mill, John Stuart. *On Liberty*. 1859. Ed. Alburey Castell. Arlington Heights, Ill.: Harland Davidson, 1947.

Miller, Laura. "How to Be Bad," *Slate*, January 28, 2019. https://slate.com /culture/2019/01/transgressive-art-political-correctness-vanessa-place -louis-ck-hannah-gadsby.html.

Mishra, Pankaj. *Age of Anger: A History of the Present*. New York: Farrar, Straus and Giroux, 2017.

——. *Bland Fanatics: Liberals, Race, and Empire*. New York: Farrar, Straus and Giroux, 2020.

Modal, Anshuman A. *Islam and Controversy: The Politics of Free Speech after Rushdie*. New York: Palgrave Macmillan, 2014.

Modern, John Lardas. *Secularism in Antebellum America*. Chicago: University of Chicago Press, 2011.

Moore, Roy, with John Perry. *So Help Me God: The Ten Commandments, Judicial Tyranny, and the Battle for Religious Freedom*. Nashville: Broadman and Holman, 2005.

Morozov, Evgeny. *The Net Delusion: The Dark Side of Internet Freedom*. New York: Public Affairs, 2011.

Mouffe, Chantal. "The 'End of Politics' and the Challenge of Right-Wing Populism." In *Populism and the Mirror of Democracy*, ed. Francisco Panizza, 50–71. New York: Verso, 2005.

Muirhead, Russell, and Nancy L. Rosenblum. *A Lot of People Are Saying: The New Conspiracism and the Assault on Democracy*. Princeton, N.J.: Princeton University Press, 2019.

Müller, Jan-Werner. *What Is Populism?* Philadelphia: University of Pennsylvania Press, 2016.

Mutz, Diana C. "Status Threat, Not Economic Hardship, Explains the 2016 Presidential Vote." *PNAS* 115, no. 19 (2018): 4330–4339. www.pnas.org/cgi /doi/10.1073/pnas.1718155115.

Nacos, Brigitte L., Robert Y. Shapiro, and Yaeli Bloch-Elkon. "Donald Trump: Aggressive Rhetoric and Political Violence." *Perspectives on Terrorism* 14, no. 5 (October 2020): 2–25.

Nancy, Jean-Luc. "Church, State, Resistance." *Journal of Law and Society* 34, no. 1 (March 2007): 3–13.

Nejaime, Douglas, and Reva B. Siegel. "Conscience Wars: Complicity-Based Conscience Claims in Religion and Politics." *Yale Law Journal* 124, no. 7 (2015): 2516–2591.

Neville-Shepard, Ryan. "Post-Presumption Argumentation and the Post-Truth World: On the Conspiracy Rhetoric of Donald Trump." *Argumentation and Advocacy* 55, no. 3 (2019): 175–193.

Ngai, Sianne. *Ugly Feelings*. Cambridge, Mass.: Harvard University Press, 2005.

Noble, Safiya Umoja. *Algorithms of Oppression: How Search Engines Reinforce Racism*. New York: New York University Press, 2018.

Noll, Mark A. *The Rise of Evangelicalism: The Age of Edwards, Whitefield and the Wesleys*. Downers Grove, Ill.: InterVarsity, 2003.

Norris, Pippa, and Ronald Inglehart. *Cultural Backlash: Trump, Brexit, and Authoritarian Populism*. New York: Cambridge University Press, 2019.

Novak, Michael. *The Joy of Sports: End Zones, Bases, Baskets, Balls, and the Consecration of the American Spirit*. Rev. ed. Lanham, Md.: Madison, 1994.

Nussbaum, Emily. "Last Girl in Larchmont." *New Yorker*, February 16, 2015. https://www.newyorker.com/magazine/2015/02/23/last-girl-larchmont.

Nwanevu, Osita. "The Willful Blindness of Reactionary Liberalism." *New Republic*, July 6, 2020. https://newrepublic.com/article/158346/willful-blindness-reactionary-liberalism.

Ott, Brian L., and Greg Dickinson. *The Twitter Presidency: Donald J. Trump and the Politics of White Rage*. New York: Routledge, 2019.

Paine, Thomas. *Common Sense*. 1776. Reprint, Mineola: Dover, 1997.

Peck, Reece. *Fox Populism: Branding Conservatism as Working Class*. New York: Cambridge University Press, 2019.

Pham, Larissa. "The Architecture of Racism at Yale University." *Guernica*, November 18, 2015. https://www.guernicamag.com/larissa-pham-the-architecture-of-racism-at-yale-university/.

Phillips, Jack. *The Cost of My Faith: How a Decision in My Cake Shop Took Me to the Supreme Court*. Washington, D.C.: Salem, 2021.

Posner, Sarah. "An Army of Christian Lawyers." *The Nation*, January 1–8, 2018.

Postel, Charles. *The Populist Vision*. New York: Oxford University Press, 2007.

powell, john a. "As Justice Requires/Permits: The Delimitation of Harmful Speech in a Democratic Society." *Law and Inequality* 16, no. 1 (1998): 97–151.

Pritchard, Elizabeth. "Seriously, What Does 'Taking Religion Seriously' Mean?" *Journal of the American Academy of Religion* 78, no. 4 (December 2010): 1087–1110.

Puar, Jasbir K. *Terrorist Assemblages: Homonationalism in Queer Times*. Exp. ed. Durham, N.C.: Duke University Press, 2017.

Ransby, Barbara. *Making All Black Lives Matter: Reimagining Freedom in the 21st Century*. Berkeley: University of California Press, 2018.

Rawls, John. *Political Liberalism*. New York: Columbia University Press, 1996.

Read, Max. "How Much of the Internet Is Fake? Turns Out, a Lot of It, Actually." *New York Magazine*, December 26, 2018. http://nymag.com /intelligencer/2018/12/how-much-of-the-internet-is-fake.html.

Reid, Thomas. *An Inquiry into the Human Mind on the Principles of Common Sense*. 1764. Ed. Derek R. Brookes. University Park: Pennsylvania State Press, 2000.

Rich, Frank. "In Conversation." *New York Magazine*, December 1, 2014. https://www.vulture.com/2014/11/chris-rock-frank-rich-in-conversation .html.

Robin, Corey. *The Reactionary Mind: Conservatism from Edmund Burke to Donald Trump*. 2nd ed. New York: Oxford University Press, 2018.

Robinson, Jackie, as told to Alfred Duckett. *I Never Had It Made*. New York: Putnam, 1972.

Rolsky, L. Benjamin. "Colin Kaepernick, Religion, and the Academic Think Piece." *Marginalia: Los Angeles Review of Books*, September 10, 2016.

——. *The Rise and Fall of the Religious Left: Politics, Television, and Popular Culture in the 1970s and Beyond*. New York: Columbia University Press, 2019.

Ronson, Jon. *So You've Been Publicly Shamed*. New York: Riverhead, 2015.

Ross, Alex. "The Frankfurt School Knew Donald Trump Was Coming." *New Yorker*, December 5, 2016. https://www.newyorker.com/culture /cultural-comment/the-frankfurt-school-knew-trump-was-coming.

Roth, Michael S. *Safe Enough Spaces: A Pragmatist's Approach to Inclusion, Free Speech, and Political Correctness on College Campuses*. New Haven, Conn.: Yale University Press, 2019.

Rousseau, Jean-Jacques. *The Social Contract and Discourses*. Trans. G. D. H. Cole. New York: Everyman's Library, 1973.

Said, Edward W. "A Clash of Ignorance." *The Nation*, October 4, 2001. https://www.thenation.com/article/clash-ignorance/.

Schaefer, Donovan. "Whiteness and Civilization: Shame, Race, and the Rhetoric of Donald Trump." *Communication and Critical/Cultural Studies* 17, no 1 (2020): 1–18.

Schonthal, Benjamin. "Environments of Law: Islam, Buddhism, and the State in Contemporary Sri Lanka." *Journal of Asian Studies* 75, no. 1 (February 2016): 137–156.

Scott, Joan Wallach. *Sex and Secularism*. Princeton, N.J.: Princeton University Press, 2018.

Seligman, Adam B., Robert P. Weller, Michael J. Puett, and Bennett Simon. *Ritual and Its Consequences: An Essay on the Limits of Sincerity*. New York: Oxford University Press, 2008.

Serazio, Michael. *The Power of Sports: Media and Spectacle in American Culture*. New York: New York University Press, 2019.

Shapiro, Ben. *Facts Don't Care About Your Feelings*. Hermosa Beach, Calif.: Creators, 2019.

Shapiro, Judith. "From Strength to Strength." *Inside Higher Ed*, December 15, 2014. https://www.insidehighered.com/views/2014/12/15/essay-importance -not-trying-protect-students-everything-may-upset-them.

Shatz, Adam. "'Orientalism' Then and Now." *New York Review of Books*, May 20, 2019. https://www.nybooks.com/daily/2019/05/20/orientalism -then-and-now/.

Sides, John, Michael Tesler, and Lynn Vavreck. "The 2016 U.S. Election: How Trump Lost and Won." *Journal of Democracy* 28, no. 2 (April 2017): 34–44.

Silverstein, Paul A. "Sporting Faith: Islam, Soccer, and the French Nation-State." *Social Text* 18, no. 4 (Winter 2000): 25–53.

Slobodian, Quinn. *Globalists: The End of Empire and the Birth of Neoliberalism*. Cambridge, Mass.: Harvard University Press, 2018.

Smith, Gregory A., and Jessica Martinez, "How the Faithful Voted: A Preliminary 2016 Analysis." *Pew Research Center*, November 9, 2016. https:// www.pewresearch.org/fact-tank/2016/11/09/how-the-faithful-voted-a -preliminary-2016-analysis/.

Smith, Jamil. "Trump, Guns, and White Fragility." *Rolling Stone*, January 23, 2020. https://www.rollingstone.com/politics/political-commentary /richmond-gun-rally-trump-impeachment-mitch-mcconnell-941512/.

Smith, Jonathan Z. *Imagining Religion: From Babylon to Jonestown*. Chicago: University of Chicago Press, 1982.

Smith, Leslie Dorrough. *Compromising Positions: Sex Scandals, Politics, and American Christianity*. New York: Oxford University Press, 2020.

——. *Righteous Rhetoric: Sex, Speech, and the Politics of Concerned Women for America*. New York: Oxford University Press, 2014.

Smith, William S. "Samuel Huntington Was Not Like Steve Bannon." *Center for the Study of Statesmanship*. https://css.cua.edu/ideas_and_com-mentary/samuel-huntington-was-not-like-steve-bannon/.

Sobieraj, Sarah, and Jeffrey M. Berry. "From Incivility to Outrage: Political Discourse in Blogs, Talk Radio, and Cable News." *Political Communication* 28, no. 1 (2011): 19–41.

Stanley, Jason. *How Fascism Works: The Politics of Us and Them*. New York: Random House, 2018.

Sullivan, Winnifred Fallers. *Church State Corporation: Construing Religion in US Law*. Chicago: University of Chicago Press, 2020.

Sultana, Farhana. "The False Equivalence of Academic Freedom and Free Speech: Defending Academic Integrity in the Age of White Supremacy, Colonial Nostalgia, and Anti-Intellectualism." *ACME: An International Journal for Critical Geographies* 17, no. 2 (2018): 228–257.

Taussig, Michael. *Defacement: Public Secrecy and the Labor of the Negative*. Stanford, Calif.: Stanford University Press, 1999.

——. "Transgression." In *Critical Terms for Religious Studies*, ed. Mark C. Taylor, 349–364. Chicago: University of Chicago Press, 1998.

——. "Viscerality, Faith, and Skepticism: Another Theory of Magic." In *In Near Ruins: Cultural Theory at the End of the Century*, ed. Nicholas B. Dirks, 221–256. Minneapolis: University of Minnesota Press, 1998.

Taves, Ann. *Religious Experience Reconsidered: A Building-Block Approach to the Study of Religion and Other Special Things*. Princeton, N.J.: Princeton University Press, 2009.

Taylor, Keeanga-Yamahtta. *How We Get Free: Black Feminism and the Combahee River Collective*. Chicago: Haymarket, 2017.

Telle, Kari. "Faith on Trial: Blasphemy and 'Lawfare' in Indonesia." *Ethnos* 83, no. 2 (2018): 371–391.

Tisby, Jemar. *The Color of Compromise: The Truth About the American Church's Complicity in Racism*. Grand Rapids, Mich.: Zondervan, 2019.

Titley, Gavan. *Is Free Speech Racist?* Medford, Mass.: Polity, 2020.

Tolentino, Jia. *Trick Mirror: Reflections on Self-Delusion*. New York: Random House, 2020.

Trudeau, Garry. "The Abuse of Satire." *Atlantic Monthly*, April 11, 2015. https://www.theatlantic.com/international/archive/2015/04/the-abuse -of-satire/390312/.

Trump, Donald J., with Meredith McIver. *How to Get Rich*. New York: Ballentine, 2004.

Trump, Donald J., with Tony Schwartz. *Trump: The Art of the Deal*. New York: Ballantine, 1987.

Tufekci, Zeynep. *Twitter and Tear Gas: The Power and Fragility of Networked Protest*. New Haven, Conn.: Yale University Press, 2017.

Vauclair, Jane Weston. "Local Laughter, Global Politics: Understanding Charlie Hebdo." *European Comic Art* 8, no. 1 (Spring 2015): 6–14.

Waggoner, Kristen. "Supreme Court Leaves Americans Guessing about the Meaning of Tolerance." *Newsweek*, July 7, 2021. https://www.newsweek.com/supreme-court-leaves-americans-guessing-about-meaning-tolerance-opinion-1607243.

Waldron, Jeremy. *The Harm in Hate Speech*. Cambridge: Harvard University Press, 2012.

Warner, Michael. *Publics and Counterpublics*. New York: Zone, 2005.

Watson, Micah. "The Damned Neighbors Problem: Rousseau's Civil Religion Revisited." *Religions* 10, no. 6 (2019): 349–362. https://doi.org/10.3390/rel10060349.

Watt, David Harrington. *Anti-Fundamentalism in Modern America*. Ithaca, N.J.: Cornell University Press, 2017.

Wenger, Tisa. *Religious Freedom: The Contested History of an American Ideal*. Chapel Hill: University of North Carolina Press, 2017.

Whitehead, Andrew L., and Samuel L. Perry. *Taking America Back for God: Christian Nationalism in the United States*. New York: Oxford University Press, 2020.

Williams, Patricia J. *The Alchemy of Race and Rights*. Cambridge, Mass.: Harvard University Press, 1991.

Wojcik, Stefan, and Adam Hughes. "Sizing Up Twitter Users." *PEW Research Center*, April 24, 2019. https://www.pewresearch.org/internet/2019/04/24/sizing-up-twitter-users/.

Wolff, Michael. *Fire and Fury: Inside the Trump White House*. New York: Henry Holt, 2018.

Worthen, Molly. "Idols of the Trump Era." In *Evangelicals: Who They Have Been, Are Now, and Could Be*, ed. Mark A. Noll, David W. Bebbington, and George M. Marsden, 256–261. Grand Rapids, Mich.: Eerdmans, 2019.

Wuthnow, Robert. *Inventing American Religion: Polls, Surveys, and a Tenuous Quest for a Nation's Faith*. New York: Oxford University Press, 2015.

Wyman, Patrick. "Local Gentry: Local Power and the Social Order." *Perspectives: Past, Present, and Future*, September 17, 2020. https://patrickwyman.substack.com/p/american-gentry.

Yelle, Robert. *Sovereignty and the Sacred*. Chicago: University of Chicago Press, 2019.

Zakaria, Rafia. "Writing while Muslim: The Freedom to be Offended." *Los Angeles Review of Books*, May 8, 2015, https://lareviewofbooks.org/article/writing-while-muslim-the-freedom-to-be-offended-charlie-hebdo/.

Zerofsky, Elizabeth. "The Illiberal State." *New Yorker*, January 14, 2019.

——. "Steve Bannon's Roman Holiday." *New Yorker*, April 11, 2019. https://www.newyorker.com/news/dispatch/steve-bannons-roman-holiday.

Zirin, Dave. "On Colin Kaepernick's Nike Ad: Will the Revolution Be Branded?" *The Nation*, September 4, 2018. https://www.thenation.com/article/on-colin-kaepernicks-nike-ad-will-the-revolution-be-branded/.

INDEX